Bib.

Also available from SCM Press:

Ethics Matters

This is an enlightening guide to those moral questions that don't go away. It should go to every politician, civil servant, teacher and bishop; not to mention the rest of thoughtful humanity!

> Dr Kenneth Wolfe, Emeritus Head of Philosophy and Religion,
> Godolphin & Latymer School, London, and
> Director, London Society for the Study of Religion

Whether one is an A-Level student wanting a more sophisticated discussion of the ethical landscape or an undergraduate needing a very clear outline of the issues, this book has the great virtue of providing just enough to understand the scholarly debates but not so much to overwhelm.

> Michael Wilcockson, A-Level Chief Examiner,
> Head of Philosophy, Eton College, Berkshire

God Matters

A must-read for Year 12 and 13 Philosophy of Religion students and their teachers, which will also be of great value for undergraduate students . . .

> Dr Paul Rout OFM, Lecturer in the Philosophy of Religion,
> University of London

God Matters is an excellent and thoroughly readable updated discussion of the arguments concerning the existence of God and the challenges to that belief. I'm sure it will be thoroughly appreciated by both sixth formers and undergraduate students of this subject area.

> Dr Vaughan Salisbury, Director of ITET Secondary Education,
> University of Wales Trinity Saint David

Bible Matters

Peter and Charlotte Vardy

scm press

Published in 2015 by SCM Press
Editorial office
3rd Floor
Invicta House
108–114 Golden Lane,
London EC1Y 0TG

SCM Press is an imprint of Hymns Ancient & Modern Ltd
(a registered charity)
13A Hellesdon Park Road
Norwich NR6 5DR, UK

www.scmpress.co.uk

British Library Cataloguing in Publication data

A catalogue record for this book is available from the British Library

9780334043935

Typeset by Mary Matthews
Printed and bound by CPI Group (UK) Ltd, Croydon, CR0 4YY

Contents

To Chris Moses,
a friend

Preface

At the age of 30, Peter sold his house, left his career as a chartered accountant and company chairman, and started reading for a Master's degree in theology at King's College, London. Lots of people asked him why! It certainly wasn't for the money or job security, and it wasn't because he suddenly 'got God'.

In 1996 Charlotte started reading for a degree in theology at Worcester College, Oxford. She chose to specialize in biblical studies, particularly the pre-exilic Hebrew Scriptures. People kept on asking her why; she didn't want to be a vicar and wasn't sure she even believed in God! She certainly wasn't keen on rowing or the union. She wasn't set on a career in the city and didn't even want to be an academic theologian.

For both Peter and Charlotte, their reason for studying the Bible was Søren Kierkegaard.

For Kierkegaard, truth is the only thing that matters and that 'truth is not a matter of knowing this or that but of being in the truth'. To anyone of moderate intelligence it is obvious that human beings cannot be the measure of all things. How human beings see things cannot be the way they really are – truth is bigger than us and our limited perspective. The only way to live truthfully is to recognize the existence of an independent absolute truth and that although we humans cannot claim to know it, we live in the face of it whether we like it or not.

This is the essence of the Bible and why it matters. As Kierkegaard said:

> The Bible is very easy to understand. But we ... pretend to be unable to understand it because we know very well that the minute we understand, we are obliged to act accordingly.

People explain their reasons for studying the Bible in many different ways. Some frame it in terms of sociology, others history, literary studies, linguistics, politics or psychology, a few religious knowledge. Few manage to communicate why the Bible *really matters*, perhaps because it is deeply countercultural in an age steeped in postmodern 'incredulity towards metanarratives'. In the end, however unfashionable or uncomfortable this might be, the Bible bears witness to the truth – *el emet*.[1]

Of course, the truth is way beyond anything that can be communicated simply, literally, directly. Truth is beyond mere words, beyond clear comprehension, but it is the very *ground of our being*. As the Bible explains, truth is even the guarantee of God's mercy, justice and power,[2] so it is ultimate, absolute reality. Studying the Bible, and studying how people have studied the Bible, gives us a window into the nature of truth and how most people have avoided understanding and acting on it.

For both Peter and Charlotte, in this sense, studying the Bible is the ultimate philosophical activity and the reason they chose to devote their lives to it. Nothing else truly matters.

Peter and Charlotte Vardy
Montbrun-des-Corbières, France
Easter 2015

---

1 'God of Truth', as in Ps. 31.5 and Isa. 65.16, Hebrew אל אמת.
2 E.g. Deut. 32.4; Ps. 100.5; John 7.17; John 8.32.

The poem in the rock and
The poem in the mind
Are not one.
It was in dying
I tried to make them so.

R. S. Thomas, 'Epitaph'

Introduction

Does the Bible really matter in today's multicultural, scientifically informed and technologically enabled world? What have the traditions of a long-dead Middle Eastern culture to offer us in the enlightened West? Do stories about the God who sent bears to dismember children (2 Kings 2.23–24), who slaughtered Egyptian babies for the crimes of their King (Exod. 12.29) and who went so far as to drown the entire world (Gen. 7.21–23) have anything to tell us about how to build a better world, whatever we might think about the evidence for God's existence?

Two centuries of intensive scholarship have made the meaning of the Bible less, not more, clear. The authority, even the importance, of the Bible has been challenged as questions about its historical accuracy have been raised and the apparent complexities of its authorship exposed. Richard Dawkins is persuasive when he says:

> To be fair, much of the Bible is ... just plain weird, as you would expect of a chaotically cobbled-together anthology of disjointed documents, composed, revised, translated, distorted and 'improved' by hundreds of anonymous authors, editors and copyists, unknown to us and mostly unknown to each other, spanning nine centuries.[1]

Yet does such a reductionist view do justice to the Bible? How and why did a 'chaotically cobbled-together anthology', if such it really is, become the bestselling book of all time? Why did demand for the Bible drive the development of printing, lead to revolution and regime change across the world? Why have tens of thousands

---

1 Richard Dawkins, *The God Delusion*, London: Black Swan, 2007, p. 268; ch. 7, 'The Good Book and the Changing Moral Zeitgeist'.

died through demanding the right to read the Bible or providing it to others? Why are concepts of God and human goodness still so shaped by the Bible? Why do its pages still exert influence on international affairs? Why do all sorts of people keep on opening the Bible and seeing in its pages something life-enhancing – how can it still inspire a Leonard Cohen to write 'Hallelujah' or a Tracey Emin to bare her soul on a wall?

Around 31.6 per cent of the world's population identify as being Christian – over 2.5 billion people. For many Christians the Bible is the focus of their faith. Because of this the Bible remains the world's bestselling non-fiction book. The Bible is available all or in part in 2,426 languages, covering 95 per cent of the world's population. In 2007 *The Economist* estimated that 100 million copies of the Bible are sold or given away each year.[1] Nevertheless, levels of biblical knowledge and understanding among Christians remain incredibly low.

A recent Gallup survey[2] found that, for all their country's apparent religiosity, less than half of Americans can name the first book of the Bible, only a third know who delivered the Sermon on the Mount and a quarter do not know what is celebrated at Easter. Further, 60 per cent could not list five of the Ten Commandments. In the same survey it emerged that 12 per cent think Noah was married to Joan of Arc! And while acknowledging that Christianity has changed,[3] the hope that most Christians in the developing world have far better knowledge of the Bible than do most Americans is not supported by much evidence.

Further, for people of faith, understanding the Bible is about far more than recognizing famous stories and quotations. The meaning of each passage has to be unpacked theologically in relation to its context and wider themes in order to make sense

---

1 See www.economist.com/node/10311317. Apparently Americans buy more than 20 million new Bibles every year (to add to the four the average American has at home).

2 Quoted in www.economist.com/node/10311317.

3 In 1900, 80 per cent of the world's Christians lived in Europe and the USA; today 60 per cent live in the developing world.

of it and know how to apply it to life and belief in the modern world. Of course, there is little agreement over how Bible texts should be read or interpreted, let alone over how their wisdom should be applied. Different theological interpretations of the Bible exist within each faith tradition as well as between them, so the extent to which a person is deemed to have understood the Bible or any passage of it may well depend on the extent to which their interpretation concurs with that adopted by the person or denomination making that judgement!

- Some Protestant Christians claim to take the Bible literally, seeing it as requiring them to denounce homosexuality – while also ignoring regulations about wearing mixed fibres or planting different crops side by side. On the other hand, most Catholics argue that the Bible has to be interpreted as a whole, by those trained in biblical interpretation. Of course, many people who see themselves as Christian see the Bible as a cultural resource like Shakespeare but never actually read or study it.
- While some Jews try to follow all 613 laws in the first five books of the Bible absolutely, others see the Bible as a complex literary document whose value lies in what it can tell us about the people and societies that contributed to its development. Some Jews keep the Torah in its original Hebrew, written on traditional scrolls, and see true Jewishness in terms of being able to chant and interpret it in the synagogue; others see this traditional approach to preserving the text as unnecessary in an age of eBooks and iPads.
- Some Muslim countries have made distributing copies of the Bible impossible, despite the fact that it contains the teaching of the second most important Muslim prophet – Jesus, *Issa* in Arabic – and many other prophets sent by Allah and fully acknowledged by the Prophet Muhammad.[4] For some Muslims the Hebrew Scriptures and Christian teaching

---

4 christianity.stackexchange.com/questions/9351/in-what-countries-is-it-legal-to-own-a-bible-the-most-banned-book-in-the-world.

prefigures most of the Prophet's teaching,[5] consequently true Jews and Christians are to be respected. For others, such as followers of Daesh – so-called Islamic State – Jews and Christians are fit only to be persecuted or even killed.

So given that knowledge and understanding of the Bible is poor even among those who profess its central importance, and bearing in mind that there is little agreement about how texts should be interpreted or applied, is there much point in continuing to study the Bible? Has it become irrelevant?

In *Bible Matters* we will argue that far from being irrelevant, studying the Bible has become *more* relevant in recent years.

First, because Bible stories and the language in which they have been told continue to underpin Western culture – although many young people do not realize this and so are ill-equipped to get the most out of cultural experiences. Hollywood films, bestselling books, works of contemporary art and architecture as well as political speeches, marketing campaigns and pop hits reference the Bible, use and manipulate its cultural power. It is no accident that many theology graduates are drawn to work in advertising, journalism and the law, when their degree has entailed studying the foundations of our culture and some of the best examples of how to communicate and persuade in human history.[6]

The relevance of Bible study goes way beyond the power of its language. The Bible represents for Western culture a repository for many of our memories, symbols, archetypal stories, morals – the essence of our collective identity and what makes our societies

---

5 'Say ye: "We believe in Allah, and the revelation given to us, and to Abraham, Isma'il, Isaac, Jacob, and the Tribes, and that given to Moses and Jesus, and that given to (all) prophets from their Lord: We make no difference between one and another of them: And we bow to Allah (in Islam)."' Surah 2.136.

6 This point was made recently by researchers from Exeter University who called for the Bible to be used to improve young peoples' writing skills. See www.telegraph.co.uk/education/educationnews/10881096/The-Bible-should-be-used-to-develop-pupils-writing-skills.html and blogs.spectator.co.uk/culturehousedaily/2014/06/the-bible-can-teach-us-and-our-politicians-how-to-use-words-properly, 6 June 2014.

what they are. As the *OSCE Toledo Guiding Principles on Teaching about Religions and Beliefs in Public Schools* concluded in 2007, knowing about the Bible and the beliefs and practices it has inspired is 'an essential part of a quality education. It is required to understand much of history, literature and art, and can be helpful in broadening one's cultural horizons and in deepening one's insight into the complexities of past and present.'[7]

Second, studying the Bible is relevant because historical claims originating in biblical texts continue to cause tension. Was the land of Israel promised to the Jewish people by God? Were the Jewish people really displaced by the Romans? Will the last judgement be heralded by the arrival of the Messiah through the Golden Gate of Jerusalem? While some people doubt the historical reliability of the Bible, others see it as our most important record of the past and an essential guide for shaping future affairs. Examining the historical status of the Bible is important if we are to understand, let alone make progress in, world affairs and if we are to deal with the political manifestations of fundamentalism and literalism that divide our world now. Forgive us the clichés, but as Confucius said, 'study the past if you would define the future'; and as George Santayana said, 'those who cannot remember the past are doomed to repeat it'.

Third, biblical quotations are often used to lend authority to moral arguments that are often designed to persuade and influence. In Apartheid South Africa, protestors quoted Galatians 3.26–29 ('There is neither Jew nor Gentile, neither slave nor free, nor is there male and female, for you are all one in Christ Jesus') against oppressors who spouted Leviticus 25.45–46 ('You may also buy some of the temporary residents living among you and members of their clans born in your country, and they will become your property. You can bequeath them to your children as inherited property and can make them slaves for life').

Outside US abortion clinics, 'pro-life' protestors shout about the sanctity of human lives created 'in the image of God' and that murder should be avenged 'an eye for an eye', while 'pro-choice'

---

7 See www.osce.org/odihr/29154, p. 14.

campaigners ask how people who claim to venerate human life can judge, reject, constrain the freedoms of vulnerable women and doctors – even physically attack them – when Jesus taught 'love your neighbour as yourself', 'judge not, lest ye be judged' and regularly forgave sinners. It is important to be able to engage with people who seek to use the Bible's authority to win arguments and change policy.

Further, some atheists have seized on apparent contradictions between specific biblical quotations, seeking to discredit the whole Bible – and through that, religions and people who respect them. In their focus on reconciling detail they often ignore the bigger picture, in which some of the apparent contradictions dissolve; yet their arguments have gained traction and convinced many people in the secular West that faith is anti-intellectual, even pernicious. In a world divided between secular and religious – and over many moral, social and political questions – it is important that people have the tools to engage with faith, to look for a bigger and more complete wisdom and stop proper scepticism becoming cynicism or even nihilism.

Finally, attitudes to the Bible reflect attitudes to truth and knowledge. In this context, biblical studies offers insights into our and other cultures and those of times past, into how disputes have developed and just maybe how they could be resolved. Sadly, few modern education systems offer young people much opportunity to reflect on the nature of truth and knowledge or attitudes to either in their own or other cultures; yet without appreciating the significance of truth, knowledge and attitudes to both, young people struggle to engage with – let alone contribute to – the modern world. At its best, religious studies, of which biblical studies is an important part, provides such an opportunity. It can anchor and give heart to the curriculum, encouraging and enabling young people to put the rest of their learning in context, to reflect, discuss, analyse and begin to evaluate fundamental existential questions and different peoples' answers to them.

As we see it, studying the Bible is an essential part of education, not just in order to appreciate the cultural heritage and languages of the Western world, not just to understand why many Christians or Jews think and behave as they do, not just to learn from historical documents or a collection of literature, but because its pages contain unparalleled insights into what it means to be human. The process of studying the Bible causes us to ask questions – often uncomfortable questions – about who and what we are, about how we live our lives, about the nature and extent of freedom and responsibility, about what we can say and what we can know, about perspective, the nature of truth and reality, the limits of certainty and human understanding, about belief and about faith. And that is without even considering the question of God's existence, which even the great atheist Sigmund Freud saw as the most important question of all.

Bible Matters attempts to show why the Bible matters, why everyone should study it and find out much more, whether or not they are religious or even believe in God. Of course, no book of this length and type can hope to explore the complexities of the subject matter. We hope only that it serves to awaken interest and start readers on a journey.

PART ONE

What is the Bible?

1

What is the Bible?

It is far from clear what the Bible is. Reading it can be a very confusing experience. Even the title is confusing. The Bible suggests *a* book; the word seems to be singular. People refer to 'the good book' and describe teachings in Scripture rather than in the Scriptures. Actually the word 'Bible' originates in the Greek and Latin words for 'books' – and this is just what it is: a collection of books that are themselves often collections of smaller texts, very much in the plural.

Further, different people might understand the word 'Bible' to refer to very different books. Leaving aside for a moment the existence of different language editions and the variation that necessarily comes with translation, Bibles in the same language with the same title on the cover might contain different words and sentences, different verses and books in different orders.

The Development of the Bible

The sense we get from the Hebrew Scriptures, from the Gospels and Acts, is that they started off in a rich oral tradition, in which stories were passed on from person to person – in the case of the Hebrew Scriptures, in families and tribal communities from generation to generation.

Different tribes' versions of stories might account for the duplication of some traditions and variations in the names of places or even people, such as references to the same mountain as both Sinai and Horeb in the Torah. In addition, stories probably changed over time as historical events made certain aspects more or less interesting. Different authors probably had different styles and concerns in putting brush to papyrus as well. Similarly, different people and different communities probably had slightly different versions of stories about and the sayings of Jesus, which might account for the variation between the four Gospels.

It seems likely that the first bits of both the Hebrew Scriptures and the New Testament to be written down were particularly sensitive to variation – poems and orations, sayings or teachings and particularly laws. Histories were probably transmitted in oral form for longer, told and retold with some variations, yet it would be wrong to assume that oral tradition was completely unreliable as a means of communicating and preserving truth. Even today, historians and journalists rely on interviewing people about what they experienced and what they have heard about significant events. Just because some of the details of a story change does not mean there are not central elements that stay the same.

By tradition, the Ten Commandments were carved on two tablets of stone and kept in the Ark of the Covenant (see Exod. 34). Moses wrote the books of law and these, perhaps along with some later historical archives, were later 'discovered' in the Temple during the reign of King Josiah in around 623 BC (2 Kings 22).

The collection of Scriptures grew during and immediately after the Babylonian exile (sixth century BC), with some new writing and a lot of editing and reworking carrying on as late as the century before Jesus, and small but potentially significant variations between editions and collections well into the early medieval period.

By tradition, Paul's letters were written between AD 50 and his death in 64, while the Gospels were written shortly after this, between AD 64 and 120. The books of Acts and Revelation, and the non-Pauline letters emerged around the end of this time. It seems likely that when leading figures in the Early Church died it became necessary to record an authoritative version first of Jesus' life and teaching and then of the works and words of the early Church leaders.

Of course, tradition is not necessarily accurate and there are good reasons to believe that traditional ideas about the authorship and date of some books of the Bible are wrong. This will be considered further in Chapters 7 and 8.

By the second century AD, within both the Jewish and Christian communities a definite sense that some texts were 'authorized' and others not had developed. It remained to produce a definitive list of authorized 'canonical' works, decide which order these should be kept in and which version of each work was deemed best, so as to avoid confusion.

The Development of the Jewish Canon

Within the Jewish tradition an 'authorized' collection of Scriptures might have existed as early as the third century BC. However, the belief that the canon was closed before the third century AD has been abandoned by historians. James VanderKam believes that 'as nearly as we can tell, there was no canon of Scripture in Second Temple Judaism'.[1]

Possibly as early as the reign of Ptolemy II (283–246 BC) the Scriptures were translated into Greek for those Jews who lived in Egypt. This translation is known as the Septuagint (LXX for short), after the 70 scholars who were supposed to have worked on the translation.[2] The Septuagint contains the Torah, a collection of Prophecy that is very similar – though not identical – to the later Masoretic collection.

By 180 BC a core of texts seems to have been collected and accepted as authoritative. This collection,[3] called simply 'the books', included Genesis, Exodus, Leviticus, Numbers,

---

1 'Questions of Canon Viewed through the Dead Sea Scrolls', in *The Canon Debate*, ed. Lee Martin McDonald, James A. Sanders, Grand Rapids, MI: Baker Academic, 2003, p. 91. See also Brian M. and Charlotte Beck, 'The Dead Sea Scrolls', in *The Oxford Companion to Archaeology*, Oxford: Oxford University Press, 1996.

2 'King Ptolemy [II] once gathered 72 Elders. He placed them in 72 chambers, each of them in a separate one, without revealing to them why they were summoned. He entered each one's room and said: "Write for me the Torah of Moshe, your teacher". God put it in the heart of each one to translate identically as all the others did.' Tractate Megillah, Babylonian Talmud, pages 9a–9b.

3 Cf. Daniel 9.2, the Mishnah.

Deuteronomy, the Torah, as well as Joshua, Judges, Samuel, Kings and Job and the Prophets Isaiah, Jeremiah, Ezekiel and the Twelve Minor Prophets in something close to their current form.[4]

The Dead Sea Scrolls, discovered in caves near Qumran in the years after 1948, contain 235 biblical and apocryphal fragments, including evidence for the existence of the Torah, some of the Prophets and some of the other Writings. Many of the fragments are quite remarkable for the degree of similarity they show with the Masoretic Text, the tradition on which most copies of the Hebrew Scriptures have been based since the tenth century AD,[5] and some of them date back to the second century BC.

Philo of Alexandria, who lived from 25 BC to AD 50, quoted the Hebrew Scriptures extensively in his works, seeing them as the source of all wisdom – but he did not quote from the books of Ezekiel, Daniel, Canticles, Ruth, Lamentations, Ecclesiastes or Esther.

In the first century AD, the Jewish historian Josephus wrote:

> For we have not an innumerable multitude of books among us, disagreeing from and contradicting one another [as the Greeks have], but only 22 books, which contain the records of all the past times; which are justly believed to be divine; and of them five belong to Moses, which contain his laws and the traditions of the origin of mankind till his death. This interval of time was little short of three thousand years; but as to the time from the death of Moses till the reign of Artaxerxes king of Persia, who reigned after Xerxes, the prophets, who were after Moses, wrote down what was done in their times in thirteen books. The remaining four books contain hymns to God, and precepts for the conduct of human life.[6]

---

4 See jewishencyclopedia.com/articles/3259-bible-canon.

5 In the first half of the tenth century AD, Aaron ben Moses ben Asher and Moshe ben Naphtali were the leading Masoretes in Tiberias. Masoretes were scholars known for their precision and accuracy in recording and copying the Scriptures. Asher and Naphtali are often seen as marking the end of a process of debate and textual development that gave us the accepted text of the Hebrew Scriptures.

6 *Against Apion* Book 1.8.

By Josephus' time the three-part arrangement of the Hebrew Scriptures – Torah followed by the Prophets (Nevi'im) and Writings (Ketuvim) – had been established and the canon had shaped up to nearly its final form, containing 22 of the 24 books of Hebrew Scripture.

The idea that the Jewish canon was finally closed and authorized at the Council of Jamnia during the late first century AD was proposed by the Jewish scholar Heinrich Graetz in 1871. For decades, Jewish and Christian scholars accepted that such a council had happened in or around AD 90. Nevertheless, today that idea has been discredited; not only is there zero evidence for any such meeting, but also close reading of the Talmud suggests that disagreements about which books and bits of books to authorize persisted between leading rabbis until at least AD 200.

The Development of the Christian Canon

In 1740 a fragment of Latin manuscript was published. It had been discovered in the Ambrosian Library in Milan by the historian Father Ludovico Muratori. Claiming to be a seventh-century translation of a Greek document, possibly written as early as AD 170, it reads:

> at which point, he [Markus?] was present and thus set them down.
>
> The third book of the gospel is the one according to Lukas ... The fourth gospel is that of Johannes, one of the students ... However, the Actions of the Envoys are included in one book. Lukas addresses them to the 'most excellent Theophilus,' ... However, as for Paulus' letters: They make it clear (to those who want to know) whose they are and from what place and why they were written ...
>
> > the first to the Korinthians;
> > the second to the Ephesians;
> > the third to the Filippians;
> > the fourth to the Kolossaeans;

7

the fifth to the Galatians;
the sixth to the Thessalonikans;
the seventh to the Romans.

Although he wrote one more time to the Korinthians and to the Thessalonikans for their correction, it is recognizable that one assembly has spread across the whole globe of the earth. For in the Revelation, Johannes writes indeed to seven assemblies yet is speaking to all.

He wrote besides these one to Filemon, one to Titus, and two to Timotheos ...

There are extant also a letter to the Laodikeians, and another to the Alexandrians, forged in Paulus' name to further Markion's school of thought. And there are many others which cannot be received into the universal assembly, for 'it is not fitting for vinegar to be mixed with honey'.

Indeed, the letter of Judah, and two entitled Johannes, are accepted in the universal assembly, along with the Wisdom, written by the friends of Solomon in his honour. We receive also the Revelations of Johannes and Peter, the latter of which some refuse to have read in the assembly.

But the Shepherd [of Hermas] was written very recently in our time by Hermas in the city of Rome, when his brother overseer Pius was seated in the chair of the Roman assembly. Therefore indeed, it should be read, but it cannot be read publicly among the people in the assembly – either as among the Prophets (since their number is complete) or among the envoys, whose time has ended.

Now we accept nothing at all from Arsinous, or Valentinus and Miltiades, who also wrote a new book of songs for Markion, together with Basilides of Asia Minor, the founder of the Katafrygians.[7]

The dating of the so-called Muratorian Canon has been disputed

---

7 See www.earlychristianwritings.com/text/muratorian4.html, trans. Frank Daniels.

(some scholars claim that it cannot have been written until the fourth century), but it certainly throws light on the development of the New Testament Christian canon and shows how a core (the four Gospels and Paul's principal letters) was widely recognized well before a definitive canon was decided. Elsewhere, Irenaeus of Lyons is widely credited with having recognized this core in the late second century.

A major step towards defining the Christian canon was taken when Athanasius, Bishop of Alexandria, listed the 27 'canonical' books of the New Testament and condemned the use of other 'non-canonical' Scriptures in his Easter Letter of AD 367. The letter reads:

4. There are, then, of the Old Testament, twenty-two books in number; for, as I have heard, it is handed down that this is the number of the letters among the Hebrews; their respective order and names being as follows. The first is Genesis, then Exodus, next Leviticus, after that Numbers, and then Deuteronomy. Following these there is Joshua, the son of Nun, then Judges, then Ruth. And again, after these four books of Kings, the first and second being reckoned as one book, and so likewise the third and fourth as one book. And again, the first and second of the Chronicles are reckoned as one book. Again Ezra, the first and second are similarly one book. After these there is the book of Psalms, then the Proverbs, next Ecclesiastes, and the Song of Songs. Job follows, then the Prophets, the twelve being reckoned as one book. Then Isaiah, one book, then Jeremiah with Baruch, Lamentations, and the epistle, one book; afterwards, Ezekiel and Daniel, each one book. Thus far constitutes the Old Testament.

5. Again it is not tedious to speak of the [books] of the New Testament. These are, the four Gospels, according to Matthew, Mark, Luke, and John. Afterwards, the Acts of the Apostles and Epistles (called Catholic), seven, viz. of James, one; of Peter, two; of John, three; after these, one of Jude. In addition, there are fourteen Epistles of Paul, written in this

order. The first, to the Romans; then two to the Corinthians; after these, to the Galatians; next, to the Ephesians; then to the Philippians; then to the Colossians; after these, two to the Thessalonians, and that to the Hebrews; and again, two to Timothy; one to Titus; and lastly, that to Philemon. And besides, the Revelation of John ...

7. But for greater exactness I add this also, writing of necessity; that there are other books besides these not indeed included in the Canon, but appointed by the Fathers to be read by those who newly join us, and who wish for instruction in the word of godliness. The Wisdom of Solomon, and the Wisdom of Sirach, and Esther, and Judith, and Tobit, and that which is called the Teaching of the Apostles, and the Shepherd. But the former, my brethren, are included in the Canon, the latter being [merely] read; nor is there in any place a mention of apocryphal writings. But they are an invention of heretics, who write them when they choose, bestowing upon them their approbation, and assigning to them a date, that so, using them as ancient writings, they may find occasion to lead astray the simple.[8]

Bishop Athanasius' letter lists 22 canonical Old Testament books – based on the canon of Hebrew Scriptures at that time – and 27 canonical New Testament books. It seems that he chose his list from a much larger collection of texts that were known and used to greater or lesser extents at the time and reflected a great variety of theological views.

In 1945 a collection of texts now known as the Nag Hammadi Codices was found buried in pots in the upper-Egyptian desert. They probably date from around the time when Athanasius wrote his letter and might even have been buried in order to comply with his version of orthodoxy. The following is a list of the Nag Hammadi codices and the contents of each.

---

8   See www.newadvent.org/fathers/2806039.htm.

WHAT IS THE BIBLE?

1

The Prayer of the Apostle Paul
The Apocryphon of James
The Gospel of Truth
The Treatise on the Resurrection
The Tripartite Tractate

2

The Apocryphon of John
The Gospel of Thomas
The Gospel of Philip
The Hypostasis of the Archons
On the Origin of the World
The Exegesis on the Soul
The Book of Thomas the Contender

3

The Apocryphon of John
The Gospel of the Egyptians
Eugnostos the Blessed
The Sophia of Jesus Christ
The Dialogue of the Saviour

4

The Apocryphon of John
The Gospel of the Egyptians

5

Eugnostos the Blessed
The Apocalypse of Paul
The First Apocalypse of James
The Second Apocalypse of James
The Apocalypse of Adam

11

6

The Acts of Peter and 12 Apostles
The Thunder, Perfect Mind
Authoritative Teaching
The Concept of Our Great Power
The Republic (Plato)
Discourse on the Eight and Ninth
The Prayer of Thanksgiving
Asclepius 21–29

7

The Paraphrase of Shem
Second Treatise of the Great Seth
Gnostic Apocalypse of Peter
The Teachings of Silvanus
The Three Steles of Seth

8

Zostrianos
The Letter of Peter to Philip

9

Melchizedek
The Thought of Norea
The Testimony of Truth

10

Marsanes

11

The Interpretation of Knowledge
A Valentinian Exposition
Allogenes
Hypsiphrone

12
The Sentences of Sextus
The Gospel of Truth
Fragments

13
Trimorphic Protennoia
The Origin of the World

Today these and similar texts are referred to as Gnostic texts because many of them suggest that they impart some sort of special knowledge (Greek *gnosis*) to readers, who will be saved because of it. Another characteristic shared by Gnostic texts is the influence of the Neoplatonic philosophy that was so popular around the Ancient Mediterranean.[9]

It seems that the popularity of mixing Christian ideas with Neoplatonic philosophy was troubling because it was clear that Jesus' message was open to being corrupted and its saving potential lost in this way. Christian leaders felt that there had to be some checks and balances on philosophical speculation so that it did not lead people into error and condemn them to hell. In the end, through the work of Irenaeus, Athanasius and other Early Church Fathers, philosophical exegesis was limited to what was consistent with central principles of faith, identified and defined through Councils of the Church. The drawn-out process of establishing a single, effective church hierarchy and authoritative doctrine necessarily involved decisions about which Scriptures to endorse – and which to relegate to pots in the desert.

The final major step in defining an agreed biblical canon for Christian use was Jerome starting to translate his Vulgate into Latin in 382. Probably following on from the Council of Rome in 381, which may have attempted to bring controversy about the canon of Scripture to an end, Pope Damasus I commissioned Jerome (his secretary) to revise the *Vetus Latina* ('Old Latin') collection

---

9   Chapter 5 contains much more detail about Gnosticism and neo-platonic philosophy.

of biblical texts then in use by the Church in Rome. Jerome was reluctant, remarking:

> You urge me to revise the old Latin version, and, as it were, to sit in judgment on the copies of the Scriptures which are now scattered throughout the whole world; and, inasmuch as they differ from one another, you would have me decide which of them agree with the Greek original. The labour is one of love, but at the same time both perilous and presumptuous; for in judging others I must be content to be judged by all; and how can I dare to change the language of the world in its hoary old age, and carry it back to the early days of its infancy? Is there a man, learned or unlearned, who will not, when he takes the volume into his hands, and perceives that what he reads does not suit his settled tastes, break out immediately into violent language, and call me a forger and a profane person for having the audacity to add anything to the ancient books, or to make any changes or corrections therein?[10]

Yet despite these objections, Jerome continued his mammoth task in translation until about 405. In Rome and later at Antioch, Bethlehem and Alexandria, he sorted through all the available manuscripts and consulted leading scholars in both Christian and Jewish traditions. Controversially, he chose to translate the majority of the Old Testament from scratch himself, directly from Hebrew manuscripts into Latin rather than relying on the Septuagint or later Greek translations as other scholars had tended to. Where Hebrew manuscripts were unavailable, Jerome translated from the best Greek, Aramaic or Old Latin manuscripts that he had access to;[11] like Athanasius he called texts that were not available in the Hebrew *apocryphal* and noted that they should be read separately and seen as less authoritative.

---

10 Jerome's Preface to the Vulgate Version of the New Testament, Addressed to Pope Damasus, AD 383.

11 The works and sections that Jerome translated from non-Hebrew sources are pretty much the same works and sections the Protestants later cut from their canon.

Jerome's Vulgate New Testament is very much as Christians would recognize today, containing 27 books – plus the Epistle to the Laodiceans, which was included with a note questioning its authenticity. Like Athanasius, Jerome chose to include only four of the Gospels that were circulating, stating:

> I therefore promise in this short Preface the four Gospels only, which are to be taken in the following order, Matthew, Mark, Luke, John, as they have been revised by a comparison of the Greek manuscripts. Only early ones have been used. But to avoid any great divergences from the Latin which we are accustomed to read, I have used my pen with some restraint, and while I have corrected only such passages as seemed to convey a different meaning, I have allowed the rest to remain as they are.[12]

By his principle that Hebrew texts are more authentic, earlier and in all cases preferable to Greek, Jerome identified Matthew with its strong Jewish themes as the earliest and first Gospel account.[13]

Jerome's translation became immediately popular; although being in Latin it was *vulgar* and was not 'authorized' until the Council of Trent in the sixteenth century. Until the Protestant Reformation, few Christians put great emphasis on Scripture as a primary authority in religion. Even if they could read the necessary language(s) and had access to a library, ordinary Christians and even ordained clergymen were seemingly barred from reading Scriptures for themselves unless and until they had 'Mastered the Arts' and completed higher courses in the philosophy of religion and Catholic theology. William Tyndale, the great translator of the Bible, complained that:

> They have ordained that no man shall look on the Scripture, until he be noselled in heathen learning eight or nine years

---

12 Jerome's Preface to the Vulgate Version of the New Testament, Addressed to Pope Damasus, AD 383. Available at vulgate.org.

13 Ibid.

and armed with false principles, with which he is clean shut out of the understanding of the Scripture.[14]

Through the medieval period, Christians who appealed directly to the authority of the Bible often found themselves at odds with the Church:

- Francis of Assisi appealed to the poverty of the disciples to criticize the wealth of the Church and call for a return to the simple faith preached by Jesus and the sort of attitude to private property that the Apostles had in Acts. In the fourteenth century, when the Franciscan movement grew popular, the Papacy and wealthy religious orders sought to attack its more extreme claims, going so far as to declare it a heresy to say that Jesus was poor![15] Some issues just won't go away; Pope Francis – his papal name is no accident – is struggling with right-wing members of the Church in the USA, who see his suspicion of capitalism and commitment to the poor as evidence of communism rather than scriptural faith.[16]

- John Wycliffe was an English philosopher and theologian who was one of the most influential teachers at Oxford University later in the fourteenth century. On the basis of Jesus' teaching in the Gospels, Wycliffe attacked the wealth and corruption of priests and practices of the Church, such as the sale of indulgences (certificates granting time off purgatory), which would later excite Martin Luther. Unsurprisingly, Wycliffe was deeply controversial; his popularity was one of the causes of the Peasants' Revolt in England.

- Martin Luther was a German theologian who sparked the

14 archive.org/stream/williamtyndalebi00dema/williamtyndalebi00dema_djvu. txt, *Practice of Prelates*, Works, Vol. II, p. 291; quoted on page 36.

15 *Cum inter nonnullos* (1323), www.franciscan-archive.org/bullarium/qinn-e. html.

16 See for example: www.cbsnews.com/news/pope-francis-defends-himself-against-communism- claims.

Protestant Reformation. Like Wycliffe, he doubted the scriptural basis of many church teachings and was prepared to confront people who he saw abusing believers with false Christian ideas. Incensed by the sale of indulgences, Luther wrote down 95 objections to practices within the Roman Catholic Church and circulated them widely, using the newly invented printing press. People flocked to hear Luther from all over Europe, and his translation of the Bible into German (1532–4) became a bestseller. He encouraged ordinary people to read Scripture for themselves and use it as their primary guide in all matters spiritual and ethical, cutting out the authority and traditional role of the Church. His ideas started centuries of bloody warfare and changed Europe for ever, setting in train patterns of thought that led to the Enlightenment and the modern world.

Luther had forthright views about the historical origins and hence spiritual reliability of some biblical books; these views impacted on his German translation and the many Protestant translations influenced by it, including the English King James Bible.[17]

Books	Protestant tradition	Roman Catholic tradition	Eastern Orthodox tradition
Matthew	Yes	Yes	Yes
Mark	Yes	Yes	Yes
Luke	Yes	Yes	Yes
John	Yes	Yes	Yes
Acts	Yes	Yes	Yes

17 The Epistle to the Laodiceans was included in some early manuscripts and is still included in some editions of the Protestant and Catholic Bibles, although with a note that it was probably not written by Paul. Luther moved Hebrews and James to the end of his Bible, making the final works Hebrews, James, Jude and Revelation; he included a note stating that these were less reliable texts.

Books	Protestant tradition	Roman Catholic tradition	Eastern Orthodox tradition
Romans	Yes	Yes	Yes
1 Corinthians	Yes	Yes	Yes
2 Corinthians	Yes	Yes	Yes
Galatians	Yes	Yes	Yes
Ephesians	Yes	Yes	Yes
Philippians	Yes	Yes	Yes
Colossians	Yes	Yes	Yes
Laodiceans	No	No	No
1 Thessalonians	Yes	Yes	Yes
2 Thessalonians	Yes	Yes	Yes
1 Timothy	Yes	Yes	Yes
2 Timothy	Yes	Yes	Yes
Titus	Yes	Yes	Yes
Philemon	Yes	Yes	Yes
Hebrews	Yes	Yes	Yes
James	Yes	Yes	Yes
1 Peter	Yes	Yes	Yes
2 Peter	Yes	Yes	Yes
1 John	Yes	Yes	Yes
2 John	Yes	Yes	Yes
3 John	Yes	Yes	Yes
Jude	Yes	Yes	Yes
Revelation	Yes	Yes	Yes

Are the Hebrew Scriptures and Old Testament the Same Thing?

The traditional order of books in the Hebrew Scriptures is not the same as the traditional order of books in the Christian Old Testament. The Jewish canon contains 24 books, divided into:

- the five books of the Torah or instruction (Genesis, Exodus, Leviticus, Numbers and Deuteronomy);
- the eight books of the Prophets (Joshua, Judges, Samuel, Kings, Isaiah, Jeremiah, Ezekiel and the twelve Minor Prophets), known as the Nevi'im;
- the eleven books of Writings (Psalms, Proverbs, Job, Song of Solomon, Ruth, Lamentations, Ecclesiastes, Esther, Daniel, Ezra, and Chronicles), known as the Ketuvim.

Whereas the Christian Old Testament divides and rearranges these books:[18]

Hebrew Scriptures (24 books)	Protestant OT (39 books)	Catholic OT (46 books)	Eastern Orthodox OT (51 books)
Bereishit	Genesis	Genesis	Genesis
Shemot	Exodus	Exodus	Exodus
Vayikra	Leviticus	Leviticus	Leviticus
Bamidbar	Numbers	Numbers	Numbers
Devarim	Deuteronomy	Deuteronomy	Deuteronomy
Yehoshua	Joshua	Joshua (Josue)	Joshua (Iesous)
Shofetim	Judges	Judges	Judges

18 Note how Samuel, Kings and Chronicles are counted as one book rather than two, how the 12 Minor Prophets are collected into a single 'Book of the Twelve' and how Ezra and Nehemiah are seen as a single work in the Hebrew Scriptures.

Hebrew Scriptures (24 books)	Protestant OT (39 books	Catholic OT (46 books)	Eastern Orthodox OT (51 books)
Rut (Ruth)	Ruth	Ruth	Ruth
Shemuel	1 Samuel	1 Samuel (1 Kings)	1 Samuel (1 Kingdoms)
	2 Samuel	2 Samuel (2 Kings)	2 Samuel (2 Kingdoms)
Melakhim	1 Kings	1 Kings (3 Kings)	1 Kings (3 Kingdoms)
	2 Kings	2 Kings (4 Kings)	2 Kings (4 Kingdoms)
Divrei Hayamim (Chronicles)	1 Chronicles	1 Chronicles (1 Paralipomenon)	1 Chronicles (1 Paralipomenon)
	2 Chronicles	2 Chronicles (2 Paralipomenon)	2 Chronicles (2 Paralipomenon)
			1 Esdras
Ezra— Nehemiah	Ezra	Ezra (1 Esdras)	Ezra (2 Esdras)
	Nehemiah	Nehemiah (2 Esdras)	Nehemiah (2 Esdras)
		Tobit (Tobias)	Tobit (Tobias)
		Judith	Judith
Esther	Esther	Esther (and additional 103 verses)	Esther (and additional 103 verses)
		1 Maccabees	1 Maccabees
		2 Maccabees	2 Maccabees
			3 Maccabees
			4 Maccabees
Iyov (Job)	Job	Job	Job

WHAT IS THE BIBLE?

Hebrew Scriptures (24 books)	Protestant OT (39 books)	Catholic OT (46 books)	Eastern Orthodox OT (51 books)
Tehillim (Psalms)	Psalms	Psalms	Psalms (and Psalm 151)
			Prayer of Manasseh
Mishlei (Proverbs)	Proverbs	Proverbs	Proverbs
Qoheleth (Ecclesiastes)	Ecclesiastes	Ecclesiastes	Ecclesiastes
Shir Hashirim (Song of Songs)	Song of Solomon	Song of Songs (Canticle of Canticles)	Song of Songs (Aisma Aismaton)
		Wisdom	Wisdom
		Sirach (Ecclesiasticus)	Sirach
Yeshayahu	Isaiah	Isaiah (Isaias)	Isaiah
Yirmeyahu	Jeremiah	Jeremiah (Jeremias)	Jeremiah
Eikhah (Lamentations)	Lamentations	Lamentations	Lamentations
		Baruch with Letter of Jeremiah as the sixth Chapter	Baruch
			Letter of Jeremiah as standalone book
Yekhezqel	Ezekiel	Ezekiel (Ezechiel)	Ezekiel
Daniel	Daniel	Daniel (and additional material)	Daniel (and additional material)

Hebrew Scriptures (24 books)	Protestant OT (39 books	Catholic OT (46 books)	Eastern Orthodox OT (51 books)
Trei Asar (The Twelve)	Hosea	Hosea (Osee)	Hosea
	Joel	Joel	Joel
	Amos	Amos	Amos
	Obadiah	Obadiah (Abdias)	Obadiah
Trei Asar (The Twelve)	Jonah	Jonah (Jonas)	Jonah
	Micah	Micah (Micheas)	Micah
	Nahum	Nahum	Nahum
	Habakkuk	Habakkuk (Habacuc)	Habakkuk
	Zephaniah	Zephaniah (Sophonias)	Zephaniah
	Haggai	Haggai (Aggeus)	Haggai
	Zechariah	Zechariah (Zacharias)	Zechariah
	Malachi	Malachi (Malachias)	Malachi

There is a lot of similarity between the Hebrew Scriptures and the Christian – particularly Protestant – Old Testament, but there are also differences in terms of the details of the text. Seemingly because there was no closed Jewish canon in the decades after Jesus' death, early Christians studied and referred to different collections of Hebrew Scriptures, including the Septuagint and later Greek translations. Because of this, early Christian collections of Hebrew Scriptures differed in some respects from each other and from the tradition that was eventually authorized by the Jewish community.

Up until 382, when Jerome began the Vulgate, leading Christians actually preferred Greek versions of the Hebrew Scriptures to the Hebrew versions, perhaps because they seemed to offer more support for Christian claims to Jesus' being the Messiah.

For example, the Septuagint has Isaiah 7.14 prophesying that a *virgin* will be with child whereas the Hebrew equivalent said only *young woman*, reducing the impact of the miracle of the incarnation.

Jerome's decision to refer back to the Hebrew, only referring to the Septuagint in order to clarify the meaning of obscure passages, was theologically significant and played a part in the division between Christians who used Latin and looked to Rome, and Christians who carried on using Greek and looked to Constantinople (later Byzantium, modern Istanbul), a division that would come to a head in the Eastern Schism of the eleventh century and the ongoing separation between the Western, Catholic and Eastern Orthodox churches.

The Apocrypha

Today Protestants call the books that were unavailable to Jerome in Hebrew the Apocrypha; they may be included in an appendix at the end of Protestant editions of the Bible or published separately. Luther argued that these works were later and less reliable, not to be relied upon in points of doctrine.[19]

Roman Catholics describe some of the same works as Deuterocanonical (literally, 'second canon') and Eastern Orthodox Christians describe some of them as Anagignoskomena (literally, 'worthy of reading'), but both Catholics and Eastern Orthodox Christians include most of the Protestant Apocrypha in their canons.

The term Pseudepigrapha, literally meaning 'falsely attributed', is used to describe all those biblical and apocryphal works said to have been written by somebody who could not have written them, probably to imbue a later text with a sense of authority it would not otherwise have had.

---

19 Arguably the books and sections edited out of the Protestant Bible by Luther could be seen to disagree with his claim that practices like praying for the dead, worshipping saints and being justified by acts rather than faith alone were unbiblical. There might have been considerations other than the historical origin of the texts when determining the Protestant canon.

Lists of pseudepigraphical works vary but often include the following:

- 3 and 4 Maccabees
- Assumption of Moses
- 1 and 2 Enoch
- Book of Jubilees
- 2 and 3 Baruch
- Psalms of Solomon.

Of course, there are works in the Christian New Testament and New Testament Apocrypha as well, which may be pseudepigraphical. These include:

- Ephesians
- Colossians
- 2 Thessalonians
- 1 and 2 Timothy
- Titus
- The Gospel of Peter
- The Gospel of Barnabas
- The Gospel of Judas
- Paul's Letter to the Laodiceans.

Conclusion

The Bible is in some sense more a library than a book. It contains works in different languages, from widely different dates (c.750 BC–AD 200) and places of origin (Babylon in modern Iraq and Rome in modern Italy), of different genres and purposes, theological and secular.

2

Translating the Bible

It is clear that translation really matters. Anyone who has studied a language will know that few words have direct equivalents. Because of this and because the concepts words evoke differ between languages and cultures that use them as well, translation is much more of an art than a science.[1] Further, failure to render the text of the Bible in a way that communicates genre, rhyme, rhythm, idiom, homophones, homographs or even the literal meaning of names can contribute to misunderstanding. Biblical literalism might be less common if English readers read about God creating 'earth-man' (Adam) and 'earth-man's' sons, 'possession' (Cain) and 'pasture' (Abel), arguing over what sacrifice might be acceptable to God – or 'without people' (Avram) being transformed into 'father of the people' (Abraham) through God's Covenant – all of this is apparent in the original Hebrew.

The sheer importance and many pitfalls of translation made the Church extremely wary of it for centuries. In part because of the wariness of the Church, early translators worked independently, producing their own version of the Bible, which reflected their own answers to the difficult questions outlined above. Because of this, early translators had a big influence on how the Bible was understood and actively shaped theology. To take just one example: in translating the New Testament into English, Tyndale made Jesus' earthly father Joseph into a carpenter (the Greek word *tekton* just means 'workman'). Given that Nazareth perches on a barren rocky hilltop, it seems unlikely that Joseph could have been a carpenter; Tyndale's choice of word encouraged English

---

1 There is a lot more detail about language issues in both Chapter 3 and the Postscript.

readers to place Christ's family as skilled artisans rather than labourers.

In part because of the influence a single translator could have, as soon as it was possible, teams of the most able scholars worked together to produce better and better versions of the text. However, translation, even by committee, remains an art and not an exact science. Good translators tread a line between word-by-word accuracy and conveying the sense of the text in a way the reader can access.

Look at an online Bible site such as www.biblegateway.com to see the number of different versions of the Bible now available in each major language. To see how translations differ, compare these different versions of the opening words of the Bible in Genesis 1:

- **Young's Literal Translation:** [1]In the beginning of God's preparing the heavens and the earth [2]the earth hath existed waste and void, and darkness [is] on the face of the deep, and the Spirit of God fluttering on the face of the waters.
- **New International Version:** [1]In the beginning God created the heavens and the earth. [2]Now the earth was formless and empty, darkness was over the surface of the deep, and the Spirit of God was hovering over the waters.
- **Common English Bible:** [1]When God began to create the heavens and the earth [2]the earth was without shape or form, it was dark over the deep sea, and God's wind swept over the waters.
- **Good News Bible:** [1]In the beginning, when God created the universe, [2]the earth was formless and desolate. The raging ocean that covered everything was engulfed in total darkness, and the Spirit of God was moving over the water.

Note how the Good News Bible is the least accurate translation, although it is probably the easiest to read. For the purposes of textual study it is important to choose a translation of the Bible that is recognized as being very accurate. Examination boards and universities usually give recommendations, but as a general rule Protestants could look for NRSV versions and Catholics for the NJB, but a widely available compromise would be the NIV, which renders the sense of the Hebrew and Greek quite accurately.

Textual Criticism

Having decided which books to include in the Bible and in which order, the next challenge to face scholars, Jewish and Christian, was to decide which *version* of each text was authoritative. Although the degree of variation between manuscripts is amazingly small, some significant variations exist even within the Hebrew tradition, and these really matter because of the degree of scrutiny biblical texts are subject to and the use they are put to in inspiring and supporting theological reasoning.[2]

Before the invention of the printing press, books were copied by hand, and scribes being human, texts gradually altered with time. When copying something out by hand it is easy to let one's eye skip between lines when they begin or end in the same way. Also, when something in the source-text reads awkwardly or as if a word or phrase is missing then it is natural for the scribe to insert words to compensate. By collecting and comparing manuscripts, textual critics look for evidence of this sort of change.[3]

Protestant scholars such as Bengel (1687–1752), Griesbach (1745–1812), Westcott (1825–1901) and Hort (1828–92) developed four rules for textual criticism, which are still in use.

1   Bengel argued that the harder reading is to be preferred – that is, that scribes have a tendency to explain or simplify a text,

---

2   See Emanuel Tov, *The Textual Criticism of the Hebrew Bible*, Minneapolis: Augsburg Fortress, 2011, ch. 1.

3   Textual Criticism has been applied to many ancient texts. Starting with the writings of Classical authors such as Homer, it was used to identify additions and annotations in Shakespeare's plays and, in recent years, has even been applied to the Qur'an: the work of Gerd Puin on the manuscript fragments of the Qur'an found in 1972 in Sana'a, Yemen, is most associated with the textual criticism of the Qur'an.

making it easier to read, rather than more difficult; therefore a text that is difficult or awkward is more likely to be original.

2   Griesbach suggested that **the shorter reading is to be preferred**; that is, that scribes are more likely to add than delete and that a concise text is more likely to be original.

3   Westcott and Hort suggested that **quality of witnesses to a text is more important than quantity**; the line of transmission must be considered when trying to identify an original text.

4   Westcott and Hort also suggested that **a text that best explains the existence of the other texts and their variations is most likely to be original**.

Textual critics use these rules to work out what the original text, the archetype, would have said. Some also try to reconstruct the 'family tree' of all the remaining manuscripts of a text, showing how each related to others and in this way arguing that one manuscript should be accepted as the original. This approach is known as stemmatics. Although it is still in use, it has been criticized for more than a century because it depends so heavily on conjecture.

Because textual criticism just seeks to clarify the original meaning of a text and eliminate anything picked up as the text has been transmitted through the centuries, it is perhaps better understood in terms of conservation than restoration. As such it is now within the bounds of acceptable practice even for very conservative Jewish and Christian scholars.

Textual Criticism and the Hebrew Scriptures

In the *Textual Criticism of the Hebrew Bible*,[4] the prominent Jewish Textual Critic Emanuel Tov[5] justifies the need for Jewish scholars to evaluate different manuscript traditions, despite the immense care with which the Scriptures have been preserved. Tov

---

4   Tov, *Textual Criticism*, pp. 2ff.

5   Tov was heavily involved in the publication of the Dead Sea Scrolls.

explains that tiny differences between the manuscript sources or copies of them can have a big impact on the apparent meaning of the text, leading to divergent translations, which matters a lot when believers do not have the language skills to understand that there are different translations and why.

For just one example, Genesis 49.10 can be translated:

- **New International Version** The sceptre will not depart from Judah, nor the ruler's staff from between his feet, until he to whom it belongs shall come and the obedience of the nations shall be his.
- **King James Bible** The sceptre shall not depart from Judah, nor a lawgiver from between his feet, until Shiloh come; and unto him shall the gathering of the people be.
- **Douay–Rheims Bible** The sceptre shall not be taken away from Juda, nor a ruler from his thigh, till he come that is to be sent, and he shall be the expectation of nations.
- **English Standard Version** The sceptre shall not depart from Judah, nor the ruler's staff from between his feet, until tribute comes to him; and to him shall be the obedience of the peoples.

In this case the differences stem from a slight difference in the vocalization of the Hebrew – a matter of a missing dot and dash, a slight gap between letters in ancient, blotchy handwritten manuscripts.

As Tov notes, interest in the written sources for the Hebrew Scriptures began with Christian scholars; Jewish scholars had always interpreted the written Torah alongside the oral Torah and did not put the same emphasis on manuscripts.

- In the third century AD Origen prepared a six-column comparison of the Hebrew text with Greek versions, which is known as the Hexapla, well before Jerome commented on the differences between Hebrew and Greek versions of the Hebrew Scriptures in preparing his Vulgate translations.

- The production of interlinear versions of the Bible in the seventeenth century reawakened interest; scholars such as Richard Simon explored the significance of variations in the source-texts.
- By the eighteenth century Johannes Eichhorn, a German scholar of oriental languages, made significant contributions to the understanding of the development of the Hebrew Scriptures; in the nineteenth century Julius Wellhausen investigated the development of their first six books exhaustively.

Manuscript sources for the Hebrew Scriptures include:

- Some 22 per cent of the texts included in the **Dead Sea Scrolls** are parts of Hebrew Scripture; they attest to the existence of all barring the book of Esther in the first two centuries BC and first century AD.[6]
- The **Nash Papyrus** is a collection of four fragments of a single sheet of papyrus – not part of a scroll; of unknown provenance but probably Egyptian and dating from 150–100 BC.
- **Codex Orientales** 4445; most of Genesis—Deuteronomy 1.33, AD 820–50 (British Museum).
- The **Cairo Geniza**[7] contained fragments of nearly 300,000 Jewish texts dated between the ninth and nineteenth centuries AD, including some fragments from the Hebrew Scriptures, particularly a manuscript of the Prophets bearing the date AD 895.
- **Codex Babylonicus Petropolitanus**; the Latter Prophets, AD 916 (National Library of Russia).
- **Aleppo Codex**; complete, *c.*AD 930 (partly destroyed in 1947, Israel Museum).

6 James C. Van der Kam and Peter Flint, *The Meaning of the Dead Sea Scrolls*, New York: HarperSanFrancisco, 2002, p. 32.

7 A geniza is a storeroom attached to a synagogue, in this case the oldest synagogue in Cairo.

- **Michigan Codex**; complete, tenth century? (University of Michigan Library).
- **Leningrad Codex**; complete, AD 1008 (National Library of Russia).
- **Codex Reuchlinanus**; the Prophets, AD 1105.
- **Erfurt Codices**; complete – E1 around fourteenth century, E2 possibly thirteenth century, E3 possibly eleventh century (Berlin).
- **Scroll 2**; dated AD 1155–1255 (University of Bologna Library).[8]
- **Damascus Keter**; complete, from Spain, 1260 AD (National Library of Israel).

Textual Criticism and the New Testament

In terms of the New Testament there are a huge number of papyrus fragments and other partial or complete manuscripts, ranging from a fragment of the Gospel of John dating to the first half of the second century AD (Rylands Library Papyrus P52, University of Manchester), to the Codex Sinaiticus, the earliest complete copy of the New Testament from the fourth century, to beautifully illuminated Latin translations.

The sheer number and range of differences between manuscripts suggests that the Gospels are more properly understood as products of years of development – much of which took place in various communities far removed in time and place from the subject matter of the Gospel records – than as copies of some original scroll.

New Testament textual criticism has raised questions over the status of the ending of Mark's Gospel (ch. 16), the status of the fourth Gospel account of the woman taken in adultery (John 7.53—8.11), over the references in Luke's passion narrative to Jesus sweating blood and in 1 Corinthians to women being silent in church. Either early manuscripts omit these sections altogether

---

8 A list – with links – to facsimiles of these ancient manuscripts available online can be found at www.animatedhebrew.com/mss/mss_facsimiles.pdf.

or literary analysis of the Greek suggests they were added by another hand.

An example of a prominent textual critic of the New Testament would be Bruce Metzger, who was Professor at Princeton Theological Seminary, served on the board of the American Bible Society and United Bible Societies and worked on both the Revised Standard Version (RSV) and the New Revised Standard Version (NRSV) of the Bible. In the UK Henry Wansbrough would be a good example of a New Testament textual critic. Currently Professor of Biblical Studies at Liverpool Hope University, he served on the Pontifical Biblical Commission and was general editor of the New Jerusalem Bible.

The Language of the Hebrew Scriptures

The spoken language of the patriarchs and their fluid oral traditions developed into written Hebrew during the biblical period. In the first instance it was a consonants-only aide-memoire, which required any reader to have been trained within a tradition of recitation and interpretation. Later, scribes added dots and dashes[9] to indicate vowel sounds, record pronunciation and reduce the possibility for poorly trained readers to confuse homonyms, which are exceedingly common in a language with only 22 consonants and a structure that requires all verbs to be made up of just three of them!

Numbers are written using letters in Hebrew. Because every Hebrew letter denotes a number, every Hebrew word also has a numerical value. For example, the word Torah (TRVH) has the numerical value 611, and famously the number 18 is very significant, because it is the numerical value of the word Chai, meaning life or living.[10]

---

9 Manuscripts suggest that there was relatively little variation in these between the last centuries BC (e.g. the Dead Sea Scrolls, found at Qumran) and the Middle Ages. However, the formalization of the so-called Masoretic Text, the tradition from which most modern Scriptures are copied, did not occur until around the tenth century AD. The Torah Scrolls are traditionally copied without vowel pointing and recited by trained people, using the text as an aide-memoire.

10 See www.jewfaq.org/alephbet.htm. Within Judaism, mystics have long been

Only tiny bits of biblical manuscripts seem to have been written in Aramaic – only 250 verses out of a total of over 23,000. Arguably, larger portions might have originated in Aramaic, being translated later into Hebrew. Aramaic was widely spoken through and after the exile and uses the same script as Hebrew, although the pronunciation of words differs. Some scholars have argued that other Ancient Near Eastern Languages such as Ugaritic or Egyptian are referenced through certain words and phrases, and that exploring this possibility might cast light on the meaning of difficult passages – although the great philologist James Barr was an opponent of those who refer to other languages without exhausting the possibilities of the original.

The Language of the New Testament

Most scholars believe that Jesus and his disciples spoke Aramaic but would have had a working knowledge of Hebrew – enabling them to read, recite and even discuss the Hebrew Scriptures – and probably also of Koine Greek, the language of the wider ancient world.

Judging by existing manuscripts, all of the New Testament texts were written in Koine Greek, reflecting the fact that most of their Christian readers would have been Greek speakers. The Koine Greek alphabet has 24 letters and is written in cursive (lower case) script rather than in the block capitals typical of classical times.[11]

The most famous inclusion of an Aramaic phrase in the New Testament is '*Eli, Eli, lema sabachthani?*' (Matt. 27.46), and it is immediately followed with a translation into Greek '(which means "My God, my God, why have you forsaken me?")'. Greek New Testament texts seem to reflect remembered conversations

---

fascinated by the possible hidden numerical meanings of biblical texts.

More recently, 'Bible Code' books have become very popular, in which (mostly) Christian authors claim to reveal messages hidden in the text, whether in the original Hebrew of the Old Testament, in the Greek of the New Testament – or even in translations of the Bible.

11 To get a sense of the Greek New Testament and issues with understanding and translating it, look at www.gospel-john.com/greek/chapter-1.html.

and sayings that were originally in Aramaic; considering the likely Aramaic words makes sense of some passages by showing that there could be wordplay or puns.

An alternative explanation would be that one or more of the Gospels was originally written in Aramaic and only later translated into Greek. Scholars have speculated about this possibility from as early as the second century, but there is little hard evidence to support the theory.

The Form of the Bible

Of course, the Bible incorporates many different types, forms or genres of text; there are long lists of laws, detailed genealogies and authentically horrible histories; there are prophetic incantations, the words of songs – even an erotic love poem (The Song of Songs). The genre of a text can have a big impact on its meaning.

Greek transliteration	Literal translation
eyn archey eyn ho logos *kai ho logos eyn pros ton theon* *kai theos eyn ho logos* *houtos eyn en arche pros ton* *theon*	In beginning was the saying and the saying was toward the God and God was the saying this was in beginning toward the God
panta di autou egneto *kai chowris autou egneto oude* *hen ho gegonen*	all through same became and apart from same became not yet one which has become
eyn autow zowe eyn *kai hey zowey en tow phows* *town anthowpown*	in same life was and the life was the light of the humans
kai to phows en tey skotia *phainei* *kai hey skotia auto ou* *katalaben*	and the light in the darkness is appearing and the darkness not same got- down

For example, when John Donne wrote 'She is all states, and all princes, I', he did not intend people to ask whether he was writing about the relationship between monarchies and the United Nations – because he was writing a poem.

Sometimes the genre of a text is unclear. Sometimes an original text has been redacted, so that in its new context its original form and genre is obscured. At other times genre gets 'lost in translation': what is quite obviously poetic in Greek might read like prose in English; what is quite obviously a legend in Hebrew might read like history in English.

Read the famous opening of John's Gospel[12] in the original Greek and it is clear that you are reading a poem or a hymn.

Yet in translation this might not be understood.

Or Genesis 1.2: 'And the earth was without form, and void; and darkness was upon the face of the deep. And the Spirit of God moved upon the face of the waters' (KJV) might seem odd to the attentive reader; there is a clear difference between God bringing form or order to formless chaos and God creating out of a void, nothingness. However, if the reader is in a position to recognize the relationship between the Hebrew words *theu* (formlessness), *beu* (emptiness), *theum* (abyss) and *emim* (waters), it is clear that the author is playing with rhyme and the relationship between the

Hebrew transliteration	Literal translation
wə·hā·'ā·reṣ hā·yə·ṯāh ṯō·hū wā·ḇō·hū,	and the earth she was without form and void
wə·ḥō·šeḵ 'al-pə·nê ṯə·hō·wm;	and darkness on the face of the abyss
wə·rū·aḥ 'ĕ·lō·hîm, mə·ra·ḥe·p̄eṯ 'al-pə·nê ham·mā·yim.	and spirit of the gods moving over the face of the waters:

---

12 If you are interested in reading the Bible in its original languages, look at www.scripture4all.org, where you can access an interlinear translation of the texts, showing the original words, transliterations, literal and finished translations.

words to suggest 'a more fluid, figurative meaning'.[13] From this perspective it seems inappropriate to try to extract precise meaning from phrases designed to evoke a sense of creation rather than recording it historically or scientifically.

Conclusion

The Bible we have today is the product of human choices – about which books to accept as authoritative, how to arrange them, which version of each book and even phrase to use – and all those before any choice about how to translate and interpret the meaning of the text is made. It is difficult – if not impossible – for modern readers of the Bible to understand its meaning in the same way as historical readers of the Bible, let alone its authors. Modern readers are likely to import or read in connotations that would not have occurred to the author or original audience – and miss the significance of other points. Nevertheless the process of studying the Bible, of telling its story and discussing the possible meaning of its texts, is immensely rewarding.

13   Christopher Hopper, 'Linguistics and the Bible', augustinecollective.org/augustine/linguistics-and-the-bible.

3

The Bible Story

Whatever version and translation we choose today, the Bible tells us probably the greatest story ever told – how God created our ordered world out of primordial chaos, how men and women betrayed him and were punished with mortality, how human history developed through the quest to regain God's trust, Eden and eternal life.

The ancient stories of the seven days of creation, of Adam and Eve and the fall, of Cain murdering his brother Abel, of the great flood and Noah's Ark, of the destruction of the tower of Babel and the division of peoples across the earth, are buried deep in our culture. They have inspired stained glass windows and Russell Crowe movies, Damien Hirst installations and Haydn oratorios, the speeches of Martin Luther King and episodes of the Simpsons. We don't even notice when we use an online translator called Babel, visit an ecological tourist attraction called the Eden Project, read about an international seedbank called the Ark or watch an old episode of *Buffy the Vampire Slayer* featuring 'Adam', but these all draw on biblical ideas and assume a level of biblical literacy.

Of course, we have all heard of Abraham, the father of the people,[1] and how he nearly sacrificed his only son Isaac; all heard of Moses, how he was called by God to tell pharaoh 'let my people go!', to lead them out of Egypt through the divided sea and across the Sinai desert to the promised land. The names of heroes such as David, the shepherd boy who killed Goliath with a slingshot and went on to be a great king, of the humble foreign widow Ruth who looked after her mother-in-law and was rewarded with a good marriage and becoming the ancestor of kings or of the Prophet

---

1 *Av* (father) *ha* (the) *am* (people) in Hebrew.

Daniel whose faith and obedience to the law kept him safe for three days and nights in the lions' den are well known. Yet the details of the Bible story are not as familiar as once they were, despite the efforts of directors such as Ridley Scott!

The Bible Story

It all began with an act of faith. Abram obeyed God's call, set out from home in his old age to start a new life and a new nation.

With his wife Sarai, Abram left from Mesopotamia, the town of Ur, the remains of which are between Basra and Baghdad in modern Iraq. After spending time in Haran (now on the Turkish border with Syria), he travelled widely in Canaan, spending time near Bethel. He visited Egypt before returning to Canaan and settling near Hebron.

Abram believed that obedience to God would be rewarded. He wagered everything he had when he left home – and his blood as well when he circumcised himself and all the men of his tribe. God had promised him descendants and a new and better land for his people to call home.

Eventually the promise was fulfilled. In her old age Sarai gave birth to Isaac ('who laughs'). Abram ('father of no people') became Abraham ('father of the people') and Sarai ('barren') became Sarah ('princess'). The covenant relationship between God and Abraham was sealed when, on the top of Mount Moriah (now under the Dome of the Rock in Jerusalem), Abraham showed that he was willing to sacrifice Isaac but also to listen when God said that human sacrifice was not demanded, only the faith that would render it.

Isaac shared in the faith of his father Abraham. His twin sons Esau ('hairy') and Jacob ('smooth') were brought up to honour God and, like their father and grandfather, they were rewarded by becoming the fathers of nations. Jacob (sometimes called Israel, 'he who wrestles with God') had no fewer than 12 sons, who went on to found the 12 tribes of Israel.

Typically, the 12 brothers did not get on. In particular the youngest brother, Joseph, was disliked because he was arrogant and his father's favourite. In the heat of an argument his brothers attacked him and threw him down a well, telling their parents he had died hunting and producing his precious coat, stained with blood, as evidence. In fact Joseph survived. He was taken into slavery and sold in Egypt but – in time – his cunning enabled him to become vizier, the pharaoh's overseer.

Famine overtook Canaan and Joseph's brothers became economic migrants in Egypt. When they discovered that their brother was alive and in a position to help them, a family rapprochement was called for! The tribes of Israel settled in the land of Egypt, a land of plenty.

For some time it seemed that their faith and obedience had been rewarded with divine protection – until a new pharaoh, who did not know Joseph, was crowned.

Under the new pharaoh the immigrant Israelite tribes, now very numerous and called Hebrews, were enslaved. Brutal laws demanding the death of all newborn male Hebrews were passed in order to control the number of Hebrews in Egypt. Nevertheless one mother managed to save her baby son. She hid him in bulrushes by the Nile, leaving his sister Miriam to keep watch.

Moses ('taken out of water') was discovered by the pharaoh's daughter, who adopted him and brought him up Egyptian in the palace. He knew nothing of Hebrew customs or beliefs but was still offended when he saw his people being mistreated. In an adolescent temper, Moses tried to defend a Hebrew slave and accidentally killed an Egyptian. He became a wanted man and had to flee into the desert.

In exile Moses learnt the virtues of his wandering ancestors. He encountered the God of Abraham, Isaac and Jacob, who spoke to him out of a burning bush. Like his forefathers, Moses showed great faith and obeyed, seemingly against all reason. Speaking out of a burning bush God – who revealed Godself as 'I AM' – chose Moses to renew the covenant by returning to Egypt on the seemingly impossible mission of freeing the Hebrews. God gave him the power to perform signs and wonders to convince Hebrews and Egyptians alike that he acted with divine authority.

When the pharaoh refused to free the Hebrews, Moses, in the name of God, brought down ten plagues on the Egyptian people. With God's help he helped the Hebrews to escape each of these plagues unscathed. When the angel of death took the firstborn son of every Egyptian family, it 'passed over' all the Hebrew homes that showed the sign of lamb's blood on the doorposts.[2] The Hebrews made haste to leave the country, escaping while the Egyptians were at their lowest ebb.

When pharaoh gave chase with his armies, following God in the form of a pillar of cloud and fire, Moses was able to part the waters of the Red Sea with his staff so that the Israelites could pass through dry-shod. God's people had been saved; through faith they were reborn, washed clean by the sea to achieve liberation and the hope of restoration to the promised land. For their part of the new covenant, all they had to do was obey God's commands.

In the desert even Moses struggled to keep the people together. In their wanderings they felt that the God of Israel had left them; they wanted to go over to worship other gods and hoped that by doing so their luck would change. Nevertheless the God of Abraham stayed with them. God revealed the Law to Moses on Mount Sinai so that henceforth everyone might know what to do without relying on prophets and priests to communicate God's wishes.

The tablets of stone on which the Law was written were placed in the Ark of the Covenant, a box covered with the smelted remains of the idols people had set up and the riches they had set aside to insure against disaster. Again the people were called to demonstrate their faith in the God of their forefathers so that the covenant relationship might be restored.

With his brother Aaron, Moses set out a form of worship that brought the people of Israel together in faith and obedience to God. A tabernacle, or portable temple, was created to house the Ark each night and on rest days; otherwise the Ark travelled ahead of

---

2 These events are remembered every year in the Jewish festival of Passover.

the people as they made slow progress towards the promised land, which Moses was allowed to glimpse once before he died.

Arriving in the promised land was one thing; taking control of it quite another. Other peoples had occupied the land, and now the people of Israel faced a series of battles and wars to get it back. Joshua was the leader of this campaign after Moses' death. He secured Jericho against great odds, using the procession of people behind the Ark as a weapon that caused the walls of the ancient city to crumble. Nevertheless it was not for many years that the conquest was in any sense complete.

Throughout this period it seemed that God only granted victory when the people obeyed God's laws and otherwise kept up their faith. The priests and leaders saw that maintaining religious and cultural purity was the key to their claim on the land.

The Israelites settled in the few cities they had seized and in rural areas, leaving other cities under the control of the Philistines, the Canaanites or Jebusites – any of dozens of local peoples, each of whom had their own culture and gods. When, as happened periodically, the Israelites suffered a setback, it was usually interpreted as God's punishment for fraternizing with or even tolerating other people in the land.

As in the time of Jacob's 12 sons, tribes settled together, each taking a portion of the land. The tribes were led by judges, who were more or less effective at securing and expanding their territory. Sometimes tribes worked together and sometimes they did not; sometimes the Israelites were in the ascendancy but at other times they were forced to pay tribute to other peoples and their kings.

The judges who were successful against the enemies of the people owed that success to obeying the law and the customs of the people, to controlling the power of the Ark – but above all to having absolute faith in one God and never worshipping any other.

There was only one Ark, and it could not be within reach of all the tribes all of the time. It was cared for by the tribe of Levi, who took care of the rituals and ceremonies demanded by custom and moved the Ark from one resting place to another. Permanent shrines sprang up to replace the old tabernacle, and each of these started to attract a permanent staff, who would carry out sacrifices and other rituals even when the Ark was not present.

People dedicated children to the service of the shrines, particularly in thanks for God's favour. They were set apart, made to follow a special diet, dress distinctively and sleep in the shrine. One such child was Samuel, dedicated by his mother to the service of God and soon in regular communication with his maker.

Samuel became pre-eminent among the leaders of Israel, but even he came to acknowledge the shortcomings of the existing system of informal government. The people begged him to ask God to give them a proper king like those of their neighbours. Samuel warned of the dangers in vesting such power in one man, but eventually acquiesced and asked God for a king.

Perhaps it was a foregone conclusion that Saul, Samuel's first choice, would fail, given that Samuel opposed the idea of a king and wanted to show that he, and God, still pulled the strings. Be that as it may, King Saul was undoubtedly a disaster, ending up mad and then dead on the battlefield – with his son by his side.

Samuel's second choice seemed just as likely to fail, though for different reasons. Where Saul was an accomplished soldier, a heavyweight from a powerful tribe, David was a shepherd from the smallest tribe, Benjamin. He was a boy with no experience or expectation of power, no qualifications beyond his gift for harp-playing and his way with a slingshot, which had brought him to the attention of King Saul.

Samuel might have had ideas of shaping David into a puppet king – much easier to control than the unpredictable megalomaniac Saul – but God works in mysterious ways and David turned out to be a brilliant leader. He was a gifted soldier, an inspirational general and a devoted servant of God. He reclaimed and rebuilt Jerusalem and then purchased the land on which Abraham had offered up Isaac (a threshing-floor on Mount Moriah, near Jerusalem), drawing up plans to build a magnificent Temple there to house the Ark of the Covenant permanently. David also secured the succession – though in age-old fashion his sons were not satisfied to await their inheritance and continually rebelled and quarrelled with each other.

Solomon, David's youngest son, fulfilled his father's promise. The kingdom was large and secure. Solomon never had to make the compromises his father had made; he was a pure and wise leader who focused on building up wealth, administering the law, building the splendid new Temple in Jerusalem and making strategic alliances.

Sadly Solomon's sons did not inherit their father's flair for kingship. His twins Rehoboam and Jeroboam divided the kingdom between them, diluted the authority of the Temple, frittered away their father's wealth and neglected his political alliances. What had been a relatively large and powerful Israelite kingdom became little more than a few city states buffeted on the fringes of empires.

Israel, centred on Samaria, fell first. In 721 BC, Sennacherib, King of the Assyrians, destroyed everything, deporting the elite and driving many of the people of the ten tribes that made up Israel south to seek shelter with the two tribes that made up Judah. Other cities were destroyed, but Jerusalem narrowly escaped, people thought because of the piety of the Judaean King, Hezekiah. Many wondered why their God had allowed this to happen to God's chosen people. Had they done something to offend God? Was the land not promised anymore? How could they restore the covenant and their fortunes?

Northern prophets such as Amos and Hosea blamed the fall of their kingdom on people's unethical behaviour, made all the worse because God had given the Israelites the law. Salvation could only come, they warned, if Israel repented and became morally pure, showing the faith of Abraham by upholding God's word even when following the law was difficult or dangerous. The Prophet Isaiah went to the court in Jerusalem, encouraging the pious King Hezekiah to resist. Amazingly, Jerusalem survived and the people were assured that God was with them if they prayed, obeyed and showed willing to fight.

The old prophet's message resounded when Judah too was threatened and then attacked, this time by King Nebuchadnezzar in

43

the spring of 597 BC. To begin with people thought their sufferings were due to the corruption of their kings but as things got worse and worse, even after the bad kings had gone, they began to blame each other, saying it was God's judgement for evil behaviour. As the prophets had said, God is just and must punish wrongdoing; everything would be destroyed by God's vengeance and only the tiniest remnant would be left.

The Assyrians had perfected the art of psychological warfare; they had a policy of deporting and resettling whole populations as a means of establishing dominance over conquered lands. In 597 BC and again in 587 and 582, thousands of Judaeans were deported and forcibly resettled; only the poorest peasants were left (2 Kings 24.14).[3]

Far from home and in their imaginations, a group of elite Judaean exiles built their homeland into an ideal of freedom and justice, in stark contrast with Babylonian society. Trained in the courts of Babylon, the generation of priests born in exile used their skills in writing, interpreting and persuading to collect or even construct important parts of the Bible at this time. In exile the songs, stories, prophecies and laws of Judah and, to some extent, Israel became the focus of attention, a way of expressing emotion, rationalizing what had happened and planning for a better tomorrow – as well as of demonstrating one's authenticity and authority as a proper 'Jew'. Hope – that God's anger would pass and that they could return, re-establish the covenant and refound the kingdom – sustained the Jews throughout this period.

Yet despite their harking back and efforts at cultural revival, the Jews were influenced both by Babylonian culture and by their new circumstances, and their religion changed very significantly as a result. Their concept of God developed philosophically, as did their ideas about justice and life after death. They began to recognize that God is everywhere, knows everything and can act

---

3 Evidence suggests that far from being a single united community in exile, the displaced people of Israel and then Judah ended up in cities as far apart as Cyrene in Libya, Elephantine in Egypt, Damascus and Antioch – perhaps even as far afield as Kerala in India.

without limits. They began to see how God can be served in life, with or without sacrificial vessels, how God may forgive and bless even non-Jewish people,[4] perhaps making up for the injustices of this life in some future sort of life, about which only God really knows.

Without a Temple or priests to sacrifice, worship focused on reciting, reading or explaining the Scriptures. Religious gatherings (Greek *synagogos*) led by the elders of the Jewish community probably date from this time and it is likely that they existed in cities across the Babylonian Empire and beyond. So Judaism developed out of Israelite religion and particularly the Jerusalem Temple cult as it was in exile.

The writing was on the wall for the Babylonians and their new King Belshazzar. The conquering Persian emperor Cyrus saw fit to release the Jews, allowing them to return to Jerusalem and start to rebuild their Temple. Perhaps inevitably, the Jerusalem they found failed to measure up to Zion, the city of their dreams. To those who returned, the local people seemed rustic and foreign, their religion crude and unfamiliar; even in town there were no suitable houses, no ritual facilities and precious little food. Work on the rebuilding was slow, back-breaking and expensive; people lost heart and abandoned proceedings time and again, sometimes returning to Babylon or pursuing opportunities elsewhere.

Those exiles who did not return, in company with those who left again, became Jews of 'the diaspora', serving God as they had in exile, by studying the Scriptures and reciting them together in meetings, keeping God's laws and offering only occasional sacrifice when they could visit Jerusalem or send funds. The returnees resented them, believing that if they joined the rebuilding project things would progress much faster, that God would be displeased by lack of commitment and that they were somehow 'letting the side down' by choosing to be bound to money, to reject the freedom of God.

After 609 BC the monarchy had begun to lose status. Despite

---

4 Books such as Jonah reflect these developments and how some people found them difficult to accept.

his righteousness and efforts to restore the covenant, the powerful reforming King Josiah died in battle and the Egyptians and the Assyrians raced to appoint his successor. In 597 BC, King Nebuchadnezzar deported King Jeconiah to Babylon and installed a puppet king, Zedekiah – but he rebelled and was defeated and maimed in 586 BC. The lineage was broken except for Zerubbabel, the grandson of Jeconiah, but his authority to rule was continually questioned, not least because the Prophet Jeremiah cursed the line of Jeconiah (Jer. 22.30).

At this time some prophets prophesied a new shoot (Hebrew *nsr*) coming from the Davidic line (e.g. Isa. 11.1; 53.1), who would be pure, serve God and the people and restore the covenant. This was wordplay: Zerubbabel's name came from the Hebrew root *zra* meaning seed, and he shared some characteristics of ancient Nazirites (Hebrew *nsr*), being a very righteous, zealous man who had trained as a priest in Babylon. The prophets hoped that, as king, Zerubbabel could rebuild both Jerusalem and its Temple, unite the monarchy and priesthood, administer the law of Moses and offer sacrifice on behalf of the people (e.g. Zech. 6). Unfortunately the prophets' inflated hopes came to nothing and Zerubbabel failed in his impossible task. Judah remained an impoverished backwater and its people divided. In time the priests took over the task of restoring the nation, shelving hopes of a new Davidic kingdom until and unless God should rule it in person.

After Zerubbabel's failure the priests added to and reworked the Scriptures as part of an attempt to unify the people. They emphasized their own importance and authority;[5] their leader Ezra was even said to have been taken up into heaven – like Moses and Elijah. Zerubbabel's role was downplayed, although some people came to see remaining references to him as prophecies relating to a future king, an anointed one (Messiah) who would achieve what Zerubbabel had not – unite the people, restore the covenant and usher in a new 'kingdom of God'.

Under the leadership of Ezra, the priests were strict in drawing a line between 'pure' Jew and 'impure' foreigner, demanding full

---

5 Chronicles – perhaps also a full 'Priestly' (P) redaction of the Torah.

ritual participation and total obedience to their authority. They were particularly ruthless in excluding the 'remnant' of people who had remained in and around Jerusalem from any future part in the life of the nation – which resulted in generations of animosity towards the Samaritans, who shared heritage and many beliefs with the Jews but who had been denounced as impure and forced to worship at a different temple.

Being able to write down, read and interpret the laws, histories and customs of the past made the priests the focus and the arbiters of Jewishness. With the fully restored, rededicated Temple the authority of the high priest increased massively. However, outside Jerusalem the synagogue continued to sustain Jewishness. It encouraged men to take responsibility in their community, to educate themselves and their sons, to uphold standards of behaviour and to honour traditions.

On the whole the people of Judah supported the priests but sometimes felt that their leadership lacked pragmatism and was out of touch with their needs. They were also suspicious of the many new ideas and customs that the priests were introducing, preferring traditional, simpler ways of doing things.

Judah slowly recovered and was largely left alone by the descendants of Cyrus the Great and then by the warring inheritors of the vast Greek empire of Alexander the Great, which subsumed Cyrus' Persian lands after the battle of Issus in 333 BC. During this period the Jews were divided over the extent to which they all needed to maintain the cultural isolationism Ezra had demanded after the exile in order to please God.

One major concern was the priestly prohibition on intermarriage between Jew and non-Jew and the definition of Jewishness focused on – female-line – inheritance rather than on faith or even ethical action. 'Historical' Writings such as Ruth and Esther reflect the controversy that developed.

Another major concern was the extent to which Jews could adopt Greek 'Hellenistic' ideas, customs and fashions, which that came to dominate the whole ancient world. Many people welcomed Greek influence; they wanted Jewish cities to provide public baths and beautiful monuments, gymnasia and schools for young men known as *ephebeion*. Many wanted to learn about the world, experiment with mathematics, rhetoric and logic, even have a say in government, but others said that all aspects of Hellenistic culture were incompatible with Jewish law, dangers to the covenant and to be resisted at all costs.

Political factions began to develop:

- The old aristocratic priestly families saw Jewishness and the leadership of the nation as their birthright and were totally against intermarriage. Any attack on the Temple, its purity, pre-eminence or assets was an attack on the 'Sadducee' faction. Nevertheless their education gave these aristocratic priests the ability to interpret the law and other parts of the Scriptures and to explain how it was compatible with elements of the modern world, including Hellenistic culture and philosophical ideas, and some Sadducees felt that so long as they maintained the rituals of the Temple and preserved the Scriptures, Jewishness was not a requirement to retreat into cultural isolationism – at least not for educated people, so long as they kept the bloodlines pure.
- The developing urban middle classes and the many less aristocratic priests saw Jewishness in ritual terms. The more the people behaved in the right way, the more they sacrificed and donated in the Temple, read the Scriptures and observed the letter of the law, then the more God might be expected to favour them and the better off everyone would be. Any attack on or attempt to change the customs and traditions of Judaea was an attack on the 'Pharisee' faction – they rejected intermarriage and were extremely suspicious of any and all Hellenistic influences.
- Local tribespeople saw Jewishness as a national phenomenon, dependent on preserving ancient customs and on military success. They wanted to recreate a powerful Jewish kingdom in the tradition of David and Solomon, crushing their enemies and ruling over them in triumph. They were ready to rebel

against foreign overlords or Jewish leaders who seemed to be collaborating with foreign powers, and fought to the end, using guerrilla tactics or even terrorism when things went against them. The Zealots and, eventually, assassins known as Sicarii ('dagger-men'), usually came from areas outside Jerusalem, particularly Galilee in the north.

Things came to a head around 175 BC. The relatively quiet period of self-rule came to an end with the death of the wise and just high priest Simon II. His sons Onias and Jason disagreed profoundly over the direction the country and its religion should take.

- Onias was a traditionalist who opposed assimilating Greek culture – but he was lazy, avaricious and incompetent.
- Jason was Greek through and through – and an effective operator.

When Onias botched his first tribute-payment to the Ptolemies, Jason seized power and started to reform the country, converting Jerusalem into a *polis*, a modern Greek city with all the trimmings – but even this did not go far enough for some in the 'Tobiad' faction, which comprised the most extreme Hellenizer-Sadducees. The Tobiads supported another priest, Menelaus, in an effective *coup d'état*. When he went to the Seleucid emperor on Jason's behalf to pay tribute, Menelaus promised Antiochus IV more tribute in return for a troop of soldiers to get rid of Jason and his supporters and, to make matters worse, when he arrived in Jerusalem he seized Temple treasure to meet his obligation – and tried to cover this up by having Onias murdered and killing witnesses who had accused him in court, or who threatened to accuse him in court.

Throughout this scandal, Antiochus IV failed to provide justice, but things soon got a lot worse. When Jason seized an opportunity to regain power, in revenge Menelaus encouraged Antiochus to march on Jerusalem, use his armies to depose Jason and plunder what was left of the Temple treasure. Antiochus ended up making the Temple into a fully Hellenistic shrine (featuring a statue of himself), totally forbidding traditional Jewish worship and forcing the priests to sacrifice to idols in order to punish the rebellious people and stamp his authority.

Unsurprisingly, war was the result – a long, bitter conflict involving empire troops.

A Jewish priest from rural Modi'in, Mattathias the Hasmonean, sparked the revolt against the Seleucid Empire by refusing to worship the Greek gods and killing a Jew who offered to sacrifice to an idol in his place. In 166 BC, Mattathias' son Judah, known as Maccabee ('the hammer'), led an army of dissidents to an incredible victory over the Seleucid dynasty. They 'cleansed' the country of all Hellenistic influence, which they associated with the supporters of the Seleucids. They destroyed pagan altars and forcibly circumcised boys, preventing them from participating in athletics and other Greek pastimes in future and marking them for life as Jews.[6]

Judah Maccabee's army fought a notorious guerrilla campaign to victory against all the odds. Eventually Maccabee entered Jerusalem and ritually cleansed the Temple, installing his brother Jonathan as high priest.[7] The Maccabees' victory was sealed when Emperor Antiochus IV suddenly died and the army returned to Syria. The Seleucid commander agreed to a compromise – possibly brokered by Menelaus – that restored religious freedom to the Jews.[8]

Following the rededication of the temple, the supporters of the Maccabees were divided over the question of whether to continue fighting or not. The war had originally aimed to end Seleucid oppression; however, many ended up wanting to continue, to conquer other lands with Jewish populations, even to convert their

---

6 By this time many Jewish parents did not circumcise their sons and some men even tried non-surgical means of restoring their foreskins, so that they could avoid the stigma associated with being Jewish when participating in Greek life – a surprising amount of which involved being naked!

7 The Jewish festival of Hanukkah celebrates this occasion. According to tradition the Maccabees could only find one small jug of oil to feed the lamp in the Temple, but it miraculously lasted the whole eight days until more oil was found.

8 It is unclear, therefore, whether the victory was entirely that of the Maccabees – or whether the restoration of the Temple was due to other factors.

peoples. This became yet another major point of division in an already shattered religio-political landscape, and would go on to fuel the rebellions in the first and second centuries AD, which led to the eventual destruction of Temple and country.

In the end the new Hasmonean dynasty lasted no longer than previous dynasties. The military talent of its kings was short lived and they were divided between pandering to the Greek-leaning aristocracy, the Sadducees, and appeasing the righteous traditionalists among the middle class, the Pharisees. In 67 BC this division widened and civil war broke out. An enterprising Idumean official known as Antipater played the situation to his own advantage; the Romans intervened and Antipater ended up running Judaea on their behalf, though a Hasmonean (Hyrcanus) was kept on as puppet king.

Antipater's son Herod, already a ruthless warlord and devious politician, was appointed to rule Galilee at the age of 25. When King Hyrcanus was deposed for a second time, Herod went to Rome, got himself appointed 'King of the Jews' and returned at the head of Roman armies to claim his prize and establish a new 'Herodian' dynasty in Jerusalem. As a 'foreign' Idumean – and possibly the distant descendant of a slave – Herod was despised by both the Sadducees and the Pharisees. His vast wealth, brutality and cosiness with the Romans didn't help win the people over. Although Judaea was peaceful and prosperous during this period, although Herod rebuilt the Temple on an epic scale, adorned the country with fabulous castles and monuments, the Jews were almost united in opposition to their king.

Herod the Great reigned from 37 BC to 4 BC, but his final years were miserable. His wives and sons plotted and were executed in turn, his health deteriorated until he was a mass of suppurating flesh and worms. When he died he was immured in one of his castles, the grave allegedly hidden in case successors tried to wreak revenge on his corpse.

Naturally Herod's surviving sons couldn't live up to their father's legacy. Rome took a more active role in Judaean politics and Antipas, Archelaus and Philip had limited power and declining authority, even though they carried the title of Tetrarchs. The real axis of power lay between the priests (whose council was known as the Sanhedrin) and the Roman Prefect (later Procurator) who administered power in the region on behalf of the governors.

The priests were anxious to maintain power in their own hands. They tried to keep the Temple 'pure' and free of foreign influence, encouraging people to buy 'pure' sacrifices with a 'pure' Temple currency and participate in elaborate ceremonies from which non-Jews were excluded forcibly. They led the Jews in refusing to offer the normal Roman military service, in refusing to worship the Emperor, in refusing to tolerate other beliefs from being practised in their cities. They encouraged people to revive Jewish traditions and observe religious laws more strictly, to pay Temple taxes on top of the Roman taxes. They were playing with fire, treading a fine line between preserving national identity and inciting rebellion, and continually tempted to play to the local audience despite Roman opinion mattering much more.

Taking advantage of being part of the Roman Empire, landowning aristocrats grew very wealthy; ordinary Jewish people struggled to serve two masters. Priests from wealthier families invested in elaborate new houses with multiple private ritual baths – suspiciously like the public baths they banned poorer people from using for being Greek. They linked their homes to Herod's new Temple with beautifully engineered Roman bridges so they didn't have to battle through hoi polloi on their way to work.

All this caused some of their poorer colleagues to baulk. What happened last time Judaism was allowed to be polluted with foreign ideas? Surely God will be angry with everybody again unless these few greedy and selfish fools listen to reason! Why should Romanized hypocrites call all the shots? Shouldn't those who actually cared about preserving the purity of the Laws and traditions of Judaism be in control of them?

But Sadducees and Pharisees working together against the Romans couldn't last for long!

Politics became more and more complex, religious leaders competed with each other for the peoples' affections and another major rebellion became a real prospect. The Roman Prefects had a terrible job keeping a lid on a bubbling cauldron of unrest and political intrigue and collecting taxes to recoup the spiralling cost of administering the province on behalf of absentee governors.

Prophets had long preached the end of days. They foretold a terrible final judgement in which God would punish all human wickedness, liberate the oppressed, reward the good and start again with a new Eden, an ideal, just kingdom. From the third century BC, through the Hasmonean and Herodian kingdoms, the end of time seemed to be drawing closer. The Temple started to feel like a house of finance rather than of prayer; the priests were more worried about power and enjoying the riches of foreign civilizations than serving God or acting in the interests of God's people.

Some people despaired of being able to live a good life in ordinary villages and towns. They felt that the polluting influence of Greek and Roman culture, the pressure of taxation and the filth of politics made it impossible to follow God's law and earn any possibility of salvation. The Essenes withdrew from ordinary life into monastic communities in the desert, where they tried to remain pure and ready for the final judgement.

Others interpreted the struggle for purity in a different way. The Zealots and Sicarii took up arms and plotted assassination, sabotage and armed revolution. They were willing to lay down their lives as testament to their faith and fervent desire to restore the covenant. Perhaps, through the blood of their sacrifice, the land could be washed clean of corruption and restored to how it was in the days of Abraham.

Popular leaders inspired revolts that were more – or usually less – successful in wresting power from the Romans. People often saw revolutionary leaders in terms of the 'Messiah', a God-given King, who they believed had been promised by the prophets to herald a new beginning in the Jewish covenant relationship with God.

At the end of the rule of the fifth Prefect of Judaea, Pontius Pilate (26–36 AD), a small group of Galileans known as Nazarenes became convinced that the Romans had just martyred the Messiah (Jesus) – but that they hadn't prevented a new Covenant from being established with God, supported by a more complete law and a firm promise of eternal life in a new kingdom.

Initially Jesus had been associated with the popular preacher John the Baptist, but soon – when John was imprisoned and then executed by the Tetrarch Herod Antipas – Jesus surpassed him. His teachings caught the public imagination, particularly in the hard-pressed villages of Galilee. Unlike other rabbis, Jesus taught with *authority* – not just stringing together quotes from Scripture (although he was perfectly capable of doing that) but making sense of them for ordinary people by using a range of colourful stories (parables), practical demonstrations (signs) and even by working miracles (driving out evil spirits and healing the diseases and disabilities that condemned many people to a life on the margins of society).

Jesus was careful not to preach against the Roman authorities directly and encouraged his followers to be peaceable, practising the sort of non-violent direct action later employed by Gandhi and Martin Luther King to such effect – of course, they both got the idea from reading the Bible. Nevertheless Jesus was a big threat because:

- He undermined the tetrarchs, priests, local scribes and rabbis who administered power on Rome's behalf, exposing their venality, corruption and how they had distorted the meaning of Scripture for their own ends.
- He had a way of getting Roman servants like soldiers and tax-collectors to repent and stop being ruthless and efficient.
- He attracted large crowds of people to leave their homes, families, farms and boats to follow him from place to place, the length and breadth of the country.
- His miracles often caused near-riots as people clamoured to get close.
- He gave hope to the marginalized and oppressed, to the poor and to women, so that they would no longer just accept being

54

treated badly, and would demand justice and publicly draw attention to injustice.

Most dangerously of all, he encouraged people not to fear death or be attached to earthly things but act together for certain heavenly reward. This was explosive stuff – just think what we call preachers who encourage people to abandon their families and earthly possessions and embrace death without fear today!

Jesus' prophecies of an imminent and awful divine judgement and his calls for repentance and the restoration of the covenant beforehand were fairly typical of the time. His habit of calling God *Abba* (Aramaic for 'father') and speaking quite confidently on God's behalf – predicting the future, describing God's kingdom, promising how God would honour promises made in Jesus'/God's name – were not, and caused real offence to some Jews whose understanding of monotheism did not include the idea of God having a son!

The polytheistic Greeks and Romans had little problem with the idea that Jesus had semi-divine status – they expected it of all powerful leaders and heroes. Perhaps because of this it was soon among non-Jews and Hellenized Jews living outside Judaea (the diaspora) that Jesus and his disciples started to attract most new followers. A few prominent, educated people joined Jesus' disciples soon after – and perhaps because of – his death.

Handed over to the Romans by the Sanhedrin on obviously trumped-up charges, Jesus displayed superhuman courage and heroic conviction on the cross; he followed through on his idea of non-violent direct action, conclusively exposing the corruption of both Jewish and Roman authorities and, by confronting and accepting the worst imaginable end with dignity and integrity, defeating death and loosing the chains of oppression that fear held most people in.

Just as in our own time the dignity of leaders such as Martin Luther King, Dietrich Bonhoeffer and Gandhi in facing danger and embracing death effected real change, in Jesus' time it enabled ordinary people to believe that death was not the end; that how they chose to live really mattered; that one man really could change the world. Whereas there had not before been a clear idea of a life after death in Judaism, it became absolutely central to Christianity – the key to its survival, expansion and eventual dominance of the Western world.

Luke, a Greek doctor commissioned to find out about Jesus and his followers by a wealthy patron, described how Saul of Tarsus, a prominent Pharisee and Roman citizen, was one of the prominent converts to the Nazarene sect. Using his Roman name, his status as a Roman citizen, his Pharisaic training and skill as a leader, 'Paullus' converted hundreds of people in towns and cities beyond the borders of Judaea – Syrians, Greeks and Romans as well as Jews of the diaspora; movers and shakers as well as poor and marginalized people. Judging by his many letters, preserved in the New Testament, he then instructed them in his own sophisticated blend of ideas gleaned from Pharisaic Judaism, Nazarene teaching and Greco-Roman philosophy, organizing his followers into churches (Greek *ekklesia*) and, in time, a new proto-religion he seems to have called 'The Way'.

Paul's Empire churches were largely independent of the Nazarene elders back in Jerusalem, who were probably headed by Jesus' brother James in the years after Jesus' death. Tension seems to have developed between early Christianity as a development of Judaism, and early Christianity as promoted by Paul.

In Jerusalem and the churches that looked to it for leadership, Christianity was focused on following the Jewish law, which Jesus had not altered by 'one jot or iota',[9] and taking inspiration from the sayings and scriptural interpretations of Jesus the 'rabbi', 'prophet', 'son of man' or Messiah, and from the teachings and personal example of his disciples.

Although despised by the priests, in Judaea early Christians were very much part of the Jewish tradition, marrying, practising circumcision and keeping kosher, closely reading Torah and engaging in rabbinic discussions. In this form, early Christianity was a sort of Protestant Judaism – a reaction against a seemingly

---

9 The smallest Hebrew and Greek letters.

power-obsessed remote hierarchy, a return to simple reading of the texts and ethical living.

In Empire cities, however, Paul encouraged his converts to focus on professing faith in a truly divine Jesus, the 'Son of God' or divine *logos*, and on possessing and accurately preserving the knowledge he passed on about how to attain salvation and on marking points of difference between followers of The Way and everybody else – including Jews. They re-enacted Jesus' final meal regularly, seeing this in terms of partaking in his martyrdom and affirming their willingness to follow suit; they preserved the highly theological letters of Paul and other early leaders and discussed the nature of God, the manner of God's creation, the principles of ethical behaviour Jesus revealed, as well as other philosophical questions.

Around AD 50, leaders of the different factions were summoned to a council in Jerusalem to decide which path Christianity would take in future. Judaean Christians were concerned about Paul's work, considering that he was misinterpreting Jesus' message and leading people, including otherwise faithful Jews, astray. Simon Peter seems to have played a pivotal role in persuading the assembled company to accept the validity of Paul's work; he had himself converted gentiles, had been credited with several miracles and visions and may have known Jesus, all of which gave him authority. James and the elders issued a letter excusing gentile converts from the practice of circumcision but insisting they refrain from idol-worship, eating sacrificed meat and sexual immorality.

They let Paul carry on with his mission – but he did not keep to the spirit of their decision.

Paul split with Barnabas and Barnabas' cousin John-Mark, who went back to Cyprus, and headed westwards into Anatolia with Silas and Timothy. They travelled around Macedonia and Greece, visiting all the wealthy cosmopolitan ports, starting churches and writing letters that displayed a more and more developed and distinctive theology, before returning to Jerusalem in AD 58. Paul's followers certainly did not take part in other religions or eat sacrificed meats – but would not keep full kosher, submit to circumcision or read the law of Moses either! They refrained from sexual immorality to the point of preferring celibacy and ignoring, even mortifying, the flesh.

News travelled before Paul; he was seen as a traitor by the Jewish Christians of Judaea and cities further east, who believed, perhaps with some grounds, that he was encouraging Jews to reject the law of Moses as well as converting gentiles to a distorted version of Jesus' message and giving people a peculiar impression of what they as Christians stood for. Only his arrest by the Roman authorities saved him. Paul revealed his Roman citizenship and was duly sent for trial in Rome (as was his right as a citizen), but not before dividing the Jews by claiming that the Jewish priests' dislike for him was because he was a Pharisee.

During his trials, Paul described himself as a follower of The Way (Greek *o hodos*), 'which they call a sect' (Greek *hairesis*), a word that is used to describe philosophical schools and political parties or factions such as the Pharisees or Sadducees and does not usually have the negative connotations of the word it gave rise to – 'heresy' or even 'sect' – in English. He was described by his accusers as a pest, stirring insurrection among the Jews and, moreover, a ringleader of the Nazarene sect. It is clear that Paul was a controversial figure who had an enormous impact on the development of Christianity, not least because he was among the first major Christian leaders to visit the Church in Rome,[10] where he was eventually executed in AD 64, a couple of years after the death of James by stoning in Jerusalem.

The early churches did not die with their first generation of leaders though – a compromise between James' Judaic sect and Paul's Empire churches was forged, probably by the Church in Rome that came to bear the name of Peter. In the next three centuries, fully fledged Christianity, a way between the extremes of Hellenistic Gnosticism and Pharisaic Judaism, developed under the leadership of charismatic bishops. It would outstrip Judaism

---

10 There is a second-century tradition that places Simon Peter's death in Rome at the same time as Paul's, but this is not well supported by evidence – see www. philologie.uni-bonn.de/philologie/personal/zwierlein/st_peter_in_rome.pdf.

and become the official religion of the Roman Empire. In that it offered salvation and hope beyond suffering and earthly death to all who chose a life of commitment and service – and showed obedience to doctrine and those with the authority to determine it – it is not hard to understand why!

Although this is not recorded in the Bible itself, events in Judaea helped this transformation along. In AD 66, Jewish protests against Roman taxation came to a head. There were attacks on Roman citizens and Rome responded violently, plundering the Temple of its ritual objects – perhaps including the Ark of the Covenant – and executing around 6,000 Jewish people.

The Jewish Wars were bloody and drawn out. In the end, divisions between the Jewish political factions or sects, including the remnant of the Judaean Nazarene sect, contributed to the downfall of Jerusalem and its Temple in AD 70. Even after that the remaining Zealots holed up in fortresses and prevented others from negotiating an end to conflict when there was no hope of survival, let alone victory. With the destruction of the Jerusalem Temple the priests and the wider Sadducee faction lost power. With the defeat of Jewish armies the Zealot and Sicarii revolutionaries were all but annihilated – the last few retreating into a prolonged siege at Masada, which ended by 74 AD with an infamous suicide pact in which nearly 1,000 people died.

In the years after AD 70 the Pharisees, who had come to dominate Jewish politics, forged a new approach to Judaism based on synagogue gatherings, reading and discussing the Scriptures. Sacrifice was now impossible, the priests and their rituals were irrelevant and the aristocratic Sadducee faction was finally ruined; the defining factor in Judaism was now following the law of Moses to the letter. Pharisaic rabbis, trained in reading and interpreting the Hebrew Scriptures for the people, led communities; their teachings eventually became the Talmud, which underpins modern Judaism.

There were those who wanted to restore Judaea by violence, vindicating their ancestors' memories. Between AD 115 and 117, hundreds of thousands of Roman citizens – and local Christians – were killed by Jewish rebels in Judaea and other provinces across the Empire. They destroyed temples, churches and other public buildings associated with Roman authority or idolatry. Legions were sent in, from Libya to Iraq, Cyprus to Egypt as well as to Judaea. Jewish rebels were executed but campaigns to put down Jewish rebellion were not decisive and spelt the end of Roman ambitions in Mesopotamia. The campaigns came to be known as the 'Kitos'[11] war and although seldom remembered today, contributed to the sense that Jews, and anybody associated with them, were potential enemies of the state.

It took the 'Bar Kokhba' ('son of a star') revolt of AD 132–6 to put an end to hope. It all seems to have begun when the Romans announced plans to rebuild Jerusalem as a Roman city, 'Aelia Capitolina', which may have included the rebuilding of the Temple. Simon Bar Kokhba, who was accepted by some as the promised Messiah and took the title *Nasi Israel* (Prince of Israel), established an independent kingdom for more than two years before the Romans could mass their armies – from as far away as Britain – to march against him. The Roman writer Cassius Dio claimed that 580,000 Jews were killed, and 50 fortified towns and 985 villages razed in the ensuing war.[12] A rabbinic Midrash claimed that, in addition to Bar Kokhba, the Romans executed ten leading members of the Sanhedrin, including the high priest, using agonizing tortures: Rabbi Akiba – who had first claimed Bar Kokhba as Messiah – was flayed, Rabbi Ishmael had the skin of his head pulled off slowly, and Rabbi Hanania was burned at a stake. The Middle East is no stranger to this sort of horror.

The remaining Jewish population was finally banished from Judaea or sold into slavery. Not until the dawn of the twentieth century did Jerusalem and its surrounding lands play a significant role in Jewish history again.

The Bible story, the story of the promised land, its chosen people and their covenant with God was well and truly over.

---

11 After the Roman general in charge, Lusius Quietus.

12 Cassius Dio, *Roman History*, Book LXIX, 14:1–2; pp. 447–51, in the Loeb Classical Library.

4

So is the Bible Story True?

We are philosophers, so we are constitutionally unable to give a straightforward answer to such a big question.

It really depends on what you mean by *truth*. The answer is far from straightforward.

Truth affects every aspect of biblical studies; it is not possible to answer a question about the meaning of a text – whether people or places really existed, which version of a teaching is the right one, whether the Bible has been interpreted and applied correctly – without having a concept of truth, stated or otherwise.

In fact 'truth' means different things to different people. The **Enlightenment** still casts a shadow over – or illuminates, depending on your point of view – the way most people think and speak today. In an Enlightenment world view, human beings, through reason, could access the truth and have objective knowledge of it. In this way:

- Columbus EITHER did, OR did not discover America in 1492;
- the universe EITHER did, OR did not have a beginning;
- the Mona Lisa EITHER is, OR is not beautiful;
- Shakespearean sonnets EITHER are, OR are not greater than sonnets by Byron;
- 2+2 EITHER does, OR does not = 4;
- democracy EITHER is, OR is not the best mode of government;
- circumcising baby boys EITHER is right, OR is wrong;
- God EITHER does, OR does not exist ...

In such a world view the meaning of any statement or claim is EITHER true OR false – unless the statement or claim is essentially meaningless. The Bible contains many claims or different types – historical, theological, ethical – and these must EITHER be true OR be false OR be meaningless.

Yet gradually popular culture is coming to terms with the demise of the Enlightenment world view and the rise of a postmodern one. In such a world view there is no way anybody can claim objective knowledge because the way each one of us sees the world is coloured by our perspective – by gender, race, religion, age, place in time and space. Truth claims can only ever be *subjective*. In this way:

- the Battle of Waterloo BOTH was a victory for liberty AND was a victory for tyranny, depending on your point of view;
- for physicists the Big Bang caused the universe AND for Christians God caused the universe;
- Tracey Emin's unmade bed can be BOTH a brilliant work of art AND a colossal joke;
- it is BOTH true that *Frankenstein* is the story of an active agent exposing and criticizing society's oppressive economic and ideological systems AND true that it is the first great science-fiction novel;
- it is BOTH true that 2+2=4 AND that 2+2=4 is an example of how mathematicians have forced the world to conform to conceptual architecture that has its roots in how the human brain operates, not how things really are;
- democracy is BOTH the best form of government to American politicians AND the worst example of Western corruption to some Muslim extremists;
- female genital mutilation is BOTH right within certain African communities AND wrong according to UK law;
- God BOTH exists within faith communities AND does not exist within atheist communities.

It is time to explore the philosophy of reading the Bible, finding out more about these two models of truth, where they came from, their strengths and weaknesses and why postmodern thinking is gradually replacing an Enlightenment thinking, so as to put different Christian, Jewish and atheistic attempts to answer to the question 'So is the Bible true?' in some sort of context.

The Philosophy of Reading the Bible

In 1781 the Enlightenment philosopher Immanuel Kant started his critical exploration of philosophy by asking 'What can we know?', a question closely related to that of truth.

Before Kant, philosophers had been divided into two camps.

Following Plato the majority of philosophers saw ultimate reality as metaphysical. Our eyes can deceive us (a stick appears to bend when it enters water), and so can our ears – all our senses in fact. Sensory experience can be faulty, differs between people, changes over time and makes no sense without being processed into ideas and concepts. For Plato, the physical world is like a shadow of an ideal world where the essence or forms of things exist timelessly, spacelessly, unchangingly, perfectly. The physical world and sense experience thus relates to reality but is not in itself ultimate reality. In order to grasp the way things truly are, people have to reflect on what they have seen/heard and so on rationally, contemplating the nature of things and the logical relationships between them to get closer to experiencing reality. It is possible to understand truth without much reference to sense experience at all, with sufficient mental effort.

- In modern terms, think of mathematicians and theoretical physicists. They don't spend a great deal of time fussing about in laboratories. They arrive at ultimate truths about the universe through mathematics, pure reason, logic, without reference to experience – though their most elegant equations can get Philae to land on a comet, make mobile phones work and model the spread of Ebola.

Following Aristotle, other philosophers rejected what they saw as metaphysical speculation and got right back down to earth. Reality is, they reasoned, what we experience, not what we might think or dream about. It is possible to conceive of unicorns and universal forms, dragons and demons – but we *never* experience them in the real world. What we see, hear, smell, touch and taste must be the ground and ultimate test of all knowledge and all claims about reality, ultimate or otherwise. Of course, people make sense of what they have observed through reason; ideas and concepts on their own cannot yield reliable knowledge.

- In modern terms, think of experimental physicists, astronomers and geneticists making painstaking observations, gathering massive amounts of data to support each hypothesis.

Kant argued for a middle way, suggesting that knowledge does start with experience, *phenomena*, things we can touch, smell or see, which offer us the most certain *practical* form of knowledge, but that mathematics or logic can take us well beyond what can be verified through the senses and open up *pure* knowledge about the way things are in general, laws of nature.

For Kant, reason is paramount and able to access something very close to ultimate reality, to bring together sensory experience and conceptual understanding. Reason uncovers a universe that is ordered, regular and able to be described – to a point. Importantly, for Kant there is no way anybody can claim to know about things beyond possible human experience, independently of the framework of time and space that confines and defines us. As he remarked, 'Thoughts without content are empty, intuitions without concepts are blind. The understanding can intuit nothing, the senses can think nothing. Only through their unison can knowledge arise.'[1]

Human beings cannot have a 'god's eye view' of the universe or truthfully claim *objective* knowledge of things in themselves (*Ding an sich*), *noumenal* existence. For Kant, all human knowledge is *subjective* because it starts with practical experience and utilizes concepts that cannot escape space or time. Human beings cannot conceive of ultimate reality beyond space and time,

---

1 *Critique of Pure Reason* A51 / B75.

beyond the fabric of reality that we perceive – but that does not mean that such ultimate reality does not exist. It must, although nobody can understand it, know or describe it.

Consider how the following three different world views relate to religious belief and attitudes to the Bible.

For Plato, ultimate reality is metaphysical; physical reality is limited, partial, imperfect and corrupt. Human beings can understand something of ultimate reality through reason, but we are held back by our physical existence. Words signify rational concepts and, when properly understood, can describe ultimate reality. It is easy to see how this fits in with religious beliefs about God's perfect metaphysical existence and human beings' relationship with God. By this approach, the Bible is witness to God's metaphysical truth; its words, when properly understood, are signposts to truth. Reading the Bible offers the truth that will set people free, giving them a way of seeing beyond, and in the end escaping, the toils of physical existence.

For Aristotle, ultimate reality is encountered through sense experience. Experience is the basis for natural laws, which explain them and govern the behaviour of all things – including human beings. There is no way that human beings can claim to know about metaphysical reality, whether the universe has a beginning or end, what might or might not exist outside it. All we can do is study our world and try to make sense of it, so that we know how best to live and flourish; this is called natural philosophy. In terms of religious belief, if God exists, God is beyond human understanding. Natural philosophy suggests that a prime mover, first and sustaining cause is necessary to explain why contingent things exist, but this would be completely other, beyond human ability to describe and certainly not some anthropomorphic deity who works miracles, speaks to people or rewards people with an afterlife. The Bible is a primitive human record of and explanation of experience, which should be replaced by better-informed records and explanations as they arise.

For Kant, ultimate reality is unknowable. God probably exists, but human beings cannot claim to have knowledge of or revelation from God. Typically, as a philosopher of the Enlightenment, Kant thought that human beings must focus on the world they experience and the rational principles evident in that experience. If anything, religion should be revised to be compatible with reason and to serve the interests of society and world peace; elements of the Bible that seem to contradict reason and might therefore obscure peoples' understanding of reality should be kept only for the purposes of study.

Kant's readers were divided in their response to his work, and there was what Michaelson has called a 'divide in the road' in philosophy,[2] which has influenced the development of biblical studies ever since and led to the existence of a range of different understandings of what truth can mean in relation to the Bible.

- On the one hand, some philosophers moved from Kant's argument that nobody can know anything beyond possible experience to saying that *nothing really exists beyond possible human experience*. Human beings are therefore the measure of all things, and truth is defined not in terms of correspondence with some state of affairs outside of human experience, but in terms of correspondence with human experience – Hegel, Feuerbach, Dilthey, Husserl (Hegelianism, phenomenology, some postmodernism).
- On the other hand, other philosophers accepted Kant's arguments about the limitation of reason as a means of providing knowledge beyond possible experience, and either accepted the need to live with doubt (as if suspended over 70,000 fathoms[3]) or looked to intuition, revelation and any other supra-rational way of engaging with ultimate reality – Schleiermacher, Kierkegaard, Barth, Bultmann, Ricoeur (romanticism, liberal theology, existentialism).

---

2 Gordon E. Michaelson, *Fallen Freedom: Kant on Radical Evil and Moral Regeneration*, Cambridge: Cambridge University Press, 1990.

3 Søren Kierkegaard's memorable phrase!

Biblical Hermeneutics

In the late eighteenth, nineteenth and early twentieth centuries a discrete branch of philosophy started to develop that was concerned with the way written words should be interpreted so as to ensure that only the *true meaning* of a text, often the Bible, was understood. Hermeneutics 'stands in the same relationship to exegesis that a rule-book stands to a game ... The rules are not the game, and the game is meaningless without the rules.'[4]

Once rules are established it should be possible to read, understand and explain the meaning of (exegesis) any piece of writing properly, avoiding reading in false meanings (eisegesis), such as those based on one's own theological concerns or contemporary insights.

Here are some questions that hermeneutics might seek to answer:

- Is there any objective meaning in a text – or is it entirely subjective?
- Who defines meaning – the author or the reader(s)?
- If the author defines meaning, what is the role of translators or editors?
- If the author of a text is dead or unknown, is the meaning of their work unknowable or lost? Is there any point in reading it in that case?
- If the reader defines meaning, can one reading be 'better' than another?
- What must the reader do in order to understand a text properly?
- Are there any 'rules' that should be followed? What are they? Why?
- Are different readings of the same text all potentially valid?

---

4 Bernard Ramm, *Protestant Biblical Interpretation*, Grand Rapids, MI: Baker, 1970, p. 11.

Gottfried Herder: The Science of Interpretation

Herder was a pupil of Kant at the University of Königsberg. He made huge contributions to the development of philosophy and theology that are often overlooked. In relation to assessing the truth of the Bible, Herder's philosophy of language and theory of interpretation is important. In *On Diligence in Several Learned Languages* (1764) and the *Fragments* (1767–8), Herder argued:

1   Thought is essentially dependent on language; without language people cannot think and people cannot think about things they can't express in language.
2   Meanings, concepts, derive from the usage of words and do not refer to any independent 'form'.
3   Because of this, concepts – even metaphysical concepts – derive from experience, which itself is made up of physical and emotional sensations.

Following on from 2 and 3, Herder argued that there are marked differences between how different individuals and people in different periods of history form concepts and understand the meaning of words. This makes it extremely difficult to know how to interpret someone else's words, though not impossible.

For Herder, interpretation was more like a science than an art. The meaning of a text is concrete and objective and must be described accurately by the interpreter, although this process is long and difficult. An interpretation is like a scientific conclusion, drawing together as many detailed observations as possible in a logical way and always mindful of the conditionality of its authority. Textual interpretations, like scientific laws, depend on the evidence and are always able to be falsified.

Evidence may be of linguistic and other types and, in part, relies on proper preparation and a process of *Einfühlung*, whereby an interpreter engages in detailed research, reads other contemporary texts, finds out more about the author's world, language and individual psychological type. This process helps the interpreter appreciate the radical difference between the author and themselves, so avoiding projecting their own or familiar ideas and genres onto the text or otherwise identifying too closely with the author. It is acceptable to go beyond the evidence and engage in some conjecture or divination, but this should be clearly acknowledged and open to being falsified.

Herder suggested that the interpretation of texts must never rely on religious assumptions or means, even when the texts are sacred ones, but must instead rely only on secular principles. In addition, interpretation must pay close attention to the genre or original intended form and aim of a text. Genres vary from age to age, culture to culture and even individual to individual. The interpreter therefore faces and needs to resist the temptation to assign a work to a genre with which they are familiar, when the true genre and thus the meaning of the text might be quite different. Further, interpreters must strive to approach texts holistically and not examine short phrases or extracts out of context.

Finally, Herder's philosophy of language had implications for translation. Given that people in different times and parts of the world have different experiences, their concepts may differ from ours and a word in one language cannot be seen to equate precisely to a word in another. The translator must therefore also be an interpreter and make careful, well-supported decisions about how to render a text into another language while retaining its sense.

Herder's Influence

Following Herder it became popular to claim that biblical texts could only be understood by those who had completely immersed themselves in the history, culture and languages of the Ancient Near East. Because of this, after the late eighteenth century many biblical scholars became classicists, archivists, archaeologists, philologists, orientalists – and vice versa.

In addition, Herder's insistence on approaching the text scientifically and with only secular principles led to biblical criticism being associated with atheism; in order to be credible, Christian critics felt obliged to assume a secular standpoint – and atheists felt they had licence to comment on what had mostly before been the preserve of believers.

Particularly – but not only – in Germany, many biblical scholars started to see themselves as scientists, keen to study the development of the folk superstition that was religion in order to show it to be at best a primitive form of cultural expression and at worst a cynical tool of political control. In studying the Bible, scholars were analysing documentary evidence of how superstitious religious ideas and practices developed, casting a cold rational eye over the beliefs and behaviours of naïve, simple people.

For many scholars of the later eighteenth and nineteenth centuries, the question 'What does the Bible mean?' was understood in terms of what it could tell them about what its authors and their communities believed, if and how those beliefs changed over time and why. Biblical scholars seem to have committed the so-called genetic fallacy of confusing meaning with origins. A student might ask 'What does Paul really mean by love in 1 Corinthians 13?; and a teacher of this type might respond:

> The only way to find out is to discover when and where Paul wrote, learn Koine Greek (and probably Hebrew as well), put yourself into his shoes and into his mind, analyse his use of the word elsewhere and the use of the word in other texts he might have read, and then you would be in a position to know.

In *Hard Times*, Charles Dickens shows the problem with identifying the meaning or essence of a thing with its origins or scientifically recorded characteristics:

> 'Cecilia Jupe. Let me see. What is your father?'
> 'He belongs to the horse-riding, if you please, sir.' ...
> 'Describe your father as a horsebreaker. He doctors sick horses, I dare say?'
> 'Oh yes, sir.'

'Very well, then. He is a veterinary surgeon, a farrier, and horsebreaker. Give me your definition of a horse.'

(Sissy Jupe thrown into the greatest alarm by this demand.)

'Girl number twenty unable to define a horse!' said Mr Gradgrind, for the general behoof of all the little pitchers. 'Girl number twenty possessed of no facts, in reference to one of the commonest of animals! Some boy's definition of a horse. Bitzer, yours.' ... 'Bitzer,' said Thomas Gradgrind. 'Your definition of a horse.'

'Quadruped. Graminivorous. Forty teeth, namely twenty-four grinders, four eye-teeth, and twelve incisive. Sheds coat in the spring; in marshy countries, sheds hoofs, too. Hoofs hard, but requiring to be shod with iron. Age known by marks in mouth.' Thus (and much more) Bitzer.

'Now girl number twenty,' said Mr. Gradgrind. 'You know what a horse is.'[5]

Factual explanations are not everything when it comes to gaining real understanding! The approach to biblical interpretation that became popular at the height of the Enlightenment often completely ignored that element of meaning that depends not on the author and historical context but on the reader(s), what a text means to them and what effect it has on their lives and beliefs.

Friedrich Schleiermacher: The Art of Interpretation

Through his *Aphorisms* (1805, 1809–10), *Compendium* (1819), notes (1828, 1832–3) and *Academy Addresses* (1829), Schleiermacher established hermeneutics as an independent and universal academic discipline, underpinning all other subjects and concerned with the particular problems in *understanding* verbal communications and particularly texts, of all sorts.

Reacting against philosophers such as Herder, who saw textual interpretation as a science, Schleiermacher argued that it

---

5 www.gutenberg.org/files/786/786-h/786-h.htm.

is more of an art. He criticized previous approaches to questions in hermeneutics as 'entirely mechanical'[6] and questioned their confidence that following prescribed rules could in any way guarantee understanding.

- On one level, the interpreter must *analyse* the language, genre and formal style of a text, as Herder suggested.
- On another level, the interpreter must somehow *intuit* a meaning that goes beyond what can be understood from analysis of grammar, vocabulary and so on alone.

For Schleiermacher, these two approaches are characteristically masculine and feminine – and both are essential to proper understanding, in the way that both good technique and creative inspiration are necessary in the production of great art.

Nevertheless, like Herder, Schleiermacher argued for:

1 the necessity of only **secular principles** being employed in biblical interpretation;
2 the process of the interpreter **stepping into the mind and world of the author** as central to understanding;
3 the process of acquiring understanding is lengthy[7] and **subject to constant revisions**, with our prior understandings, which Schleiermacher called *Vorverständnis*, being refined and, in time, the interpreter being transformed by the text.

Beyond getting into the mind of the author in question by becoming familiar with his entire *oeuvre*, his preoccupations and influences, the interpreter of the New Testament must enter into the world of the Early Church and come to understand the origins of the author's intentions and how the author's work would be received by its first readers better than the author himself. Schleiermacher

---

6 Friedrich Schleiermacher, *Hermeneutics: The Handwritten Manuscripts*, ed. Heinz Kimmerle, Atlanta, GA: Scholars Press, 1977, p. 175 (see also Aphorism 49 and pp. 176–95).

7 'The Task is Infinite', ibid., p. 112.

famously wrote: 'Each part can be understood only out of the whole to which it belongs and vice versa.' This came to be known as Schleiermacher's hermeneutical circle.

While taking the business of studying the origins of biblical texts seriously, the biblical critic following Schleiermacher would not confuse these origins with the true meaning of the Bible. There is a need for creativity, even inspiration in biblical interpretation. A variety of readings could be entertained and there is no way any one reading could comfortably claim to be true, yet there is no sense that there is no truth or that human beings are the measure of all things either.

The approaches of Herder and Schleiermacher, though different, shared in the Enlightenment optimism about the existence of truth and about the possibility of advancement, however slow, towards it. Their work could be said to be characteristic of a hermeneutic of innocence.

Wilhelm Dilthey: Hermeneutics as Truth in Itself ...

Reacting against Kant's world view, in the 1880s Dilthey set out to develop his own systematic philosophy in which human life (*Leben*) and experience (*Erlebnis*) were the centre, the measure of all things. His approach contrasted with that of Schleiermacher in many respects.

In Dilthey's *Hermeneutical Philosophy*, understanding – *Verstehen* – develops in peoples' minds and to begin with is subjective, but gradually it acquires an independent, objective reality. Understanding is translated into habit, custom and finally institution. Dilthey argued that it is possible to study humanity scientifically by identifying how people express their experiences, by engaging in a *hermeneutical* study of all forms of human expression. Comparing how an individual seems to understand their experience with how other people seem to understand similar experience(s) gives the human-scientist an evidence-based insight into the psychology of the individual and the particular characteristics of their society[8] and enables changes and developments over time to be identified and, perhaps, explained.

Strikingly, Dilthey wrote: 'Only by comparing myself with others and becoming conscious of how I differ from them can I experience my own individuality.'[9]

In his response to the Kantian world view that limited how much of the truth human beings could claim to know, Dilthey had definitely started down the road towards denying the existence of a truth independent of how human beings see things.

In his response to the Kantian world view that seemed to diminish the individual self and his lived experiences, Dilthey raised questions about the possible independence of the self that would end in postmodern scepticism about anyone really existing or experiencing life independently, acting actively or responsibly at all.

Edmund Husserl: Phenomenological Hermeneutics

Despairing of traditional metaphysics, which seemed to see existing things as atoms in a void, Husserl was interested in early psychology, such as in the work of Franz Brentano, which suggested that things might only really exist within the human mind. He rejected this idea but agreed that the idea that we can analyse how things exist as if from a third-person standpoint is ridiculous. For Husserl (like Dilthey), how we experience things from a first-person perspective must be the beginning of philosophy and all human knowledge.

Husserl proposed phenomenology, a new science of human consciousness, to describe and categorize how people really *experience* the world, free of any intellectualizing. In terms of hermeneutics, Husserl was convinced that human beings can come to know the truth and that the beginning of the process was to

8 The relationship between Dilthey's philosophy and that of Hegel is clear to see, although Dilthey takes Hegel's ideas much further than Hegel would have accepted. Hegel's ideas are outlined in Chapter 8.

9 Dilthey, 'The Development of Hermeneutics', in *Dilthey: Selected Writings*, ed. H. P. Rickman, Cambridge: Cambridge University Press, 1976, p. 246.

be clear about what we experience, getting rid of all manner of assumptions, habits of thought, linguistic inferences and so on to arrive at 'pure experience'. A process of analysing phenomena follows, creating a universal understanding of the essential features of each thing, based on how people experience it directly; this yields 'essential essences'. On the basis of pure experiences and essential essences, the philosopher can then construct a phenomenological description of reality.

The significance of Husserl's phenomenology for reading the Bible is that it encouraged scholars to identify the true meaning of the text with their own experience of it. The idea that a text could have an objective meaning independent of how people understand it started to recede.

Martin Heidegger: A New Hermeneutical Circle

Building on Schleiermacher's work but also influenced by Husserl and Dilthey, Heidegger developed the concept of the hermeneutical circle in the 1920s. In order to understand any text or other work of art, the interpreter has to enter into the world in which it was created, in terms of the mind of the artist, influences on them and the nature of the creative act.

For Heidegger, works of art – including texts – are BOTH ordinary things AND have deeper allegorical and symbolic significance; there is a sort of dualism at play that resists logical explanation. It follows that the validity of an interpretation depends on the interpreter understanding BOTH the ordinary world that produced and contains a text AND the language of symbol and allegory that it employs and references, appreciating the text as the product of a creative, artistic imagination.

Against Husserl, Heidegger stood up for a form of existence independent of how people experience things. He embraced aspects of phenomenological method but argued that studying how we experience things can *point us towards* understanding the way things are in themselves, although a complete understanding is difficult to the point of being impossible.

Heidegger influenced Rudolph Bultmann in his work on New Testament interpretation from the 1930s. Consequently Bultmann came to argue that studying how Jesus' message was received originally and over time, through detailed analysis of the New Testament, could point us towards understanding the true essence of what that message means to human beings.

Hans-Georg Gadamer: Understanding Truth is Complicated!

Gadamer was a pupil of Heidegger. He identified the tendency for scholars to confuse the truth with what could be described of the truth, following Kant's division of the two, and sought to address this confusion, contrasting 'method' (philosophical attempts to categorize truth, which always ended up distorting it) with 'truth' (his own attempt at 'describing what is the case').[10]

Gadamer compared communication and the art of understanding it with a game. To explain the analogy, every player and every spectator appreciates that the game exists and is bigger than any one of them, yet without players and spectators it is nothing. The game draws people in to play by the rules yet while following the rules the play of each participant is theirs, with distinctive style and characteristic moves. The movements of an individual player cannot be understood except by understanding that they are playing the game, understanding the aims and rules they are following and thus appreciating how they are playing.

In writing, authors have an aim and certain rules or literary conventions in mind and these – consciously or subconsciously – determine how and what they write. In reading, interpreters compare the writings of one author – in relation to their perceived aims, rules and conventions – with other similar writings, making judgements about the writing much as a spectator might make judgements about a footballer. According to the rules of soccer, an attacking player is skilled if they pass the ball and create or take opportunities to score; a defender would not be praised if they failed to mark and kept running up the field trying to score.

---

10 Hans-Georg Gadamer, *Truth and Method*, 2nd rev. edn from the 5th German edn, London: Sheed & Ward, 1989, p. 512.

Similarly a scholarly argument or literary creation can only be judged if we know the rules by which the author is playing and have some understanding and experience of them.

In relation to biblical interpretation, Gadamer's approach to hermeneutics would suggest that the interpreter must, as Herder, Schleiermacher and Heidegger suggested, immerse themselves in the author's world – but without neglecting the principle that the world depends on the author's contribution as well as the other way round, and the principle that any interpretation proposed will necessarily be relative to the game one considers the author to have been playing and one's broader experience of that game being played by others.

Truth as Coherence

Throughout the twentieth century the work of Dilthey and Husserl gave rise to a whole range of human sciences, which sought to identify and analyse the truth about human understanding as objectified in habits, customs and institutions. Hermeneutics came to be understood as the basis for and framework of truth claims in the human sciences, just as epistemology was the basis for and framework of truth claims in the natural sciences.

In the 1950s and 1960s, the Italian philosopher Emilio Betti built on Dilthey's ideas and reacted against those of Heidegger and Gadamer (see below). For Betti, hermeneutics was the methodological basis for all the humanities and social sciences – interpretations could be judged valid or invalid in relation to the truth that had been objectified through the general usage of a community. In basic terms, if an interpretation fitted in with or served – cohered with – accepted ideas then it was true, and if it did not then it was not true.

Betti's approach encouraged scholars to look beyond themselves, to pay attention to other people's ideas. As Gadamer explained: 'Subjectivity and self-consciousness ... lost their primacy. Now instead, there is an Other.'[11] Following Betti, the

---

11   Hans-Georg Gadamer, 'Foreword' to Jean Grondin, *Introduction to*

biblical scholar cannot work in isolation, aim at contradicting received wisdom or make a name for themselves just by being distinctive. This postmodern approach promotes the virtues of listening, collaborating, tolerating; it was radically different from the typical Enlightenment approach, in which individuality and an adversarial approach to academic study was encouraged.

Paul Ricoeur: The Story of Truth

Ricoeur's approach to hermeneutics was influenced by his experience as a Nazi prisoner of war, during which time he read widely and reflected deeply, not least on the writings of Sigmund Freud.

Ricoeur was constantly aware of double meanings, whereby people express one idea in terms of another – either consciously or subconsciously – and saw that the art of the interpreter is to identify and explain these double meanings for the reader. As he put it, 'Hermeneutics seem to me to be animated by this double motivation: willingness to suspect, willingness to listen.'[12]

The interpreter, whether of a biblical text or other literary work, must always be suspicious and look beyond the superficial meaning for a possible double meaning arising from the author's own interests and/or the traditions of their community. Further, the interpreter must also be aware of the probable effects of their own interests and community traditions on their proposed interpretation.

More interesting still is Ricoeur's work on narrative. Building on ideas of Aristotle (*Poetics*) and St Augustine, Ricoeur suggested that as symbols give rise to isolated thoughts and as metaphors give rise to individual insights, narratives have the potential to project whole worlds in which '[D]isparate elements acquire coherence and intelligibility through plot.'[13] Stories can be true even if the

Philosophical Hermeneutics, New Haven, CT: Yale University Press, 1994, p. x.

12 Paul Ricoeur, *Freud and Philosophy: An Essay in Interpretation*, New Haven, CT: Yale University Press, 1970, p. 27.

13 Anthony Thistleton, 'Biblical Studies and Theoretical Hermeneutics', in John Barton (ed.), *The Cambridge Companion to Biblical Interpretation*, Cambridge: Cambridge University Press, 1998, p. 106.

characters and events they reference are entirely fictitious. That is not to say that truth does not exist, just that stories, like symbols and metaphors, gesture towards a truth beyond themselves, a truth that cannot be captured by clumsy everyday words and can only be hinted at through the special language of double meaning. Just as you would be mad to take 'my love is a red, red rose' literally, trying to take a certain type of story literally misses the point, misses the truth that it contains.

None of the approaches of Heidegger, Bultmann, Gadamer or Ricoeur denies the existence of truth, although all embrace scepticism towards the Enlightenment idea that it can be understood and described. These might broadly be described as existentialist approaches to hermeneutics.

Why does this Matter?

For the Bible story to be true could mean quite different things:

- For an **Enlightenment** thinker, a story is EITHER true OR false. A true story is one in which all the details *correspond* with actual historical events. The story is an honest human attempt to record what happened, what was said and done. By identifying and studying authors we can come a bit closer to what actually happened by allowing for the effect of perspective.
- For a **postmodern** thinker, a story could be BOTH true AND false. A true story is one that speaks to the reader(s), fits in with the way they look at the world or has some sort of strategic value, helping people to develop their thinking in a direction that is useful. Because nobody can claim to anything more than a subjective perspective, there is no such thing as objective truth. Scholars are bound by their own perspective, so there is no way that they can really understand the authors or their intentions.

Typically enough, few scholars are clear about where they are coming from in writing books and articles about the Bible, which makes answering the question about whether the Bible is true very tricky.

- One scholar might say the Bible contains deep truth while thinking that it probably contains a host of historical inaccuracies.
- Another scholar might say that the essential features of the Bible story are borne out by archaeological research, while doubting the substance behind its theological and ethical teachings.

So Where do We go From Here?

In Part Two we will consider the historicity of the Bible, both the extent to which it can be said to give a true record of events, people and places and what the internal evidence suggests about when it was written, why, by whom and to what end. The development and application of historical techniques, including archaeology, source criticism, form criticism and redaction criticism, will be described and explained.

In Part Three we will explore alternative approaches to truth and meaning in the Bible, examining different Christian uses of the Bible and approaches to its meaning, giving separate consideration to feminist and political approaches, before ending by considering an alternative perspective on the truth of and meaning in Scripture.

Following that the Conclusion revisits this question of truth in the Bible story – and asks again why the Bible matters.

PART TWO

The Bible and Historical Truth

5

Digging up the Bible

The most obvious and most ancient way of investigating the historical truth of the Bible is to find independent external evidence of what happened, when and involving whom, which could either corroborate or question the accuracy of the Bible story. The importance of entering into the world of the biblical authors in order to understand the meaning of their work was emphasized by Herder, Schleiermacher and Heidegger, so since the eighteenth century many Christians have seen archaeological and historical research as part of deepening their faith.

Today the discovery of inscriptions or sources that seem to reference the Bible is big news, with websites, newspapers and television channels rushing to turn the spotlight on any archaeologists or historians who claim to be able to answer the question 'So is the Bible true?' – however slight their discovery, however tendentious their interpretation of its meaning and significance.

Of course, archaeology can support the belief that many details of biblical stories are plausible, that events could have happened as described. Many of the historical references already described are inscriptions, reliefs, stela or fragments of papyri; they depend on archaeological context and analysis to establish their authenticity and date. Beyond inscriptions, finds – ranging from a hilltop shrine of similar dimensions to Solomon's Temple to a pavement that could match the description of where Jesus was tried – can help us understand the Bible story better, can help interpreters get into the mindset of biblical authors and understand what they were trying to say more effectively.

However, archaeology can never really prove that the story in all its complexity is true, let alone that it was written at or even very close to the time. How could anyone dig up proof that a group of Israelites passed through the Red Sea or that the sky darkened when Jesus died? What would constitute physical evidence that Moses wrote Genesis or that David wrote the Psalms, beyond later manuscripts – which can always be disputed – claiming such authorship? Even if a team were to discover the remains of a giant picnic of bread and fish by the shores of lake Galilee, there would be no way to establish that it really involved 5,000 people, that they had not brought their own supplies or that Jesus was present! The evidence of archaeology is often circumstantial.

It is important to remember that however exciting finds may seem and however sensationally they are reported in the media, the interpretation of stones and bones is never straightforward. For every expert claiming an advance and a certain interpretation there will be others claiming that none has been made and that another interpretation is more likely. The fact that many of the scholars engaged in archaeological excavation and interpretation are Jews, Christians or avowed atheists raises questions about the scientific objectivity of much work that is undertaken. Further, the fact that historical and religious claims to the land are bound up together and highly significant to politicians in the region and further afield adds to this sense.

When assessing the credibility of expert witnesses, it is standard practice to ask whether they are *neutral* and whether they have a *vested interest* in what they are attesting to. When somebody has definite beliefs they may be inclined to interpret the evidence as supporting them. This was observed by the philosopher David Hume and later by Gottfried Herder. The difficulty of approaching archaeology in the Bible lands impartially has definitely damaged the value of its conclusions as support for the truth of the Bible story, though that will not stop people digging or making claims.

The History of Archaeology in the Bible Lands

The Roman Emperor Constantine, who first converted the Empire to Christianity, gave his mother Saint Helena unlimited access to the imperial treasury in order to locate the relics of Judeo-Christian tradition. In 326–8 Helena undertook a trip to Palestine, where she is said to have uncovered the site of Calvary, the remains of three crosses, a number of nails and Jesus' tomb under the Roman Temple that the Emperor Hadrian had constructed outside the Jewish Temple in Jerusalem, still called Aelia Capitolina at that point. She collected a wide variety of other 'relics' on her travels, which made their way into European churches and museums.

Throughout the Middle Ages relics of Christ, the apostles and saints were in demand to lend their authority to rulers, religious orders, churches and towns. They were often credited with miracles. The trade in relics drove some of the earliest pilgrimages to the Bible lands and impromptu excavations there.

The Crusades provided ample opportunities for further amazing 'discoveries' to be made, seemingly confirming the truth of the Bible. For example, the holy lance that pierced Christ's side while he was being crucified was allegedly discovered in Antioch on 15 June 1098. The fact that it was a timely discovery, which gave hope to the demoralized Christian army and enabled them to break the siege against all the odds, could either be interpreted as a miracle or as damning evidence that the artefact was forged, depending on your point of view![1]

By the time of the Protestant Reformation it had become abundantly clear that few, if any, of the claimed relics had any connection whatsoever with figures mentioned in the Bible. Martin Luther 'wondered how there could be 26 apostles buried in Germany, when there were only 12 in the entire Bible!'.[2] A deep scepticism towards biblical artefacts and those who claimed to have discovered them developed and, arguably, still affects European attitudes to biblical archaeology.

In the nineteenth century, when Palestine was part of the

---

1 www.historytoday.com/richard-cavendish/discovery-holy-lance.

2 Robert H. Brom, 2004, www.catholic.com/tracts/relics.

British Empire, Victorian scholars saw themselves rectifying the mistakes of the past by using the new science of archaeology to study the land and establish objective facts concerning it. They were deliberately cautious, usually aiming to uncover a context for the Bible story rather than prove specific events. Nevertheless early archaeologists were influenced by German biblical criticism, which suggested that the Bible dated from a long time after the events it recorded and so was not historically accurate.[3] Some set out to find evidence to support this suggestion – while others set out to refute it, so showing that the Bible could be a historical document.

The seeds of a later division were sown, between biblical and Levantine or Ancient Near Eastern archaeologists; those who started from a position of scepticism and their opponents, who often started from a position of faith.

In 1865 Queen Victoria became patron of the Palestine Exploration Fund, which sponsored some huge digs. Major discoveries around the Temple precinct were made by Edward Robinson, Charles Warren and Charles Wilson, which cast some light on those aspects of the Gospels that refer to events in Jerusalem.

During this period archaeological method was refined and discoveries started to be recorded properly, enabling dates to be assigned to them and more reliable interpretations to be developed.

Some of the archaeologists working in the Bible lands between 1890 and 1947 included the following.

Sir William Flinders-Petrie and his wife Hilda spent many years excavating sites across the Levant. As a strict Protestant Christian and trained surveyor, Petrie is best known as an Egyptologist, but he excavated in Palestine from 1890 and retired to Jerusalem.

Unlike his predecessors, Petrie was methodical and careful in his excavations, enabling smaller finds to be made and plans to be kept of where things were uncovered and how they related

---

3 The development and findings of German biblical criticism will be discussed in the next chapter.

together. He used pottery types to date layers or *strata* of remains for the first time. Petrie's most famous find is the Merneptah Stele dating from 1213–1203 BC and containing the first possible Egyptian reference to the tribe or people of Israel, reading 'Israel has been wiped out ... its seed is no more.' He found this in 1896 while excavating in Luxor.

Frederick Jones Bliss was an American trained under Petrie and applied his methods to excavations across the central region of Palestine before 1902.[4] Excavations in Tell el-Hasi, Tell es-Safi, Az-Zakariyya, Tell ej-Judeideh and Tell Sandahannah tried to establish the locations of biblical towns and a system of chronology.

Ernst Sellin was a German Protestant theologian. As a great example of how historical criticism and archaeology were intertwined during this period, Sellin set out to explore the background to Luke 18.35 (Jesus heals a blind man on the way into Jericho) and Mark 10.46 (Jesus heals a blind man while leaving Jericho) and so clarify his understanding of the New Testament. He discovered that Jericho was in fact twin cities; the old city was that mentioned in the book of Joshua, the new city was Roman, about a mile away. Confusingly, both were called Jericho! Jesus could, therefore, have left Luke's Jericho and was arriving at Mark's Jericho when the miracle took place – meaning that the texts would not contradict each other.

William Ramsay (1851–1939) is another example of a scholar who set out to establish the historical credibility of particular biblical passages by digging in places they referenced. Ramsey started by digging in Asia Minor (Turkey) to establish the veracity of the book of Acts before turning to the letters of Paul, which he argued were all authentic and consistent with the evidence.

Kathleen Kenyon excavated in Samaria (1931–4) Jericho (1951–8) and Jerusalem (1961–7), pioneering the use of reconstructive drawings in archaeology and becoming world

---

4 Rachel Hallote, *Bible, Map and Spade: The American Palestine Exploration Society, Frederick Jones Bliss, and the Forgotten Story of Early American Biblical Archaeology*, Piscataway, NJ: Gorgias Press, 2006.

famous for her finds. Kenyon had no doubt the sites she excavated were linked to the Old Testament narrative.

William Foxwell Albright, an American archaeologist and biblical scholar, was the acknowledged founder of the modern biblical archaeology movement. Although steeped in radical German historical criticism, Albright became convinced that the biblical accounts of Israelite history were largely accurate. Excavations at Tell el-Ful (1922–3) and Tell Beit Mirsim (1926, 1928, 1930, 1932) enabled him to refine his expertise in ceramics and develop a detailed chronology for the sites. He taught G. E. Wright, Joseph Fitzmyer, Frank Moore Cross, Raymond Brown, David Freedman and John Bright, all of whom became leaders in the field and exponents of Albright's approach.

In 1948 the British mandate in Palestine came to an end and the State of Israel was founded. The Israeli government invested in huge archaeological projects in order to demonstrate to the world that their claim to the land was authentic.

Nelson Glueck, an American rabbi and archaeologist, was a personal friend of David Ben Gurion and Golda Meir. He first excavated in Palestine in the 1920s and was involved in discovering 1,500 significant sites through his long and distinguished career. In particular, Glueck became an expert in Ancient Near Eastern pottery, which is often used to date sites. As a rabbi, Glueck said that his faith was not based on evidence or rational argument and that a literal interpretation of the Bible was unnecessary for religion.

Benjamin Mazar was a historian of the Assyrian period and father of Israeli biblical archaeology. Mazar directed the excavations south and south-west of the Temple Mount in Jerusalem, uncovering extensive remains from the Iron Age through the Second Temple period to Jerusalem's Islamic Period – including the great staircase leading into Herod's Temple. For decades Mazar served as the chairman of the Israel Exploration Society and of the Archaeological Council of Israel (which he founded as the authority responsible for all archaeological excavations and surveys in Israel).

Mazar's son and grandchildren have carried on his work in

the field, becoming leading archaeologists in their own right. For example, Amihai Mazar excavated Timnah, the supposed site of King Solomon's mines in the Negev desert during the 1970s and 1980s, as well as the important site Beit She'an in the 1990s.

Yohanan Aharoni was an Israeli archaeologist and historical geographer who joined many excavations, including Be'er Sheva, Hazor, Lachish and the Bar Kokhba caves near the Dead Sea.

Ruth Amiran was an Israeli archaeologist whose 1970 book *Ancient Pottery of the Holy Land* is still a standard reference for archaeologists working in Israel.[5]

Nahman Avigad worked on the excavations of Masada and was involved in the exploration of caves in the Judaean desert, where the Dead Sea Scrolls were found. In 1969 Avigad excavated the Jewish Quarter in the Old City of Jerusalem, devastated by the 1948 war. He found an early depiction of the great Temple Menorah and the Burnt House, apparently destroyed during Titus' suppression of the great Jewish Revolt described by Josephus. The dig also unearthed villas belonging to the Herodian upper classes, remains of a Byzantine Church and Jerusalem's Cardo, a fifth-century road connecting the Church of the Holy Sepulchre and the Byzantine Church. Avigad also uncovered the remnants of the Broad Wall built to defend Jerusalem during the reign of King Hezekiah in the late eighth century BC, mentioned in Nehemiah. Nearby he also unearthed the Israelite Tower, a remnant of Jerusalem's Iron Age fortifications attesting to the Babylonian sack of Jerusalem in 586 BC.

Yigael Yadin, previously Chief of the Israeli Defence Forces and an active figure in Israeli politics from the 1950s to 1981, was one of the first translators of the Dead Sea Scrolls and led excavations at Qumran, near where the scrolls were found. In the 1950s and 1960s, Yadin led digs at Megiddo and Gezer. At Gezer he identified as Solomonic a wall and gateway identical in construction to remains excavated at Megiddo and Hazor. He later conducted his legendary excavation of Masada, before writing

---

5 Ruth Amiran, *Ancient Pottery of the Holy Land: From its Beginnings in the Neolithic Period to the End of the Iron Age*, New Brunswick, NJ: Rutgers University Press, 1970.

stirring accounts of his discoveries – which served a political as well as scientific purpose.

David Ussishkin, the grandson of prominent Zionist Menachem Ussishkin, was an expert on the Iron Age. He led important excavations at a number of sites, including Lachish, Jezreel and Megiddo, and with the assistance of his colleague Gabriel Barkay undertook the first complete survey of the rock-cut tombs of the Jerusalem First Temple period necropolis at Silwan in 1968–71.

Inspired by Yigael Yadin's successes between the 1950s and 1970s, biblical archaeology became enormously popular around the world. Many saw the role of archaeologists in the region as being 'to illuminate, to understand, and, in their greatest excesses, to "prove" the Bible'.[6] Unsurprisingly, this attracted considerable criticism from mainstream archaeologists. From the 1970s a new generation of archaeologists tried to be more open-minded, scientifically rigorous and to take a position of scepticism towards the texts. Nevertheless few religious Jews or Christians could or would accept this position, so in practice it attracted secular and atheist archaeologists who seemed to be searching for disproof of the Bible on as much of an ideological bent as their predecessors searched for proof. Because of this, in the 1980s and 1990s biblical archaeology became divided between 'maximalists', book and trowel archaeologists who saw the evidence as supporting the essential historicity of the Bible, and 'minimalists', secularists and atheists who interpreted the evidence as suggesting that the Bible contains almost nothing historical at all.

Eliat Mazar, granddaughter of Benjamin Mazar, is a good example of a modern maximalist and Israel Finkelstein, the co-director of excavations at Megiddo, is an example of a minimalist.

* In 2005, Mazar made public claims to have unearthed King David's palace, to have confirmed the biblical account of a powerful united kingdom based in Jerusalem during the tenth

6 Quoted by Lynn Tatum in her review of William G. Dever, 'Recent Archaeological Discoveries and Biblical Research', in *The Jewish Quarterly Review* 85:3/4 (1995), pp. 464–6.

century BC, following excavations funded by the City of David Foundation and the Shalem Center, both organizations dedicated to the assertion of Israel's territorial rights.

• Finkelstein was sceptical! Generally critical of scholars who read the results of their excavations as confirming the biblical narratives of conquest, he has described Jerusalem in this period as a 'small hill town'.[7] The *National Geographic* reports him saying of Mazar's claims: 'Of course, we're not looking at the palace of David!' Finkelstein roars at the very mention of Mazar's discovery: 'I mean, come on. I respect her efforts. I like her – very nice lady. But this interpretation is – how to say it? – a bit naïve.'[8]

Both sides have their supporters. Mazar's confidence about the historicity of the Bible is shared by archaeologists such as Yosef Garfinkel (excavator of an important site in the Valley of Elah) and Thomas Levy (excavator of a vast copper-smelting operation at Khirbat en Nahas). Finkelstein's scepticism about the Bible is shared by most mainstream archaeologists, including Norma Franklin and William Dever.

William Dever, who has emerged as the major figure of recent decades, is controversial, with his alternative account of the history of the land as being dominated by polytheism and particularly by worship of the goddess Asherah.[9] Yet he has been critical both of extreme minimalists and of maximalists, writing:

I am not reading the Bible as Scripture ... I am in fact not even a theist. My view all along – and especially in the recent books – is first that the biblical narratives are indeed 'stories,' often fictional and almost always propagandistic, but that here and there they contain some valid historical information. That hardly makes me a 'maximalist.'[10]

7 See ngm.nationalgeographic.com/2010/12/david-and-solomon/draper-text/1.
8 Ibid.
9 William G. Dever, *Did God Have a Wife? Archaeology and Folk Religion in Ancient Israel*, Grand Rapids, MI: Eerdmans, 2005.
10 William G. Dever, 'Contra Davies', *The Bible and Interpretation* (January 2005).

The division between maximalism and minimalism in biblical archaeology is not always purely professional. David Ilan remarked that Garfinkel 'has an agenda – partly ideological, but also personal. He's a very smart and ambitious guy. Finkelstein's the big gorilla, and the young bucks think he's got a monopoly over biblical archaeology. So they want to dethrone him.'[11]

There is, of course, an economic motivation to factor in as well. Doron Spielman freely admits: 'When we raise money for a dig, what inspires us is to uncover the Bible – and that's indelibly linked with sovereignty in Israel.'[12]

Archaeologists are academics, and academics secure funding by demonstrating impact. Part of impact is column inches, which are generated by stories many people find compelling. Given that Christianity is the largest world religion, that several wealthy foundations that might fund digs were founded by Jewish philanthropists and that the Israeli government and its supporter the US government have a political interest in demonstrating the authority of the Bible and through it the Jewish peoples' claim to the land, it doesn't take much to imagine the effect on the planning and reporting of excavations. Similarly, secular, atheist and liberal-leaning organizations and publications have a lively interest in reporting stories that cast doubt on Zionist claims or evangelical literalism in equal measure!

Moderate minimalism is the mainstream position in Middle Eastern archaeology today; it starts from a position of secular scepticism but is not necessarily opposed to believing the Bible's chronology if and where the evidence is clear.

What Can Archaeology Tell Us About the Historicity of the Bible?

Part of any scholarly analysis of the historicity of the Bible involves exploring independent evidence that might corroborate events, people and places recorded in the Bible.

---

11 Ibid.
12 Ibid.

Some examples of important sources uncovered by archaeologists and archivists that seem to support the historicity of the Bible include:

1   **Egyptian stele** confirm the existence of an area called Israel from 1209 BC and the existence of towns such as Shechem, Rafah and Megiddo before 925 BC. They also give the names of pharaohs who might be those referred to in the Bible.

2   **The Mesha Stele** refers to the House of Omri (King of Israel based in Samaria) and possibly to the House of David; it also uses the name YHVH. It dates from $c.850$ BC.

3   **Akkadian cuneiform inscriptions** confirm regional names given in the Bible, including Canaan (1500 BC), Philistia/Palestine, Tyre, Sidon, Edom and maybe Israel ($c.800$ BC), Judah ($c.733$ BC).

4   **The Siloam Inscription** in paleo-Hebrew/Phoenician records the construction of a water shaft in Jerusalem, which seems to be described in 2 Kings 20.20 as occurring during the reign of Hezekiah ($c.715$–686 BC).[13]

5   **Assyrian Cuneiform inscriptions** might confirm the existence of King Ahab ($c.850$ BC; cf. 1 Kings 16—22), King Jehu ($c.825$ BC; cf. 2 Kings 9—10), and Assyrian campaigns in Palestine $c.800$ BC.

6   **The Deir 'Alla Inscription** found in Jordan in 1967 is 'the oldest example of a book in a West Semitic language written with the alphabet and the oldest piece of Aramaic literature'.[14] Dating from $c.840$–760 BC, it recounts visions of the Prophet Bala'am, son of Be'or, who may be the same Bala'am mentioned in Numbers 22—24 although in the inscription he

---

13   Ronny Reich and Eli Shukron, 'The Date of the Siloam Tunnel Reconsidered', *Tel Aviv* 38 (2011), pp. 147–57; Alon De Groot and Fadida Atalya, 'The Pottery Assemblage from the Rock-Cut Pool near the Gihon Spring', *Tel Aviv* 38 (2011), pp. 158–66.

14   Allan Millard, 'Authors, Books and Readers in the Ancient World', in J. W. Rogerson and Judith M. Lieu (eds), *The Oxford Handbook of Biblical Studies*, Oxford: Oxford University Press, 2006, p. 554.

is associated with Ashtar, a god named Shgr and Shadday gods and goddesses rather than YHVH.[15]

7 **The Tel Dan Stele** might refer to the House of David *c*.800 BC.

8 **The Lachish Relief** depicts the Assyrian siege of Lachish in 701 BC. Carved between 700–681 BC, it was originally used to decorate King Sennacherib's Palace in Nineveh (near modern-day Mosul in Iraq).

9 **The Azekah Inscription** refers to the Assyrian campaign against and defeat of King Hezekiah of Judah (*c*.701 BC).

10 **The Annals of Sennacherib** record the same events in 701 BC and also refer to the siege of Jerusalem.

11 **The Lachish Letters** were written to Joash, apparently the commander of Lachish, from Hoshaiah, a military officer stationed close by shortly before Lachish fell to the Babylonian army in 588/6 BC (Jer. 34.7). They confirm that people worshipped a God with the name YHVH.

12 **The Babylonian Chronicles** date the fall of Jerusalem to 597 BC and seem to confirm 2 Kings 24.7–17, although some scholars question whether they really do date from the period they describe.

13 **The Ketef Hinnom Scrolls** date from some time after *c*.600 BC and contain a phrase that bears some similarities with texts such as Exodus 20.6, Deuteronomy 5.10, 7.9 and the priestly blessing from Numbers 6.24–26 in paleo-Hebrew script.

14 **The Jehoiachin Inscriptions** were found near the Ishtar gate in Babylon. They seem to confirm the presence of the Judaean royal house as prisoners in Babylon.

15 **The Eliakim Seal** bears the inscription 'The property of Eliakim, steward of Jehoiakin'.

---

15 J. Hoftijzer and G. van der Kooij, 'Aramaic Texts from Deir Alla', *Documenta et Monumenta Orientis Antiqui* 19, Leiden: Brill, 1976; P. Kyle McCarter Jr., 'The Balaam Texts from Deir 'Alla: The First Combination', Bulletin of the Schools of Oriental Research 237 (1980), pp. 49–56.

16 **The Gedaliah Seal** was found at Lachish and bears the inscription 'Gedaliah, who is over the house'. Gedaliah was the name of the man the Babylonians had appointed as governor of Judah after the destruction of Jerusalem (2 Kings 25.22).

17 **The Cyrus Cylinder** describes King Cyrus' treatment of religion and displaced peoples in his empire, also described in Ezra, Nehemiah and Chronicles.

18 **The Elephantine Papyri** from Egypt span a period of 1,000 years from *c*.650 BC. One fifth-century BC fragment names Darius II, Sanballat the Horonite and Johanan the high priest, all mentioned in Nehemiah.[16]

19 **Hasmonean coins** have been discovered in various places.

20 **Herod's Temple Platform** is still intact; the most famous part of it is the western (wailing) wall.

21 **The Temple Inscription** (discovered 1871) reads (in Greek): 'No foreigner may enter within the balustrade around the sanctuary and the enclosure. Whoever is caught, on himself shall he put blame for the death which will ensue.'

22 **The Pilate Stone** was discovered at Caesarea Maritima in 1961. It reads (in Latin): 'To the Divine Augusti [this] Tiberieum ... Pontius Pilate ... prefect of Judaea ... has dedicated [this] .'

23 **The Arch of Titus** next to the Colosseum in Rome dates from AD 82. The relief carvings show plunder from the sack of Jerusalem in AD 70 being carried back to Rome in triumph. The great menorah, trumpets and what might be the Table of Showbread are depicted.

24 **Roman coins** to celebrate the destruction of Judaea were minted in 70 AD; these have been found in various places.

---

16 Interestingly the form of Jewish worship practised at Elephantine until the fourth century BC, although in many ways similar to that practised in Jerusalem during the First Temple period, included worship of Anat-Yahu, who seems to have been the wife of YHVH. Robert Karl Gnuse, *No Other Gods: Emergent Monotheism in Israel*, Edinburgh: T. & T. Clark, 1997, p. 185.

25   **Greek texts** attest to some of the events referred to in the Bible, including **Josephus** *Antiquities* XI–XVIII and XX, *Against Apion* Books I–II, *Jewish Wars* Books I–VII and the writings of **Philo** of Alexandria.

26   **Latin histories** confirm the order of events described in the Bible, Apocrypha and Pseudepigrapha, from the reign of Cyrus the Great to the reign of the Emperor Hadrian.[17] In very broad terms these sources confirm that events happened as the Hebrew Scriptures suggest. Early references to the existence of Jesus and the emergence of early Christianity can also be found in Tacitus, Suetonius, Pliny the Younger, Lucian of Samosata, Thallus and Celsus.

27   **There are references in the Talmud** and Mishnah that suggest a variety of similar long-lived oral traditions existed among ordinary Jewish people independent of the written Scriptures.

28   **The philosopher Mara Bar Serapion** wrote a letter in Syriac in or shortly after AD 73. It reads:

> What advantage did the Jews gain from executing their wise king? It was just after that their kingdom was abolished. God justly avenged these three wise men [Socrates, Pythagoras and the 'Wise King of the Jews]: the Jews, desolate and driven from their own kingdom, live in complete dispersion. But Socrates is not dead, because of Plato; neither is Pythagoras, because of the statue of Juno; nor is the wise king, because of the 'new law' he laid down.[18]

This passage might refer to Jesus.

---

17   There are relevant references in Herodotus, Solinus, Syncellus, Eusebius, Quintus Curtius, Tacitus, Polybius, Diodorus, Plutarch, Pompeius Trogus, Porphyry, Strabo, Cassius Dio, Cicero, Livius, Marcellinus, Florus, Pliny, Plutarch and Appian, Macrobius, Eutropius, Suetonius, Sulpicius Severus, Philostratus, Spartinius and Cornelius Fronto – listed by Samuel Mercer in *Extra-biblical Sources for Hebrew and Jewish History*, New York: Longmans & Co., 1913.

18   Robert E. Van Voorst, *Jesus outside the New Testament: An Introduction to the Ancient Evidence*, Grand Rapids, MI: Eerdmans, 2000, pp. 53–5.

From the range of independent historical sources that attest to events, places, peoples and even individuals mentioned in the Bible, it seems clear that the Bible at least refers to history.

In addition to direct references to events, places, peoples and individuals mentioned in the Bible, important historical *parallels* for the Bible include the following.

From Assyria

1   **The Enuma Elish** (*c*.1120 BC) has been seen to parallel aspects of the Genesis creation stories and other references in the Bible to creation, including Psalm 74.[19]

2   **The Epic of Gilgamesh** (dating from well before *c*.650 BC) tells the story of a man Enkidu who was created from the earth by a god. He lives among the animals in a natural paradise until he is tempted by a woman, Shamhat. He accepts food from this woman and is forced to leave the place where he lives after becoming aware of his own nakedness. Later in the epic he encounters a snake, which steals a plant of immortality from him. Gilgamesh also contains an account of a hero Utnapishtim surviving a world-destroying flood that shares many details with the biblical story of Noah.

3   **The Code of Hammurabi** (*c*. seventeenth century BC) is a list of clear rules said to have been handed down by a deity. Some of the regulations are exact parallels with the Ten Commandments or other laws in the Bible; others duplicate shared cultural and social values in a more general way.

4   **Middle Assyrian law codes** dating to the sixteenth to thirteenth century BC have parallels with Deuteronomy 22.22–29 on sexual impropriety and reflect the practice of married women wearing a veil and prostitutes not (cf. 1 Cor. 11.4–16). Laws regulating ownership and transfer of land, property and slaves are also similar.

---

19   The full text of the Enuma Elish, in English, can be found at www.cresourcei.org/enumaelish.html.

From Canaan

The Ras Shamra texts give scholars an insight into the religion of the Canaanite people, often referenced in the Bible; there are 89 references to the god Baal, 40 to the goddess Asherah and 10 to the goddess Ashtoreth in Hebrew Scripture.

1   Among them, the **Baal and Anat Cycle** probably dates to 1400–1200 BC. It seems to offer a parallel for the Hebrew Scriptures, particularly for Genesis 1, Psalms 29, 74, 89 and 104 and passages in Habakkuk, Isaiah, Daniel and Zechariah.

From Persia

The Avesta (the Persian Scriptures of the Zoroastrians, tenth century BC) tells the story of how Ormuzd created the world and the first two humans in six days and then rested on the seventh. The names of these two human beings were Adama and Evah.

From Egypt

1   **The Egyptian Book of the Dead** (*c*.2600 BC) refers to an eternal god creating the Word and simultaneously being the Word. This work also contains a sort of negative parallel for the Ten Commandments in chapter 125.

2   **The creation legend of Khnum** (*c*. fourth century BC) has the god creating man out of clay, a parallel with Genesis 2.7 and Isaiah 64.8.

3   **The Ausar/Auset/Heru Allegory** (*c*. late fourth century BC) has some striking similarities with the gospel story. In both, the central character has a supernatural conception and divine birth, proceeds to struggle against an enemy in the wilderness and eventually experiences resurrection from death to eternal life.

4   **The Auset Myth** and the story of the Virgin Mary have some similarities; both were able to conceive without male impregnation. Auset (Isis) was revered as the Virgin Mother.

5   **The Aten Hymn** (*c*. fourteenth century BC), composed

in honour of the Aten (single sun-god) by the Pharaoh Akhenaten, shares its sequence and images with Psalm 104.

6 **The Instruction of Amenemope**, dating from $c.1300-1075$ BC, contains wisdom texts very similar to those in the book of Proverbs.

7 **Manetho's** *Aegyptica* listed pharaohs and divided Egyptian history into dynasties to make some sense of the complex relationships of Egypt's rulers. The date and apparent political motivation of Manetho's history are of interest to scholars of the Hebrew Bible as they might suggest that the narrative histories in the Bible were of a similar date and could have had a similar motivation in terms of trying to establish a new ruler's grip on power and integrate different cultures.[20]

From Greece (and the Hellenized World)

Plato ($c.428-347$ BC). Plato's philosophy was enormously influential. As described in the previous chapter, he saw ultimate reality in metaphysical terms and the physical world as a mere shadow of the world of the forms. In *The Republic* he used the allegory of the cave to explain the political difficulties faced by anybody who understood the true nature of things. A group of prisoners are kept underground in a cave, chained together and facing the rockwall. The only light comes from a fire behind them; it casts a variety of mysterious shadows on the wall. To the prisoners the shadows are their only reality. A prisoner escapes and feels his way out of the cave. Confronted by daylight and the three-dimensional reality of the real world, he chooses to return and tell the prisoners that their reality is but a world of shadows. The prisoners, still chained in the cave, do not believe him and kill him to shut him up.[21]

---

20 Manetho was a historian, probably working as a priest of Ra at the great temple at Heliopolis during the third or second century BC. Most of his works have been lost but his major history of Egypt is preserved, in part in the writings of Josephus. He was probably influenced by the work of the fifth-century BC Greek historian Herodotus, and commissioned to write his history by the Ptolemaic dynasty as part of their attempt to bring unity to Egypt and justify their own power.

21 See *The Republic* Book VII, classics.mit.edu/Plato/republic.8.vii.html.

Plato's philosophy dominated the Hellenistic world and spawned a wide variety of Neoplatonic philosophies. In particular these were characterized by a focus on reason, disdain for the physical world and the body, and a belief that knowledge of ultimate reality was dangerous and must be kept secret, only shared with those who could be trusted to make proper use of it.

Philo of Alexandria (25 BC–AD 50) was an aristocratic philosopher with connections with leading Jewish families in Judaea and who visited Jerusalem at least once. He tried to bring Greek philosophy – particularly Stoicism – together with Jewish thought. In particular Philo brought together Jewish belief in a creator God and Platonic teaching about the transcendence of God, by describing God's creation in terms of *Logos*. God creates through *Logos*, which is both separate from the world and all-pervading in it. For Philo, it is *Logos* that communicates God's will and enables human minds to comprehend God's existence and the moral imperative. The *Logos* is in some sense God's emissary and an advocate for human beings, who have fallen away from God and need restoring to God's favour.

Some scholars have suggested that John's Gospel and parts of Paul's letters were influenced by the ideas of Philo.

Religions that Might Offer Parallels to Christianity

In the third and second centuries AD a dizzying variety of religious and philosophical ideas were developed in and near Ptolemaic Egypt, some of which contributed to what can be broadly described as Hermeticism and some of which to what can broadly be described as Gnosticism.

Some time during the late third or second centuries BC, legends about Hermes Trismegistus ('the three-times-great Hermes') began to circulate in Egypt, probably as a result of attempts to show that the Egyptian god Thoth was the same as the Greek god Hermes. Both were gods of writing and magic in their respective cultures, both were responsible for guiding souls in the afterlife.

As it developed, the cult suggested that Hermes' writings, which were thought to include the Hermetic Corpus, the Emerald Tablet and the Perfect Sermon, offered people insight into the workings of the universe, a way of living and an understanding of what happens after death.[22] In particular they taught that:

- There is one single, transcendent God, existing outside the material universe.
- God created the world and everything in it through an act of will; separated the elements earth, air, fire and water and ordered them into seven spheres of heaven, which govern destiny. 'The Word' (Greek *Logos* or *nous*) set the spheres in motion and brought forth life, including human life, an androgynous man made in God's image.
- Human beings are both mortal in body and immortal in spirit and are torn between their two natures. In being slave to our physical natures we lose The Word and our understanding of how to escape from earthly existence, which is like a prison.
- Intermediary divine beings such as angels explain the interaction of God and the world and account for supernatural events.
- There is a single true theology within all religions, originally given to human beings by God.
- There is a relationship between what happens on small and on universal levels – 'that which is below corresponds to that which is above, and that which is above corresponds to that which is below'.
- Reason and knowledge (Greek *nous*) are the basis of morality, making good or evil choices possible. God is in a sense pure reason and as such is unlimited, immaterial and the origin of goodness; demons are limited, material, the origin of evil in the universe. If people choose to focus on material things they turn away from God.
- God somehow feels betrayed by God's creation and

---

22 In fact it is unlikely that any of the writings predate the second century BC, and there is little basis for believing that Hermes Trismegistus ever really existed.

particularly by humankind, and wishes to punish people for being materialistic and evil. He offers them a way back though, through revealing the secrets of the universe and how to progress towards perfection through the practice of alchemy, astrology and theurgy.[23]

At the same time a collection of other cults and philosophies were developing that today are often described as Gnostic – from the Greek *gnosis*, 'knowledge'. Like Hermeticism they revolved around the idea that special knowledge had been revealed to them, often through a prophet-like figure who went on to write the knowledge down in a mysterious, symbolic form. Common Gnostic beliefs included:

- There is a remote, supremely powerful God and divine beings, *Aeons*.
- There is a secondary creator-god or *demiurge*, an emanation of the supreme God.
- The world is an 'error' or shadow of higher-level reality, only ever as good as its material nature allows.
- The body is sinful and a prison for the soul – bodily urges, particularly sex, are evil and hold us back from fulfilling our spiritual potential.
- A divine element 'falls' to earth and dwells within certain human beings; it may return to the divine realm through awakening.

Around the time of Christ we know that a Gnostic religion known as Mandaeism existed on the borders of Israel.[24] There are still Mandaeans today.

---

23 In practice, alchemy and astrology are ways of studying, understanding and mastering the operation of the natural world and theurgy is natural theology – understanding how we should live in order to fulfil God's will.

24 There were still around 70,000 Mandaeans living in Iraq until the outbreak of war in 2003; only 5,000 remain, many having fled to other countries or been killed.

- They claim to be descended from Adam and recognize Abel, Seth and Enoch as prophets.
- They also see themselves as descendants of Noah and his sons Shem and Ram, who split away from Judaism when Abraham demanded circumcision.
- They reject Moses as a false prophet, Jesus as a false Messiah and revere John the Baptist as an important teacher.
- They see the Holy Spirit as an evil force.

Nevertheless Mandaeans share many traditions and ideas familiar from the Hebrew Scriptures and were seen as 'people of the book' along with Jews and Christians by the Prophet Muhammad. They even claim to have been resident in Egypt for a while – their name for the devil is Ptahil, which might have been derived from the name of the Egyptian god Ptah, perhaps combined with the name of the Canaanite god El.[25]

Right at the end of the period in which New Testament texts were being finalized, the Iranian Prophet Mani wrote seven works that were heavily influenced by Gnosticism and drew on the teachings of Jesus, the Buddha and Zoroaster.[26] His ideas spread and soon came to compete with Christianity in Syria, Egypt, Greece and Rome. Like other Gnostic religions, Manichaeism upholds a dualist philosophy that sees good and evil locked in battle for dominance over the world.

---

25   The name Mandaeism is derived from the Aramaic from knowledge, *manda*, and the name Sabianism is derived from the Aramaic for baptism, *sabi* – this sums up the essential features of the religion, which is centred on secret knowledge revealed through the prophets and sees baptism as a means of attaining salvation. Mandaean writings are essentially dualistic, seeing the world locked in a struggle between good and evil.

Scholars such as Bauer and Bultmann suggested a connection between Mandaean ideas and the New Testament, particularly the prologue to the Gospel of John, which seems unduly concerned with John the Baptist and shot through with gnostic and dualist ideas.

26   Sometimes called 'Zarathustra' (e.g. Nietzsche), Zoroaster was the ancient Iranian founder of Zoroastrianism, a religion that still exists today. The Yazidis who have recently been victim to persecution by Daesh (IS) follow a religion related to Zoroastrianism. Both Baha'i and Ahmedi Muslims accept Zoroaster as a prophet.

While Manichaeism was too late to influence much of the Bible, it shows how Gnostic ideas developed in parallel to Christianity and Judaism in the first to third centuries AD. It certainly influenced early Christian thinkers and shaped the ideas of leaders who would play a part in defining the biblical canon. Augustine converted from Manichaeism to Christianity as a young man.

When the Dead Sea Scrolls were discovered and later published it became apparent that some of the Essene writings contained ideas similar to those identified with Gnostic cults, suggesting that comparable ideas pervaded the whole ancient world in the period from the second century BC to the second century AD. The Scrolls also contained a range of texts that never made it into the biblical canon – a rich source of parallels for some historical and theological content of the Bible.

Conclusion

Today biblical archaeology offers mixed support to the historicity of the Bible story.

Finds – such as clay seals that show that Jerusalem might have been a prosperous centre at the time of King David; pools that match the Gospel descriptions of the location of a miracle; first-century tombs that match the description of that which Jesus was placed in before the resurrection – have been seen to support the plausibility of the Bible story by maximalists, although minimalists often dispute the interpretation of such finds.

Inscriptions and references in ancient manuscripts offer a surer possibility of corroborating the Bible story, although the content of each is very limited, maybe confirming a date, a name, a practice rather than the sense of the Bible story.

Little evidence has been or could ever be found to support or really date the Exodus, the conquest of the land under Joshua and the early judges or the life of Jesus. Some minimalists have suggested that this is because the story is just that: a much later literary concoction. Others see it as evidence of the limitations of this whole approach to assessing the historicity of the Bible.

Exploring parallels for elements of the Bible story from other cultures offers scholars another way of dating it, checking that it could indeed be as old as believers think and so is potentially 'authentic'. On the other hand, the existence of multiple parallels for elements of the Bible casts doubt on its originality and uniqueness and could offer support to those who see it as the product of its culture rather than divine revelation.

Archaeologists and historians exist on a spectrum from extreme sceptical minimalism to the view that the Bible is an essential guide to digging and interpreting the ancient past of the whole area, trowel in one hand and translated text in the other. These positions are not always formed after and as a result of the evidence they discover; it seems that pre-existing opinions often colour what is looked for, where and how what is found is interpreted.

6

The Development of Historical Criticism

Biblical criticism is an umbrella term covering various techniques for applying critical methods to analyse and study the Bible, uncovering *internal evidence* relating to its origins and development through time.

To be clear, the word 'criticism' is not to be taken in a negative sense; it simply refers to the scholarly approach of studying, evaluating and assessing the Bible in order to understand it better, both in terms of its historicity and origins on the one hand (sometimes called 'higher criticism' or 'historical criticism') and its meaning and proper interpretation on the other (sometimes called 'lower criticism' or 'textual criticism').

Erasmus

At the dawn of the sixteenth century, across Europe, change really started to happen. Desiderius Erasmus of Rotterdam was a true renaissance man – educated in the best monastic schools in the Netherlands, he focused on the Classics. His Latin was widely admired and, unusually, he had command of Greek as well. He was excused from following his monastic vows on account of his learning and was able to focus on academic study at Paris, Leuven and Cambridge.

Erasmus turned his attention to the New Testament in 1516, in stages publishing the first printed edition of the Greek text along with a complete revision of the Vulgate Latin translation and annotations, explaining how study of the Greek elucidated the meaning of the Latin. Erasmus was bold in his use of textual criticism, such as by deleting words from 1 John 5.8 on the basis that they are not found in any Greek manuscript before the fourteenth century and appear only in later copies of the Vulgate translation. He applied humanistic techniques in textual criticism, translation and interpretation that had been developed by students of classical texts and was not afraid to polish and improve the style of the Latin, so that it could compete with the great literature with which his readers were now familiar.

Erasmus' work was different and highly controversial, although because of his style and choice to write in Latin, it did not reach a wide audience. While he shrewdly dedicated his work to the Pope, Erasmus seems to have encouraged other scholars to translate his Latin into German and English. Access to even parts of the Bible in different languages added fuel to the dispute that became the Reformation – ordinary people could not find in the text any support for major practices and doctrines of the Church. Where were the verses confirming the Church's authority to sell indulgences? Where was the demand for priests to be celibate? Where were the references to sacraments such as the last rites, or to purgatory?

The Age of Enlightenment

At the dawn of the Enlightenment in Europe, the philosophers Thomas Hobbes and Baruch Spinoza asked questions about the origins of the Hebrew Scriptures, particularly the Torah. They prized reason and were not satisfied with the traditional justification for the authority of the Genesis creation stories, the Ten Commandments or other aspects of the law – that they were revealed to and written by Moses. Examining the texts in detail they noticed that the evidence suggested more than one author or source.

Thomas Hobbes

Hobbes opened chapter 33 of his *Leviathan* (1651) by stating:

> Their antiquity, who were the original writers of the several Books of Holy Scripture, has not been made evident by any sufficient testimony of other History, (which is the only proof of matter of fact); nor can be by any arguments of natural Reason; for Reason serves only to convince the truth (not of fact, but) of consequence. The light therefore that must guide us in this question, must be that which is held out unto us from the Books themselves: And this light, though it show us not the writer of every book, yet it is not unuseful to give us knowledge of the time, wherein they were written.[1]

He argued that the Pentateuch must have been written after Moses' death, referring to passages such as Deuteronomy 34.6, 'no man knoweth of his [Moses'] sepulchre unto this day', to make his point, and used internal evidence in other books of Hebrew Scripture to suggest that traditional ideas about authorship and dating were false. Books such as Job and Jonah should, Hobbes argued, not be understood as works of prophecy to be dated at the time they are set – both are better understood as treatises on theological themes that could have been composed later by writers inspired by the stories of characters from the histories or traditions of their people.

By Hobbes' reasoning, books of the Bible should properly be dated thus:

- somewhere around 623 BC for the Torah (although it contains fragments of Moses' much earlier writings, e.g. Ten Commandments);
- some Psalms might be Mosaic or Davidic but others date from the Babylonian exile – the collection was probably made after 500 BC;
- well after 450 BC for Joshua, Judges, Samuel, Kings and Chronicles, Ruth, Ezra and Nehemiah.

---

1 See literature.org/authors/hobbes-thomas/leviathan/chapter-33.html.

Hobbes concluded that 'it is manifest enough, that the whole Scripture of the Old Testament, was set forth in the form we have it, after the return of the Jews from their Captivity in Babylon.'[2] And although he accepted that 'the writers of the New Testament lived all in less than an age after Christ's Ascension, and had all of them seen our Saviour, or been his Disciples, except Paul, and Luke; and consequently whatsoever was written by them, is as ancient as the time of the Apostles', he made it clear that 'the time wherein the Books of the New Testament were received and acknowledged by the Church to be of their writing, is not altogether so ancient' and pointed out that:

> some of those Books which are called Apocrypha, if left out of the Canon, not for inconformity of Doctrine with the rest, but only because they are not found in the Hebrew. For after the conquest of Asia by Alexander the Great, there were few learned Jews that were not perfect in the Greek tongue ... But it is not the Writer, but the authority of the Church, that maketh a Book Canonical.

Hobbes subjected religious authority and the Scriptures it relied on to clear, rational analysis and found that it was not so well supported as might have been assumed. He argued that while reason can support certain aspects of religion, such as rules that coincide with natural laws, where it cannot, religious authority cannot be held absolute.

Richard Simon

The French priest Richard Simon (1638–1712) was in some sense the forerunner of modern biblical criticism. From careful reading of different versions of the texts in their original languages, he concluded that the Hebrew Scriptures are composite documents, reliant on multiple historical sources that had been preserved in the archives of Israel and Judah. The long process of editing, perhaps dominated by Ezra, produced the double narratives and odd

---

2 See literature.org/authors/hobbes-thomas/leviathan/chapter-33.html.

variations of style so apparent in close readings of the Pentateuch, even in translation. Simon doubted that Moses could be the author of any fragment of the Bible.

Baruch Spinoza

Spinoza went much further than Hobbes. In *Tractatus Theologico-Politicus*, published anonymously in 1670, he tried to reveal the truth about the Bible and thereby undercut the political power exercised in modern states by religious authorities.[3] Obviously, at the time this was somewhat controversial!

Although of a Dutch–Jewish background, Spinoza dismissed the biblical claim that the Jews are the chosen people of God. As he saw it, their kingdom and proof of God's favour were long gone. He concluded: 'At the present time there is nothing whatsoever that the Jews can arrogate to themselves above other nations.'[4]

For Spinoza, true faith is universal and accessible to anyone through the free exercise of reason, regardless of religion, belief or lack of it. God, who Spinoza understood in terms of the single necessary substance of the universe, cannot perform arbitrary miracles in time or speak to individual prophets. Accounts of God's actions or words in the Bible have therefore to be seen as the products of human imagination and interpreted as such. He wrote:

> It will be said that, although God's law is inscribed in our hearts, Scripture is nevertheless the Word of God, and it is no more permissible to say of Scripture that it is mutilated and contaminated than to say this of God's Word. In reply, I have to say that such objectors are carrying their piety too far, and are turning religion into superstition; indeed, instead of God's Word they are beginning to worship likenesses and images, that is, paper and ink.[5]

---

3 Steven Nadler, 'Baruch Spinoza', *The Stanford Encyclopedia of Philosophy* (Fall 2013 Edition), ed. Edward N. Zalta – http://plato.stanford.edu/archives/fall2013/entries/spinoza, Part 3.

4 *Tractatus Theologico-Politicus*, ch. 3, G III.56/S 45.

5 *Tractatus Theologico-Politicus*, ch. 12, G III.159/S 145–6.

Spinoza aimed to show that both the peace of society and faith are actually endangered by the suppression of the freedom to philosophize, think, speak and write without prejudice, taboo or restraint.

Looking closely at the texts he saw that 'the Torah as we have it, as well as other books of the Hebrew Bible (such as Joshua, Judges, Samuel and Kings), were written neither by the individuals whose names they bear nor by any person appearing in them.'[6] Spinoza argued that the whole Jewish history was composed by a single historian, and that this was most likely Ezra, writing *c*.450 BC – further, that Ezra's work was later added to, amended and otherwise altered by unknown scribes, translators and interpreters. Like Hobbes, Spinoza noted that canonization occurred a long time after the texts were written and that at this point biblical texts were chosen from a multitude of others, not always for sound reasons. What we now possess, then, 'is nothing but a compilation, and a rather mismanaged, haphazard and "mutilated" one at that'.

Richard Dawkins couldn't have put it better!

In the 1670s these views were enough to make Spinoza a marked man, whose very life was in danger according to Gottfried Leibniz.

Gottfried Leibniz

Although personally ambitious and willing to bend his ideas to suit the times, Leibniz became privately obsessed with Spinoza's ideas, wrote him clandestine letters and met him secretly in 1676.[7]

Leibniz developed Spinoza's ideas but tried to make them more acceptable. He distinguished between faith and reason, defining faith as 'the object of faith is the truth, which God has revealed in an extraordinary way'.[8] For Leibniz, miracles and

---

6 Nadler, 'Baruch Spinoza'.

7 For a detailed but highly readable exploration of the thinking of Spinoza and Leibniz, focused on this meeting, see Matthew Stewart, *The Courtier and the Heretic: Leibniz, Spinoza, and the Fate of God in the Modern World*, New Haven, CT: Yale University Press, 2007.

8 PD §1/GP VI 49, quoted in Paul Lodge and Benjamin Crowe, 'Leibniz, Bayle,

revelations are not strictly impossible, although they should be understood to have been planned by God as an exceptional feature of God's creation rather than enacted spontaneously. Faith cannot be maintained in opposition to reason but does not need to be based entirely on reason.

Interestingly, Leibniz argued that the historicity of the Bible, like the authenticity of miracles, is a matter beyond the scope of normal arguments to prove or disprove. We can only decide what is more *probable*, that the Bible is historically reliable or not, that a miracle happened as told or not. For Leibniz, it is more probable that the Bible is historically reliable than it is not. Generations of people believed and trusted in it, and Leibniz explains that although the Bible appears to describe improbable events, even when it comes to miracles, 'they have nothing in them of absurdity. Thus, demonstrations are required if they are to be refuted',[9] and the Bible cannot be demonstrated to be false. Leibniz concludes that:

> It is a matter of no difficulty among theologians who are expert in their profession that the motives of credibility justify, once and for all, the authority of Holy Scripture before the tribunal of reason, so that reason in consequence gives way before it, as before a new light, and sacrifices thereto all its probabilities.[10]

Leibniz's views were highly influential and enabled many Protestant scholars to maintain a public faith while philosophizing in the best Enlightenment tradition. Essentially, in answer to the question 'So is the Bible true?', Leibniz would say that an answer is impossible but as it cannot be proven false and as probability seems to indicate its truth, it may be taken as such.

---

and Locke on Faith and Reason', *American Catholic Philosophical Quarterly* 76:4 (2002), pp. 575–600.

9 Quoted ibid. PD §28/GP VI 67.

10 Quoted ibid. PD §29/ GP VI 67.

David Hume

Building on the empiricist, atheistic tradition of Hobbes, Hume developed an argument that undermined the authority of the Bible in *An Enquiry Concerning Human Understanding* (1748), in chapter 10 of which he attacked the idea that any testimony about miraculous events should be taken seriously because:

- The evidence for a miracle will always be outweighed by the evidence against it. By definition a miracle is an occasion on which laws of nature are broken by God, but surely laws are laws for a reason! When 99.9999 per cent of our experience attests to people sinking when they climb out of a boat and attempt to walk, the one report of a man walking on water is an anomaly, very probably false.
- Witnesses are unreliable, prone to exaggerate their experiences and claim them as miraculous. For example, a healing whips up a sense of euphoria and people soon exaggerate the object's condition before and the effect of the cure, partly in the hope that others might be healed.
- Those with existing religious beliefs are particularly likely to report events falsely that serve their beliefs, however unconsciously and however well meaning they might be. How convenient that Jesus was able to make six ever-full jars of wine, when Elijah made only one jar of flour and one of oil! Couldn't it just be that one of Jesus' followers created the story to support their belief that Jesus was greater than Elijah?
- The fact that miracle stories, including the biblical narratives, originate in 'ignorant and barbarous nations' confirms that they should not be taken seriously. Ignorant people are more likely to be credulous, believing the reports of others uncritically even when good judgement and wide experience would suggest they are probably false.

Hume went on to explore the social and human origins of religion in his *Natural History of Religion* (1757). This pioneering work, which pre-empted some of the ideas of Feuerbach, Weber and

Durkheim, saw religion as a response to human weakness, fulfilling social and personal need, evolving as those needs changed over time. Hume saw polytheism and idolatry as the first stage of religiosity, gradually replaced by monotheism and then a purer form of theism as human understanding grew to encompass the world as a whole and curiosity about the general order of things developed. Hume concluded:

> Examine the religious principles, which have, in fact, prevailed in the world. You will scarcely be persuaded, that they are anything but sick men's dreams. Or perhaps will regard them more as the playsome whimsies of monkeys in human shape, than the serious, positive, dogmatical assertions of a being who dignifies himself with the name of rational.[11]

It is clear that Hume had little time for such religious beliefs as originated in and depended on the Bible, although the Bible is still an interesting and useful historical document, which truly charts the development of a society and the human origins of its religious beliefs if not precise dates and orders of events.

Immanuel Kant

Hume's extreme scepticism influenced the German philosopher Immanuel Kant. For Hume and for Kant, we cannot know things as they really are, just how they appear to be – to believe otherwise is dogmatic. If God exists then God is beyond time and space and the limitations they impose. There is no way that we can argue from our limited experience to God or prove God's existence; and similarly, the idea that God can act spontaneously in time and space, even to respond to a prayer or particular situation, is ridiculous. Given this, the Bible cannot be seen in terms of direct revelation; neither can its testimony of miraculous events and revelations be taken literally.

---

11 *The Natural History of Religion* (1757), in *A Dissertation on the Passions, The Natural History of Religion: A Critical Edition*, ed. T. L. Beauchamp, Oxford and New York: Clarendon Press, 2007, section 184.

While Kant did not involve himself on either side of the developing German academic debate about the Bible's historicity, he was well aware of it and his work had obvious implications for biblical studies going forward. For Kant, there is no way in which human beings can claim to have knowledge of God who is by nature beyond our understanding. He saw the only reason to believe in God was to explain the essential order of the universe, the existence of human reason and freedom, the moral law and an afterlife such as would make up for the injustice of bad things happening to good people. Such a belief could only be based on a sensible *postulate*, never on proof.

It follows that for Kant any suggestion that the universe is not orderly and predictable actually undermines the sense of believing in God. Miracles, religious experiences, any instance the laws of nature being broken would be bad news for faith. Consequently the Bible should not be understood as a historical record of supernatural events but as a book designed to teach morality that might otherwise be understood from reason and experience. Religion should exist within the boundaries of reason and should never teach people what cannot otherwise be supported by proper argument.

For Kant – like Hume – the historicity of the Bible is questionable and its claim to be revelation or record revelations is inauthentic. Nevertheless, for Kant the Bible story could be 'true' in yet another sense, in that it describes and commends universal moral principles.

Hermann Samuel Reimarus

An expert in the Roman writer Cassius Dio, whose histories covered much of the period also chronicled by the Hebrew Scriptures, as a philosopher Reimarus developed the thinking of Leibniz's follower Christian Wolff and was, therefore, a deist. God, although perhaps necessary to explain the universe, could not be seen to act in time to effect miracles or reveal God's will to prophets.

In the unpublished *An Apology for, or Some Words in Defense of, Reasoning Worshipers of God*, Reimarus applied his reason to the Bible. He concluded that the Hebrew Scriptures are entirely worthless because their writers were ignorant of the immortality of the soul. He pointed out how full of historical and moral errors the text is, how gross an example it sets readers and how little use it is as a guide to doctrine. Much later, Albert Schweitzer wrote of Reimarus' work that:

> [t]he monograph on the passing of the Israelites through the Red Sea is one of the ablest, wittiest, and most acute which has ever been written. It exposes all the impossibilities of the narrative in the Priestly Codex, and all the inconsistencies which arise from the combination of various sources.[12]

Historical Criticism and Atheism

It is clear that the application of historical criticism to the Bible began with the Old Testament (particularly the 'Mosaic' Pentateuch, the Jewish law), and it was some time before the books of Prophecy (on which Jesus' messianic claim depended) and the books of the New Testament were subjected to the same degree of scrutiny. Mainstream Western scholarly opinion advanced quite quickly towards the conclusion that the Old Testament is an ahistorical compilation of material assembled for past political rather than genuine theological reasons. Whereas mainstream scholarly opinion reserved judgement about the New Testament and in some sense still shies away from drawing the same conclusions about the New Testament as it does about the Old Testament.

In part the difference in the treatment of Old and New Testaments was due to the power exercised by the Church in early modern Europe, which deterred scholars from being too outspoken on texts closely related to tenets of Christian doctrine. However, there is little doubt that it was also due to scholars' willingness to

---

12   Albert Schweitzer, *The Quest of the Historical Jesus*, ch. 2, www.early christianwritings.com/schweitzer/chapter2.html.

doubt the value in texts venerated by people against whom they had a deep-seated and all-pervasive prejudice. For many Jews the development of historical criticism was and is seen as being motivated by blatant anti-Semitism, and there is a real sense in which this is right. Take for example the *Catholic Encyclopaedia* entry on biblical criticism:

> [A] capital distinction is to be made between criticism as applied to the Old and as applied to the New Testament. The two have followed different courses. O. T. criticism has been developed along the lines of linguistic and historic research. Philosophico-religious prejudices have been kept in the background. But in respect to the New Testament, criticism began as the outgrowth of philosophic speculations of a distinctly anti-Christian character and, as exercised by rationalists and liberal Protestants, has not yet freed itself from the sway of such a priori principles, though it has tended to grow more positive – that is, more genuinely critical – in its methods.[13]

Is it fair to say that philosophico-religious prejudices have been kept in the background in relation to Old Testament studies – or is it just that those prejudices are more acceptable than such prejudices as might question the authority of the Church? Might not Old Testament studies be seen as an outgrowth of philosophic speculations of a distinctly anti-Semitic character? We will return to that question later on.

As doubt about the historicity of the Old Testament became widespread:

- Many Christians started to stress how no doctrine of the Church *required* belief in the complete or even partial Mosaic authorship of the Pentateuch, and to focus on passages in the New Testament that denigrated 'the Jews', their laws and

---

13 See www.newadvent.org/cathen/04491c.htm.

history, seeing Jesus and his followers as the true heirs of Abraham and possessors of divine favour.

- Others argued that it is possible to see elements of the Old Testament as being divinely inspired without accepting they were physically written by Moses, David or the prophet named at the beginning of the book. After all, the Bible contains no claims about its authorship.

- Others still denounced the scholarly approach that had led to the Bible being seen as fragmentary, arguing that biblical criticism was an atheistic enterprise designed to undermine faith. They emphasized the fact that the Bible has much more stylistic, historical and theological integrity than critics allow, and focused on smooth, holistic accounts, readings and interpretations of the text.

However, by the second half of the eighteenth century, historical criticism had become clearly associated with atheism, with anti-religious or even revolutionary ideas. One example of a well-known biblical critic from this period is Baron d'Holbach.

Baron d'Holbach

Well known for his literary salon in Paris, d'Holbach brought together some of the greatest minds of his age, including Denis Diderot, Jean-Jacques Rousseau, Adam Smith, David Hume, Horace Walpole, Edward Gibbon, David Garrick, Laurence Sterne and – probably – Benjamin Franklin. He was an avowed atheist and published a series of vehemently anti-religious works – under pseudonym in the Netherlands.

Christianity Unveiled (1761) sets out d'Holbach's position quite clearly. After summarizing his moral objection to religion and his argument that it holds back progress, d'Holbach provided a skilful précis of the histories of the Jewish and Christian religions and of Christian beliefs about God, designed to reduce them to absurdity.[14] He exposed the illogicality of a religion that appeals to reason insofar as believers have to read and understand the word of God but then denounces reason when it asks questions of this revelation. He attacked the idea that an almighty unchanging God could work miracles and echoed Hume's argument against accepting as valid any testimony concerning miracles.

D'Holbach observed:

> The Bible, every word of which Christians believe to have been dictated by inspiration, is composed of an incongruous collection of the sacred writings of the Hebrews, called the Old Testament; to which are added, a number of works, more recent indeed, but of equal inspiration, known by the name of the New Testament. At the head of this collection are five books which are attributed to Moses, who ... betrays at every word a profound ignorance of the laws of Nature. God, according to Moses, created the sun, which, in our planetary system, is the source of light, several days after he had created the light. God, who can be represented by no image, created man in his own image. He creates him male and female; but, soon forgetting what he had done, he creates woman from one of the ribs of the man ... It appears, at once, that the cosmogony of the Hebrews is only a tissue of fables and allegories, incapable of giving any true idea of things, and calculated to please only a savage and ignorant people, destitute of science, and unqualified for reasoning. In the rest of the writings of Moses, we see little but a string of marvellous and improbable stories, and a mass of ridiculous and arbitrary laws. The author concludes with giving an account of his own death.

---

14 *Christianity Unveiled* is accessible and well worth reading in the original; if you enjoy Richard Dawkins' bombastic style and forthright views then you are sure to enjoy *Christianity Unveiled*. See www.gutenberg.org/files/40770/40770-h/40770-h.htm.

Moving on to the New Testament, he wrote:

> Four historians, or fabulists, have written the marvellous history of the Messiah. Seldom agreeing with respect to the circumstances of his life, they sometimes contradict each other in the most palpable manner. The genealogy of Christ, given us by Matthew, differs widely from that given us by Luke. One of the evangelists says, that Christ was carried into Egypt; while, by another, this event is not even hinted at. One makes the duration of his mission three years, while another represents it as only as many months. We do not find them at all better accord respecting the facts in general which they report. Mark says that Christ died at the third hour, that is to say, nine o'clock in the morning: John says that he died at the sixth hour, that is, at noon. According to Matthew and Mark, the women who, after the death of Jesus, went to his sepulchre, saw only one angel; whereas, according to Luke and John, they saw two. These angels were, by some, said to be within the tomb; by others, without. Several of the miracles of Jesus are also differently reported by the evangelists. This is likewise the case with his appearances after his resurrection. Ought not all these things to excite a doubt of the infallibility of the evangelists, and the reality of their divine inspirations?

D'Holbach concluded by asking:

> By what fatality does it happen that Christian revelation, the foundation of a religion on which depends the eternal felicity of man, should be unintelligible, subject to disputes, and often deluge the earth with blood? To judge by effects, such a revelation ought rather to be thought the work of a malign spirit, a genius of darkness and falsehood, than of a God desirous to preserve, enlighten, and beautify mankind.

Conclusion

The development of historical criticism and Enlightenment thinking took place at the same time. It is not unreasonable to connect the two and suggest both that Enlightenment thinking influenced scholars in questioning the historical truth of the Bible and that the questions scholars raised about the historical truth of the Bible in some sense liberated Enlightenment thinkers from accepting religious authority as they might otherwise have done.

It is important to appreciate the relationship between the model of truth adopted by Enlightenment thinkers – who commonly saw truth as *out there*, to be discovered through the senses and concepts built out of sense experience – and the assumptions made by historical critics. Historical critics thought that by investigating what happened when, and which bits of the Bible were earliest in date, they would discover the truth about what underpinned religion, whether that was God's revelation or more human activities. The truth, for historical critics, is out there to be found in the mists of time, discovered under layers of textual redaction. A statement or belief would therefore be true if it corresponded with actual historical events – or otherwise the original words of those involved – and false if it did not.

7

Historical Criticism and the Hebrew Scriptures

Jean Astruc

The French doctor Jean Astruc was outraged by the atheistic doubts that had been cast on the historicity of the Bible. A Catholic convert working in the France of the Counter-Reformation, he sought to defend the traditional view that Moses was, essentially at least, the author of the Pentateuch. Nevertheless, in 1753, despite his good intentions his book *Conjectures on the Original Documents that Moses Appears to have used in Composing the Book of Genesis. With Remarks that Support or Throw Light upon these Conjectures* (catchy title!) had to be published anonymously and in relatively liberal Brussels.

Astruc applied methods well established in the study of the Classics for assessing manuscripts to the books of Genesis, Exodus, Numbers, Leviticus and Deuteronomy. He concluded that the text had originally been four smaller texts or sources, later combined into a single narrative, creating the effect of the repetitions and inconsistencies highlighted by Hobbes and Spinoza. Astruc saw that the name used for God was a particular indicator of what source a unit of text should be assigned to. He divided the texts that referred to YHVH and those that referred to ELOHIM into two columns, noting that stories in one column appear to have parallels or doublets in the other, which could suggest that both narratives originally had a similar shape.

Astruc's reading of the Hebrew Scriptures as the product of the redaction of four sources was highly influential and seems to pre-shadow the famous Documentary Hypothesis advanced by Graf and then Wellhausen well over a century later.

Ironically, far from achieving its intended end, Astruc's analysis ended up being used by several German biblical critics to support their own historical analyses of Hebrew Scripture, which aimed to demonstrate its lack of historical credibility and religious authority.

Alexander Geddes

A Scottish priest with liberal, revolutionary sympathies, having returned from being educated in Paris, Geddes turned his attention to the Hebrew Scriptures, applying techniques in historical and literary criticism similar to those used by Friedrich August Wolf to analyse the works of Homer. Writing in 1800 he was the first to suggest that the Pentateuch and Joshua should be seen together in terms of a Hexateuch and that all six books were composed of multiple fragmentary sources, some of which may have been written by Moses, edited together in the reign of Solomon. This was later called the Fragmentary Hypothesis. Geddes was effectively unfrocked for advancing these views and, when he died, fellow priests were barred from saying Masses for his soul.

Johann Eichhorn

Between 1780 and 1812, Eichhorn continued Richard Simon's stylistic analysis of the Bible, arguing that it supported Astruc's model whereby the Pentateuch was the product of four separate source-texts, edited together into a single narrative.[1] This went on to influence De Wette, Graf and Wellhausen in the development of the Documentary Hypothesis.

Johann Vater

Geddes' Fragmentary Hypothesis was introduced into Germany by Johann Vater, who applied it systematically in his three-volume

---

1 *The International Standard Bible Encyclopedia: A–D*, ed. Geoffrey W. Bromiley, Grand Rapids, MI: Eerdmans, 1959, p. 820.

Commentary on the Pentateuch (1802–6). Vater's work went on to influence a generation of German scholars, including Wilhelm De Wette.

Wilhelm De Wette

De Wette was described by Julius Wellhausen as 'the epoch-making opener of the historical criticism of the Pentateuch'.[2] He is particularly remembered for his 1805 doctoral dissertation, which argued that Josiah's late-seventh-century BC reforms (2 Kings 22—23; 2 Chron. 34—35) must have been motivated by Deuteronomy. This was widely accepted and influenced the development of Old Testament historical criticism through the nineteenth and twentieth centuries.

De Wette used Astruc's approach to try and isolate a core of what he took to be the most ancient, historical material in the Hebrew Scriptures. Whereas the fragmentary hypothesis advanced by Geddes and Vater suggested lots of tiny units of text being edited together in one go, De Wette concluded that a core of text (part of Deuteronomy, which he identified with the scroll found in the Temple during the reign of King Josiah in 2 Kings 22.8–20) had been supplemented later with additional material in several stages of editing. This was the basis of what was later called the Supplementary Hypothesis.

De Wette also argued that the author of Deuteronomy, or his influence, could also be seen as responsible for the editing of Joshua, Judges, Samuel and Kings. Comparing Kings and Chronicles, De Wette doubted the historical reliability of the books of Chronicles. His conclusions 'eventually became cornerstones of modern biblical scholarship and established de Wette as one of the great biblical scholars of the nineteenth century'.[3]

---

2 See https://en.wikisource.org/wiki/Encyclop%C3%A6dia_Britannica,_Ninth _Edition/Wilhelm_Martin_Leberecht_De_Wette.

3 See www.jewishvirtuallibrary.org/jsource/judaica/ejud_0002_0021_0_20866. html from the *Encyclopedia Judaica*, 2008.

Karl Heinrich Graf

An expert in oriental languages, Graf used the tool of source criticism that had been pioneered by Astruc, Eichhorn and De Wette to advance the theory that the Pentateuch went through several phases of development over a period of more than 500 years, ending in the post-exilic period.

For Graf, the Pentateuch was the result of the combination of no fewer than four separate sources. This theory, later developed by Julius Wellhausen, was known as the Documentary Hypothesis, or sometimes the Graf-Wellhausen Hypothesis.

Graf identified a separate 'Priestly' (P) tradition in Exodus, Leviticus and Numbers, which he saw as much later than the 'Deuteronomistic' tradition (D, mostly in the book of Deuteronomy). There were, in effect, two complete law-codes in the Pentateuch, each with subtly different concerns.

Graf also explored the dating of the Jahwist (J) and Elohist (E) sources, identified by Astruc. He concluded that the sources should be dated in the order J – E – D – P, and this became widely accepted during the late nineteenth and twentieth centuries.[4]

Julius Wellhausen

Wellhausen brought together and developed existing work in German biblical criticism to produce his landmark *Prolegomena to the History of Israel* in 1882, the same year in which he resigned his position as professor of theology because he could not, in conscience, prepare students for the priesthood. He later became Professor of Oriental Languages at Halle.

In his *Prolegomena* Wellhausen developed the Documentary Hypothesis, and it was his version of it that came to dominate biblical criticism. He proposed that the Torah was originally four complete sources, each dealing with the same incidents and characters in its own characteristic way. The four sources were later edited together into a single narrative, and then edited again

---

4 Graf's principal work was *Die geschichtlichen Bücher des Alten Testaments* (1866).

by 'redactors' who tried to keep as much as possible of the original documents. Accepting Graf's order, according to Wellhausen the sources can be reconstructed and dated as follows:

- Jahwist (J) source = $c.950$ BC, shortly before the split into Northern and Southern Kingdoms. The J source provides the history of the Kingdom of Judah through half of Genesis and half of Exodus and parts of Numbers. J has an eloquent style and an anthropomorphic concept of God, who is often referred to as YHVH. For the Jahwist, YHVH is like a super-powerful tribal leader, who demands unquestioning obedience, provides protection and advantages to favoured individuals.
- Elohist (E) source = after 850 BC, during the two-kingdoms period before the destruction of the Northern Kingdom in 721 BC. The E source provides the history of the Northern Kingdom of Israel through a third of Genesis, half of Exodus and parts of Numbers. E is less eloquent, and provides a less anthropomorphic, more impersonal idea of God, who is often referred to as ELOHIM and who inspires awe and fear. For the Elohist, God's will is revealed through visions, dreams, prophets and angels; priests and prophets as well as rituals have a more important part to play in the relationship between God and God's people.
- Deuteronomist (D) source = $c.625$ BC, during the reign of King Josiah. Like De Wette, Wellhausen identified the D source (Deuteronomy) with the scroll of law found in the Temple in 2 Kings 22.8–20. He reasoned that because what Josiah read in the scroll caused him to insist on the exclusive worship of YHVH and destroy all cultic centres outside Jerusalem, this scroll would have the same theological concerns as Deuteronomy.
- Priestly (P) source = early post-exilic period, $c.500$ BC. The Priestly author is, unsurprisingly, concerned with the importance of priests and the Jerusalem Temple. Consisting of Genesis 1 and about 20 per cent of the rest of Genesis,

bits of Exodus and Numbers and almost all of Leviticus, the Priestly author sees God as distant and vengeful and stresses the need for priests to interpret God's will and conduct rituals – including circumcision – to appease God. The Priestly author tends to include lists, genealogies and significant numbers and sees YHVH's name as a special charm – the literary style is dry and uninspiring.

Wellhausen was radical in proposing a late date for the Priestly source; at the time, other scholars saw P as either the first or an earlier source. Nevertheless Wellhausen's Documentary Hypothesis and his order J–E–D–P was scholarly orthodoxy well into the 1990s.

Herman Gunkel

Gunkel refined Wellhausen's approach and developed form criticism, which allowed him to identify smaller – and older – sources used by the authors of the Old Testament. Gunkel started by considering each unit of text or pericope and trying to reconstruct its original context or *Sitz im Leben*, paying particular attention to its probable form or genre.

Form criticism became immensely influential in Germany and Europe during the twentieth century; it is fair to say that 'the influence of the methods pioneered by Gunkel upon subsequent Old Testament study can scarcely be overestimated'.[5] Form-critical methods were soon applied to New Testament texts and yielded important new insights into the development of the Gospels in particular.

Albrecht Alt

Reflecting on the Pentateuch in the light of insights provided by Wellhausen and Gunkel, Alt sought to reconstruct the religion of the Patriarchs in order to throw light on the theological concerns

5   Ernest Nicholson, 'Foreword: Hermann Gunkel as a Pioneer of Modern Old Testament Study', in *Hermann Gunkel, Genesis*, trans. Mark E. Biddle, Macon, GA: Mercer University Press, 1997, p. 9.

of the authors and editors of the original sources. Alt argued that Israel's formation as a nation rested upon the union of the different tribes in the worship of YHVH.[6]

Comparing the traditions recorded in Wellhausen's J and E sources, Alt noticed that there was no Jahwistic equivalent for the Elohistic tradition of God revealing God's name to Moses at the burning bush. For Alt this was the climax of the most ancient tribal tradition, retained with only minor alterations by the later Priestly editor who otherwise sought to combine the traditions of different tribes in such a way as to show their essential similarity. The various tribes that later became Israel, he reasoned, started off with paternal deities such as 'the God of your father Abraham'– they moved to naming God when unrelated (though similar) groups came together to form a new political (and religious) unity.[7]

Alt argued that underneath the present literary reworking of the material, traces of the pristine tradition are discernible. For example, he believed that at least three separate cults of the gods of the Fathers persisted into the period in which J and E were writing. At Bethel was the Jacob cult, at Beersheba the Isaac cult and at Mamre that of Abraham. The great project that the Jahwist, Elohist and later Priestly writers were engaged in was to create a unifying narrative that explained the relationship between neighbouring peoples and allowed them to develop a national rather than tribal sense of identity.

Alt has been criticized for his uncritical acceptance of Wellhausen's Documentary Hypothesis, his unbounded confidence in his critical method and for the apparent subjectivity of his approach.[8] His work is typical of that which attracted criticism in the mid-twentieth century for 'reading in' modern values and

---

6   Albrecht Alt, *Der Gott der Väter: Ein Beitrag zur Vorgeschichte der israelitischen Religion*, Stuttgart: Deutsche Bibelgesellschaft, 1929, p. 1.

7   The habit of referring to God as 'the God of' and the name of an ancestor did not die out quickly, however, and throughout the Pentateuch there is evidence of the authors identifying YHVH or ELOHIM with the ancestral deities to be sure of the authority of what they were saying.

8   Edward J. Young, 'The God of the Fathers', *Westminster Theological Journal* – available online at www.biblicalstudies.org.uk/pdf/wtj/fathers_young.pdf.

ideas; this sort of criticism eventually caused scholars to despair of using historical-critical techniques to provide credible insights into the development of the Bible.

Gerhard von Rad

One of Albrecht Alt's doctoral students at Leipzig, von Rad approached the text as the product of a particular religious and cultural community; in order to understand the text, one has to understand where it came from. As Victor Premasagar wrote, 'the Bible for von Rad, in the final analysis, is neither history nor literature, but rather the confessions of a community'.

In order to further his understanding, von Rad studied Semitic culture and became a competent archaeologist before being appointed as professor at the University of Jena in 1934.

Unfortunately Jena soon became the focus of Nazi attempts at 'de-Jewing' (German *Entjudung*) academia and establishing a scholarly basis for Hitler's ideology – the university was declared an official bastion of National Socialism.[9] The theology department was central to the Nazi project. It was incredibly embarrassing for Hitler that Christianity, a vital part of German culture and history, was dependent on Judaism. He wanted to establish the independence of Christian theology and edit any reference to Jewish ideas out of church worship. He felt that German theologians could use their influence to change Christianity in this respect, as they had changed it during the Reformation and Enlightenment.[10]

With Nazi supporters occupying key positions at Jena,

---

9 Karl Astel, a leading SS scientist specializing in eugenics, served as rector from 1939 until his suicide in April 1945. Nazi supporters were appointed to key positions, and close links were established between, for example, the medical school and the nearby concentration camp at Buchenwald.

10 Bernard M. Levinson, 'Reading the Bible in Nazi Germany: Gerhard von Rad's Attempt to Reclaim the Old Testament for the Church', provides a lot more detail on von Rad at Jena; www.academia.edu/346328/_Reading_the_Bible_in_Nazi_Germany_Gerhard_von_Rad_s_Attempt_to_Reclaim_the_Old_Testament_for_the_Church. See also Susannah Heschel, *The Aryan Jesus: Christian Theologians and the Bible in Nazi Germany*, Princeton, NJ: Princeton University Press, 2008.

Hebrew was soon eliminated from the curriculum, along with the requirement to study any element of the Old Testament. New courses in 'racial science' and 'the Jewish question' were developed. Dissertations were rejected when they disagreed with Nazi ideas, such as by arguing that Jesus must be understood in the context of Old Testament theology. Von Rad's colleagues edited the New Testament, the hymn book and the catechism so as to eliminate Hebrew words, Old Testament references and all links between Jesus and Judaism.

Von Rad was no Nazi sympathizer; he had enormous respect for the culture that gave rise to the Old Testament but realized that making this clear would cost him his career and maybe his life. He chose to use his talents to subvert Nazi ideology, arguing that the Old Testament and the Jewish roots of Christianity could not reasonably be edited out of theology or worship.[11]

Von Rad kept on holding lectures and seminars on Old Testament theology, seemingly choosing topics that would discomfort the Nazis – the book of Jeremiah, the Psalms, Exodus – even when almost no students turned up.[12] His books and articles from the period, on Deuteronomy and the wider Old Testament, should be seen in this context; they are less works of straightforward exegesis than parts of a polemic against National Socialism.

Building on Gunkel's work in form criticism, von Rad argued that Deuteronomy was not a book of law but a collection of sermons delivered by travelling Levites (priests), meant to encourage and inspire the people, to help them remember God's grace. He explored the form of the Priestly sermon (German *Gattung*) that had been identified by Ludwig Koehler from the University of Zurich.[13] He saw that this was relatively common

11 Walter Brueggemann noted that von Rad's concept of salvation history represents a polemic against National Socialist ideology: 'The ABC's of Old Testament Theology in the US', *Zeitschrift für die alttestamentliche Wissenschaft* 414:3 (2002), pp. 412–32. See also Jean Louis Ska, *Introduction to Reading the Pentateuch*, Winona Lake, IN: Eisenbrauns, 2007.

12 Only eight out of 155 students attended any of von Rad's lectures in 1935–6.

13 Ludwig Koehler, *Old Testament Theology*, Louisville, KY: Westminster Press, 1957.

in the Old Testament, particularly in Chronicles and the first part of Deuteronomy, and that it was important for understanding the original meaning of such passages.

Theologically, von Rad 'recognized' a '*"protestantische" Atmosphäre*'[14] in Deuteronomy; he ignored or explained away passages that seemed to make salvation dependent on works and obedience to the law, and argued that the covenant demonstrated Israel's unconditional election to salvation. Why? Because he was clearly concerned to show that the roots of Lutheranism lay deep in the Old Testament; that the German Christian Church's attempt to gloss over its importance was ridiculous.

Von Rad was true to the spirit of Enlightenment Jena in using the language of dialectic to express his understanding of Deuteronomy. He used antithetical statements a lot; that is, Deuteronomy is not X but it is Y. Jean Louis Ska connected this approach with the dialectical theology of von Rad's contemporary Karl Barth.[15] Barth was largely responsible for the writing of the Barmen declaration in 1934, which argued that the Church's allegiance to the God of Jesus Christ should make it resist the influence of other lords, such as Adolf Hitler.[16] It may be that von Rad was subtly declaring his sympathy for Barth's anti-Nazi theology through his textual commentaries.

Von Rad was largely responsible for keeping Old Testament studies alive between the wars in Germany, but his importance was not only in resisting Nazi whitewashing of theology and retaining some semblance of credibility for German biblical criticism going forward. Henning Graf Reventlow wrote that 'a number of von Rad's innovative papers prepared the way for the blossoming of

---

14 Gerhard von Rad, *Studies in Deuteronomy*, trans. David Stalker, 2nd edn, London: SCM Press, 1956, p. 68.

15 Ska, *Introduction to Reading the Pentateuch*, pp. 116–23.

16 Barth mailed this declaration to Hitler personally and it became one of the founding documents of the Confessing Church, of whose leadership council Barth was elected a member. Barth was forced to resign from his professorship at the University of Bonn in 1935 for refusing to swear an oath to Hitler. He then returned to his native Switzerland, where he assumed a chair in systematic theology at the University of Basel.

Old Testament studies in Germany during the first decennia after the Second World War.'[17] John H. Hayes wrote that:[18]

> In his theology, with its challenge of previous methodologies and with its new proposals, von Rad inaugurated a new epoch in the study of Old Testament theology. He argued against any organization of Old Testament theology along the lines of central concepts, pervasive topics, assumed structures of Israelite thought or world of faith, or systematic theological categories which had been characteristic, in one way or another, of all the theologies of the twentieth century, since this was to impose an alien structure on the material.

Von Rad recognized – and seems to have used – the prevalence of *eisegesis* (reading in one's own ideals and values) in biblical interpretation, and tried hard to arrive at 'the truth' about the Old Testament and the community that produced it, though in the end truth proved elusive.

Martin Noth

Martin Noth, influenced by Gunkel and particularly Albrecht Alt, was known as an advocate of tradition history. Like von Rad, he used form criticism to show that the Pentateuch was composed of blocks of traditional material added through oral tradition around some key historical experiences.

Noth's theory that from the time of the settlement Israel was organized into a twelve tribe confederation on a Greek model was highly influential; he felt that virtually nothing can be known about pre-settlement history.[19]

In 1943 Noth proposed that Genesis, Exodus, Numbers,

---

17 Quoted in *Symposia: Dialogues Concerning the History of Biblical Interpretation*, London: Equinox, 2007.

18 John H. Hayes and Frederick Prussner, *Old Testament Theology: Its History and Development*, London: SCM Press, 1985, p. 233.

19 Martin Noth, *Das System der zwölf Stämme Israels*, Stuttgart: W. Kohlhammer, 1930.

Leviticus, Deuteronomy and Joshua had originally formed a Hexateuch and argued that the Deuteronomistic redaction was largely the work of a single individual in the seventh century BC. In 1948 he presented the idea that Wellhausen's J and E sources go back to a common source, G (*Grundlage*).

Biblical Studies and Archaeology

In the mid-twentieth century, Old Testament studies were strongly influenced by the growth of biblical archaeology. The line between the textual scholar and the archaeologist was constantly blurred. Both von Rad and Noth were keen archaeologists – Noth even died on expedition to the Negev. William Albright and later his student John Bright divided their time between expeditions and research in US universities, and their books about Old Testament history made constant reference to sites and strata.

The effect of the close relationship between archaeology and biblical criticism was to ensure that the growing schism in archaeology between maximalists and minimalists would carry through into biblical criticism in the second half of the twentieth century.

Some scholars were optimistic about the extent to which the archaeological record supported scholars in reading the texts as history. For scholars like William Albright and John Bright, archaeology confirmed that the scepticism of the source critics and form critics, their tendency to see the Pentateuch and Histories as later propaganda, was unnecessary. For example, Albright noted evidence of destruction and resettlement in towns and villages, which might correspond with the settlement of the land and later with the destruction wrought by Assyrians and Babylonians. He felt that the Bible had been shown to be true in terms of its record of historical events.

Following Albright a generation of biblical critics felt at liberty to approach the Bible as a historical document and take its chronology more or less at face value. Conservative scholars such as Edward J. Young saw Albright's research opening the door to a more holistic reading of the texts and a more traditional understanding of their origins. Others tried to account for both the essential historicity of the Bible narrative and the textual evidence of multiple redactions by hypothesizing historically plausible contexts for the redacting to have taken place – the Deuteronomist working in the reign of King Josiah or the Priestly writer responding to the reforms of Nehemiah.

Other scholars disagreed with Albright's optimistic assessment of the evidence to support the Bible's historicity. They suggested that the archaeological record necessitated a totally new understanding of the history of the land and its people and a new approach to biblical criticism. For minimalists, including William Dever, Israel Finkelstein and following them to an even greater extent Thomas L. Thompson, Niels Peter Lemche, Philip R. Davies and Keith Whitelam, little in the texts can be supported by the evidence of stones and bones and so it seems at least possible that traditions and histories were early propaganda or works of fiction.

For example:

- The cities supposedly destroyed by Joshua and the Judges in a sustained military campaign against, for example, the Canaanites and Jebusites show no evidence of destruction during the relevant centuries.
- Jerusalem shows no sign of being a prosperous capital at the time of David and Solomon.

This sort of archaeological evidence is cited by minimalists to support their revisionist accounts of history and their argument that the Bible is historically inaccurate and probably the product of much later wishful thinking or propaganda.

John Van Seters

In *Abraham in History and Tradition* (1975), Van Seters argued that no convincing evidence existed to support the historical existence of Abraham and other patriarchs or to support the historical reliability of the Israelites' origins in Mesopotamia, the sojourn in Egypt, the Exodus or other major events in the Bible story. He criticized both the biblical archaeology school of Albright – which had already come under fire from Thomas L. Thompson and others – and the tradition history school of Alt and Noth, suggesting that the Pentateuch was less history than political treatise.

In the second part of the book, Van Seters went on to put forward his own theory on the origins of the Pentateuch, arguing, with Martin Noth, that Deuteronomy was the original beginning of a history that extended from Deuteronomy to the end of 2 Kings. However, against Noth and others he held that the so-called Yahwist source – usually seen as the oldest literary source in Genesis, Exodus and Numbers – was written in the sixth century BC as a prologue to the Deuteronomistic history, and that the so-called Priestly writer of the Pentateuch wrote a later supplement to this history. In doing so, Van Seters questioned the dominant Documentary Hypothesis, returned to the old Supplementary Hypothesis and developed it in a distinctive way.

Van Seters, along with Rolf Rendtorff and Hans Schmidt, suggested that advocates of the Documentary Hypothesis were wrong in their chronology; they saw the Deuteronomist as the first and original text *c*.600 BC, the Jahwist *c*.540 BC and the Priestly writer *c*.400 BC redacting and adding supplements to the work of the Deuteronomist and not writing independent documents. They questioned the very existence of an Elohist source.

Norman Whybray

Where Van Seters and Rendtorff provide revisionist accounts of how the Bible came to be written, Norman Whybray provided a detailed analysis of the evidence for the dominant Documentary Hypothesis. In *The Making of the Pentateuch* (1987) he showed how the Documentary Hypothesis rested on shaky foundations. His method was empirical: he demanded strong evidence to support claims and found that in many cases the evidence was simply absent. Other scholars had already suggested that the Documentary Hypothesis was in serious trouble,[20] but how and why had not been shown so clearly before. Whybray's alternative proposal – that the Pentateuch was essentially the work of a single author who drew upon multiple sources and disregarded, or was ignorant of, modern notions of literary consistency and smoothness of style and language – was widely criticized, but the importance of his work never lay in his alternative proposal, rather in offering a complete and thorough critique of the Documentary Hypothesis.

Conclusion

By the 1990s, in relation to the Hebrew Scriptures or 'Old Testament', historical criticism had reached the point where the shortcomings of the whole approach were apparent. The long dominance of the Documentary Hypothesis was over but no convincing alternative was forthcoming. It was clear that radically different explanations for the development of the texts could be put forward with equal passion and with more or less equal amounts of textual evidence. Similarly, overriding confidence that the historicity of the texts could be supported by archaeology had been shaken by the work of successive scientists. As technology advanced it became less and less possible for any scholar to be a master of both archaeological interpretation and biblical criticism, even if the validity of setting out to dig, Bible in hand, could be defended.

---

20   E.g. Joseph Blenkinsopp.

8

Questing for the Historical Jesus

The application of historical criticism to the New Testament rather lagged behind its application to the Hebrew Scriptures, and to begin with was split between textual critics (concerned to establish the authentic text of the New Testament, translate and interpret it better) and atheists with an anti-Christian agenda who sought to raise doubts about the historical basis for Christian beliefs.

Johann Jakob Griesbach

Griesbach was primarily a textual critic, working at the universities of Halle and Jena, but today he is chiefly remembered for his work on the synoptic problem, trying to work out the relationship between Matthew, Mark and Luke and their respective dates. The Griesbach Hypothesis (the basis for the modern two-source hypothesis) suggests that Matthew was written first by the apostle Matthew, sometimes called Levi, an educated Jew. Luke was written next by a Greek doctor who spent some time with Paul and his followers and had been commissioned to provide an account of Christian origins. Mark was written last as a sort of *pocket Matthew*, a stripped down Gospel aimed at Roman Christians with limited education.

Hermann Samuel Reimarus

Reimarus, a German rationalist philosopher of the Enlightenment, followed the ideas of Spinoza, Leibniz and Wolff. Like them he was essentially a deist but unusually he was quite forthright about his reasons for rejecting conventional Christianity and all forms of superstitious religion. As a philosopher, Reimarus was convinced that natural theology provides evidence for the existence of God and for moral laws; there is no need for revelation and, in fact, claims about revelations distract people from interpreting natural evidence and lead them to believe and do what is inconsistent with reason. Interestingly, Reimarus was just as critical of atheism, claiming that atheists ignored natural evidence and reason just as much as the claimed recipients of religious revelations.

In the 1770s, after Reimarus' death, Gotthold Lessing published extracts of his work, which became known as the Wolfenbüttel Fragments. These became highly influential, particularly because they cast serious doubt on the historical credibility of the Gospel accounts of the life and work of Jesus. Albert Schweitzer wrote: 'Seldom has there been a hate so eloquent, so lofty a scorn; but then it is seldom that a work has been written in the just consciousness of so absolute a superiority to contemporary opinion.'[1]

Reimarus started by highlighting the degree and nature of difference between the Gospel accounts, concluding that in any other case it would suggest that the authors were unsure of most of what happened in themselves and were relying on copying others and filling in gaps from their imaginations. Reimarus made a clear distinction between the teaching of the disciples and the teaching of Jesus, and argued that Jesus' teaching must make sense without knowledge of the resurrection because there was no way that Jesus, if fully human as believers claim, could be certain of what would happen before time – unless we are all predestined, which is contrary to the teaching of the Church. Given that much of what is ascribed to Jesus in the Gospels would not make sense without knowledge of the resurrection, we must see it as a later invention and not authentic.

For Reimarus, historians have to put themselves in the position of those who listened to Jesus: first-century Jews with no knowledge of Jesus' special identity – if any – and a particular understanding of concepts such as 'the kingdom of God', which could and should be reconstructed from other sources. Having analysed the Gospels thus, Reimarus claimed that:

1 Albert Schweitzer, *The Quest of the Historical Jesus: A Critical Study of its Progress from Reimarus to Wrede*, Mineola, NY: Dover Publications, 2005, p. 15.

- Jesus' simple message was 'Repent for the kingdom of God is at hand.'
- Jesus shared in Jewish ideas about racial exclusivity and, far from dispensing with the Mosaic law, enforced it with enthusiasm.
- Jesus' only real originality lay in his demand that morality applied to thoughts and words as well as deeds.

Reimarus claimed that although some apparent healings might be records of historical events, larger miracles are almost certainly a product of later exaggeration or theological wishful thinking. Further, the parables were almost certainly later constructions. He cast doubt on Jesus' intention to found a religion, to establish sacraments such as baptism or the Eucharist, and claimed that the resurrection was an invention born of pragmatism on the part of the disciples and spiritual and political necessity. He went so far as to refer to the New Testament 'hoax' – no wonder he chose not to publish in his lifetime!

Lessing, Eichhorn and Herder

In publishing the Wolfenbüttel Fragments, Gotthold Lessing sought to address the issues that Reimarus identified. In particular he suggested that the Gospel story might originally have been written down in several Aramaic *Urgospels*, each later translated into Greek to become the Gospels we know today.

Somewhat predictably, given his contribution to Old Testament studies, Johann Eichhorn suggested that there were in fact four intermediate documents, which would explain the similarities and differences between the Synoptic Gospels.

Georg Herder argued that the *Urgospels* were more likely to be oral than written. He referred to the development of Homeric epic, suggesting that the Gospel story might have been told and retold and that particular points – such as Jesus' sayings – only gradually became fixed in an essentially fluid tradition.

Karl Friedrich Bahrdt

Bahrdt was a colourful character, to say the least! The son of a leading churchman, he became a talented professor of biblical philology but also got into trouble trying to raise the spirits of the dead, to found a secret society or cult, was imprisoned for debt and ended up scraping a living by keeping a tavern and writing semi-pornographic stories.

In terms of biblical criticism his most important contribution was a translation of the New Testament into modern German that tried to make its teachings compatible with Enlightenment thought – a Bible for Kant's *Religion within the Bounds of Reason Alone* perhaps. Needless to say, *Neueste Offenbarungen Gottes in Briefen und Erzählungen* (1773–75) raised a storm of controversy and served to highlight the growing gulf between the ideas of rationalist philosophers and mainstream Christian teachings.

Johann Semler

Semler spent most of his career at the University of Halle and argued that the traditional canon of Scripture and agreed text of the Old and New Testaments had no divine authority because both were works of human beings.

Semler speculated about the date and authorship of the Gospels, revived doubts as to Paul's authorship of Hebrews, doubted Peter's authorship of 1 Peter and dated 2 Peter to the end of the second century. He thought Revelation was so late that it should be removed from the canon altogether.

Ferdinand Christian Baur

An acknowledged founder of the Tübingen School of biblical criticism, Baur was an expert on mythology, writing on Manichaeism, Neoplatonism and Gnosticism.

Following the ideas of fourth-century Gnostics, Baur argued that Paul had been a heretic, the founder of what had been a breakaway sect that held views antithetical to the ideas of mainstream Jewish Christianity as led by Peter. Baur saw references to Simon Magus in Acts 8.9–24 and elsewhere as actually referring to Paul. He argued that the dominance of the Roman Church, which became the Catholic Church, was the result of a synthesis or rapprochement between Pauline Christianity and the remains of Jewish Christianity, of which Peter had been a prominent leader. He saw John's Gospel as a product of this second-century reconciliation, designed to support the fiction that Peter and Paul had been co-founders of the Roman Church, both having been martyred in Rome on the same day, and to attract followers of both traditions to recognize the authority of the Roman institution.

Friedrich Schleiermacher

Schleiermacher was the first Calvinist invited to teach at Halle (1804). An ardent ecumenist, he championed the Prussian Union of Lutheran and Reformed churches. Later, Schleiermacher was closely associated with Wilhelm von Humboldt in founding the University of Berlin in 1810.

Von Humboldt's vision for a liberal university, which combined teaching and research, swept Europe and went on to become the dominant model for universities worldwide throughout the nineteenth and twentieth centuries. He appealed to the examples of Ancient Greece and Rome, contrasted the innovation of the classical world with the stagnation of the medieval Christian world and placed reason ahead of revelation or unthinking deference to authority.[2]

As professor of theology at the new University of Berlin, Schleiermacher was hugely important to the development of New Testament studies.

From 1819 he gave a series of lectures on the life of Jesus, much later reconstructed from students' notes and published as *The Life of Jesus*. He stressed the irreconcilable historical

---

2 Von Humboldt's model for western education and its broader effects on attitudes to Judaism and Christian interpretation of the Old Testament will be referred to in Chapter 15.

differences between the Synoptic Gospels and the Gospel of John but, unusually, he argued that John provided the better insight into Jesus. For Schleiermacher, John seems to have been written by an eyewitness, able to write a coherent and sustained account of his experience, whereas the Synoptic Gospels were stitching together various different second-hand reports.

Schleiermacher's lectures on the life of Jesus later inspired David Strauss to write his controversial *The Life of Jesus: Critically Examined*, although Strauss rejected what he saw as Schleiermacher's conservatism and applied historical-critical techniques with little restraint.

In *On the Witness of Papias about our First Two Gospels* (1817), Schleiermacher suggested that the author of the Greek Gospel of Matthew – which he saw as the first Gospel to have reached its final form – drew on an earlier collection of Hebrew sayings ascribed to the apostle Matthew. Similarly he distinguished the Gospel of Mark from the source that Papias ascribed to an associate of Peter.[3]

Schleiermacher's wider work was also significant to New Testament studies. He changed the whole philosophical and theological framework within which scholars worked, making it somewhat easier for them to say things that seemed to challenge the historical authenticity of the Gospels.

First, Schleiermacher's major work, *Der christliche Glaube nach den Grundsätzen der evangelischen Kirche*, argued that religious feeling – and not creeds, Scripture or rational argument – is the source and basis of Christian faith. He wanted to put an end to the extremes of supernaturalism and rationalism, to deliver religion from dependence on perpetually changing systems of philosophy but, in effect, he made it easier for biblical scholars to follow the evidence and raise questions about the historicity of the New Testament while remaining within the mainstream Church.

---

3 See www.earlychristianwritings.com/text/papias.html. Similarly, *c.*AD 110–40, he distinguished the Gospel of Mark from the source that Papias ascribed to an associate of Peter.

Using Schleiermacher they could argue that questions about historicity of Scripture or the rationality of believing in events that cannot be shown to have happened as recorded are immaterial – because faith is not based on either Scripture or rational argument but on religious feeling, entirely independent of either.[4]

Second, in terms of hermeneutics (as we saw in Chapter 3), Schleiermacher argued that only through exhaustive efforts to engage with the world and mind of the New Testament authors can interpreters understand the true meaning of their writings and, by implication, Christ's true saving message. In this way, engaging with historical criticism was part of the duty of any faithful Christian and certainly not just the preserve of the atheist.

Albrecht Ritschl

Ritschl saw himself continuing the work Schleiermacher had started in exploring and explaining the life of Jesus. He stood against the influence of rationalist, scholastic philosophy and argued that knowledge based on faith is more complete than knowledge based on purely logical categories. For Ritschl, Jesus should be understood as the perfect manifestation of God's will for humanity. Founding the Church, which brought believers into God's family, was Jesus' personal vocation and the highest expression of love for God and neighbour. With Schleiermacher, Ritschl went on to influence Adolf von Harnack in his interpretation of Jesus.

---

4 Tensions between the state (and the Church it defended) on one hand and universities (with their outspoken academics questioning central principles of Christianity) on the other continued throughout the main part of the nineteenth century in Prussia and neighbouring countries, coming to a head in the revolutions of 1848 and subsequent repressive measures against the freedom of expression. It became more and more important for scholars to be able to confess orthodox Christian beliefs in public while continuing their research without ideological obstacles in private! Over time this became a common approach among Lutheran Pietist scholars and clergymen. Its effects can still be seen in the work of modern biblical critics of the Reformed school, who argue that their historical deconstruction of the New Testament has no impact on their faith.

Christian Weisse

In 1838, building on Schleiermacher's work, Weisse was the first theologian to propose the two-source hypothesis (1838), which suggests that the Gospel of Mark was the first to be written and was one of two sources to the Gospel of Matthew and the Gospel of Luke, the other being Q, a lost collection of Jesus' sayings.

Heinrich Holtzmann

In his work *The Synoptic Gospels: Their Origin and Historical Character* (1863), Holtzmann developed Christian Weisse's hypothesis to argue for the priority of Mark. He saw Matthew using Mark and a 'collection of Sayings' and Luke using Mark and Matthew in their final forms.

Georg Friedrich Hegel

Hegel became professor of philosophy at the University of Berlin in 1818, becoming rector of the university in 1830, four years before Schleiermacher's death. Hegel was primarily a rationalist philosopher, and it is fair to say that he and Schleiermacher did not get on!

Hegel's work in philosophy and theology is of great significance for the development of biblical criticism, particularly in relation to the New Testament.

One of Hegel's earliest works was his Life of Jesus, *Das Leben Jesu*. It is really an essay on morality – Hegel suggests that Jesus' ethic was very similar to Kant's categorical imperative, and presents Jesus as a rationalistic philosopher, opposed to the superstition of Pharisaic Judaism. For Hegel, Jesus' miracles should be understood as signs or metaphors explaining his philosophical ideas and should not be understood literally. Hegel did not return to his discussion of the life of Jesus or the Gospels later in his career, however, focusing on other aspects of Christian theology; this omission was significant in terms of how others developed his work.

In his broader *Theology and Philosophy*, Hegel was influenced by the writings of the controversial Lutheran mystic Jakob Böhme and by the events of his lifetime – the French Revolution and Napoleon's conquest of Europe – as well as by classical philosophy and Enlightenment thinkers such as Kant.

Developing the idea of Heraclitus, he saw existence in a constant state of flux and reality as dynamic. What is real is what is *becoming*, not what is statically, abstractly being or nothing. Truth is not static, it is dynamic. It could follow from this – and some of Hegel's followers argued that it did follow from this – that religious insights should be dynamic and that if they remain static, they lose their claim to truth. Christianity, in failing to change and adapt, will be and should be superseded by another religion that is more in tune with the *Zeitgeist*.

Developing the idea of Anaxagoras and like Hermetic and Gnostic thinkers at and before the time of Christ, Hegel saw God in terms of *nous*. For Hegel, truth and reality is being thought by God, is dynamically becoming and not static in being or not being a particular way. Human thought is the reflection of God's thought, so God is not beyond human understanding but can be understood by an analysis of human thought and of reality as we encounter it.

It could follow from this – and again some of Hegel's followers argued that it did follow from this – that no static, literal interpretation of ancient Scripture can reveal God's truth so much as philosophy can.

For Hegel, humanity gradually progresses towards a state of absolute knowledge through a process of dialectic. Kant had distinguished two kinds of logic:

1   Analytic logic, which focuses the data of sense experience to yield knowledge of the natural phenomenal world.
2   Dialectical logic, which operates independently of sense experience and – falsely – seems to give knowledge of transcendent 'things in themselves', objective reality.

145

Hegel disagreed with Kant's focus on analytic logic, seeing it as too limited for philosophy. Further, he thought that Kant had misunderstood the nature of reality when he located it in the noumenal, transcendent, unknowable realm. For Hegel, true reality concerns the totality of existence and encompasses BOTH objective existence AND subjective existence. Things exist both in themselves and for others simultaneously, and it is wrong to focus on only one aspect when total existence includes both. For Hegel, dialectic reason is not concerned with Kant's 'transcendent' but with reality as a totality; it can yield true, complete, absolute knowledge.

Hegel's followers developed his ideas to describe the development of understanding towards truth in terms of a three-point cycle. A theory is proposed (THESIS) and then opposed (ANTITHESIS) before a middle line develops (SYNTHESIS). In time the synthesis becomes the new thesis and attracts its own antithetical opposition – although Hegel never used these terms, the 'Hegelian' idea that truth, although elusive, is best accessed through a PROCESS of argument, of paradigm and paradigm shift was enormously influential.

In terms of religious studies, Christianity and biblical criticism, the Hegelian doctrine of dialectic was of huge significance because it encouraged philosophers such as Strauss, Feuerbach and later Marx and Freud to think that Christianity was a stage in the development of humanity; that it was natural and right that Christianity should be challenged and replaced. In terms of Scripture, it encouraged scholars to see it as a record of how human beings conceived of the truth in the past – interesting historically, but of little value in terms of revealing the truth today. Perhaps pragmatically in conservative Prussia, Hegel never *said* any of this, but his philosophy could be taken in that way.

David Strauss

Strauss approached his study of the New Testament from a position of general Enlightenment scepticism, doubting any and all supernatural claims made about Jesus and his actions. Thoroughly steeped in Hegelian philosophy as a young man, Strauss' most famous work, also entitled *Das Leben Jesu*, took Hegel's ideas to what he believed to be their logical conclusion in the sphere of biblical studies. Showing no reverence, he analysed the texts with the aim of reconstructing the life and teachings of the 'historical Jesus' by stripping away the effects of superstition, ignorance and myth-making. Controversially, he sought to explain miracles and prophecies in terms of the general attempt by his followers to establish Jesus' claim to being the Messiah rather than as events with either naturalistic or supernatural causes.

Hegel's followers were quick to disassociate themselves from Strauss' ideas, claiming that they had nothing at all to do with Hegel and that Hegel did not endorse them. This was probably more to do with the need to put political distance between Strauss and mainstream Hegelianism than with any real philosophical distance that existed between them. As Bruno Bauer explained, there was a spectrum of opinion within Hegelian philosophy from the 'right Hegelians', who supported every aspect of Christian doctrine, through the centre ground to the 'left Hegelians', who asserted the primacy of rational philosophy and upheld very progressive views about the value of Scripture.

Let us consider the relationship between Hegel's and Strauss' thought in more detail.

For Hegel, philosophic or 'scientific' thought has the goal of revealing truth by creating a coherent discourse. The philosopher tries to describe the way things really are, which involves clarifying the nature of knowledge. Hegel was precursor to the phenomenological approach of Husserl and Heidegger. Similarly, for Strauss biblical criticism was a science that aimed to reveal philosophical truth by setting up parameters for discussion, orientated according to philosophical insights into the possible nature of truth.

For Hegel, human ideas are based on subjective experience (*Vorstellung*) and religion is part of our way of categorizing and understanding how we encounter the world. Religious ideas are therefore plural and partial, at most pointers to the truth and certainly not truth in themselves. Similarly, for Strauss religious ideas – whether in the New Testament or nineteenth-century Protestant doctrine – cannot be seen as more than pointers to the truth and are mostly the products of people trying to explain their experience of the world.

For Hegel, human beings are capable of accessing higher ideas, a purer form of understanding (*Begriff*), when they realize that things cannot really just be as we subjectively experience them, nor can they really exist objectively, independently of our subjective experience, rather they really exist only in the interface between subject and object. Similarly for Strauss, it is possible to move beyond primitive religious ideas towards a higher appreciation of the truth by recognizing their and our own limitations.

For Strauss, the New Testament was a collection of community responses to Jesus and to the huge desire his followers had for him to be the fulfilment of Jewish history and prophecy. The texts are best understood as myths, containing a very small basis in history and a lot of the authors' attempts to make sense of their experiences. It is for 'scientific' analysis to expose this state of affairs and set up a discussion that can move people beyond a *Vorstellung* of Christianity and towards appreciating its *Begriff*.[5]

Strauss was probably unwise to be quite so free in his application of Hegelian ideas; Prussia was a conservative Lutheran state where church influence continued to extend into all walks of life. Having left his job at the seminary in Tübingen aged just 27 following the publication of *Das Leben Jesu*, Strauss was forced to get by as a writer and with temporary Classics teaching jobs.[6]

---

5 A detailed account of Strauss' argument can be found in Albert Schweitzer's eminently readable *The Quest of the Historical Jesus*, ch. 8 – www.earlychristianwritings.com/schweitzer/chapter8.html.

6 First translated into English by Marian Evans (George Eliot), it caused uproar in Victorian England – the Earl of Shaftesbury reputedly called it 'the most pestilential book ever vomited out of the jaws of hell'. Part of the text is available at www.earlychristianwritings.com/strauss.

He tried to get a professorship at the radical new freethinking university in Zurich. Turned down in 1837 he tried again in 1839 and was appointed – but a petition with nearly 40,000 signatures and the threat of bloody revolution forced the university to pension him off before he took up the chair. He was actually burned in effigy during the Shrove Tuesday festival![7]

For all this, Strauss' ideas were hugely influential. As Albert Schweitzer wrote:

> He was not the greatest, and not the deepest, of theologians, but he was the most absolutely sincere. His insight and his errors were alike the insight and the errors of a prophet. And he had a prophet's fate. Disappointment and suffering gave his life its consecration. It unrolls itself before us like a tragedy, in which, in the end, the gloom is lightened by the mild radiance which shines forth from the nobility of the sufferer.[8]

In the German-speaking world his work played a major part in undermining the dominance of the Protestant churches in states like Prussia and Switzerland. Secular rulers, who relied on the Church to provide order and support their authority, were faced with revolutionary uprisings. Other radical philosophers, including Feuerbach and Marx, were inspired to press their cases. In another way, Strauss' critique of the historical basis for Christianity contributed to the development of liberal varieties of Christianity such as Unitarianism, which focused on Jesus' ethical teaching rather than on claims about his divine status. Of course, it also led to some Christians losing their faith altogether and having to think afresh about how to orientate their lives and be good without God.

---

7 Douglas R. McGaughey, 'On D. F. Strauß and the 1839 Revolution in Zurich' – www.chora-strangers.org/files/chora/mcgaughey_1994.pdf.

8 *The Quest of the Historical Jesus*, ch. 7 – www.earlychristianwritings.com/schweitzer/chapter7.html.

Bruno Bauer

Bauer first came to prominence as the spokesman of the Hegelians against Strauss after 1835; at 26 to Strauss' 27 it is little wonder their group acquired the nickname the Young Hegelians. Apart from taking apart Strauss' claim to being an heir to Hegel in his philosophy, in relation to the New Testament Bauer criticized Strauss' suggestion that a community could produce any sort of coherent narrative. He argued that only a single author could be responsible for a Gospel and that Mark's Gospel was probably the earliest. He thought that a version existed when Josephus wrote and that it was later completed and refined during the reign of Hadrian (117–38 AD), significant literary themes being added at this stage. Mark was subsequently used by the other Gospel writers. Distinctively, Bauer explored the influence of Stoicism on New Testament literature and, controversially, he suggested that all the Pauline Epistles were Greco-Roman forgeries.

Over time Bauer became convinced that the authors of the Gospels – particularly the author of Mark's Gospel – had a significant creative role in recording the story and teachings of Jesus. His work in biblical criticism became more and more sceptical about the historicity of the New Testament, and by the time he reached middle age he became a mentor to the young Friedrich Nietzsche, whose own ideas on Christianity were nothing if not extreme! Nevertheless despite this, Bauer blamed Strauss for the 1841 ban on Left Hegelians teaching in Prussian universities issued by King Frederick William IV, and was bitter for much of his career.

Ludwig Feuerbach

Although not a biblical scholar in the conventional sense, Feuerbach's work had a huge impact on the development of New Testament biblical criticism. Like Strauss and Bauer he was a Young Hegelian and a Left Hegelian; his work influenced Marx, Nietzsche and Freud in their different rejections of Christianity.

In *The Essence of Christianity* (1841), Feuerbach approached

Christianity from an anthropological perspective and came to see it as a projection of the early Christian Church – a system of ideas that satisfied their subconscious needs and desires. The early Church was dominated by oppressed people; Christianity provided them with a means of escaping their situation, a sense that they were cared for and loved as individuals and that their choices actually mattered. He then explored the role of psychology in religion, seeing that God fulfilled in human beings their individual needs and desires, and concluding that God is simply a projection, having no positive independent reality.

Feuerbach noted that both the individual projection of God – and more broadly people's projection of religion – can have negative consequences. Continuing to believe in God past the point where people become sufficiently self-aware to realize their role in creating God erodes people's 'sense of truth'. Feuerbach argued that faith is anti-intellectual 150 years before Dawkins and several years before Marx labelled religion 'the opium of the masses'. Belief in sacraments nurtures superstition and immoral behaviour – people trust in sacraments to undo what they could have chosen not to do in the first place.

Adolf von Harnack

In the final decades of the nineteenth century, von Harnack came to represent the apogee of the quest for the historical Jesus. He disregarded John's Gospel altogether, claiming it as totally ahistorical, and saw Jesus as an unorthodox and passionate preacher who threatened the Jewish authorities by speaking sense to their dogma. He only *appeared* to work miracles. For von Harnack, Jesus' message was misunderstood and later corrupted through the process of turning it into doctrine and then trying to analyse it philosophically. In returning to the text, the job of the Protestant scholar is to cut away layers of ecclesiastical dogma and doctrine and see what – if anything – is left of the original Jesus-message.

Note how closely von Harnack's Jesus resembled von

Harnack – an anti-establishment rationalist, not afraid to expose the flaws in accepted religious wisdom, and with little time for dogma!

Johannes Weiss

Weiss' exegesis of the Gospels from an eschatological perspective was particularly influential. Like Reimarus, Weiss saw passages in which Jesus refers to an imminent end to history as the most probably authentic. It followed that when the end of the world did not come about, Jesus' followers had to explain away his imminent eschatology; their attempts to do so explain much about how the New Testament developed. Weiss also concluded that the authentic teachings of the historical Jesus would be inapplicable to those who did not hold his first-century apocalyptic world view.

Weiss was also an early adopter of form criticism in relation to the New Testament, using it to argue that the First Letter to the Corinthians is an anthology of several letters from Paul, not a single whole letter. In applying source criticism to the New Testament, trying to resolve the synoptic problem and explain the levels of similarity and difference between the Gospel accounts, Weiss gave the name 'Q'[9] to the collection of Jesus' sayings that could have been used by the authors of Matthew and Luke.

William Wrede

Wrede developed many of Bruno Bauer's original ideas about the New Testament. In particular he agreed with Bauer that the author of the Gospel of Mark had a big role in creating early Christianity. His book on *The Messianic Secret in the Gospels* (1901) suggested that Jesus' instructions to keep quiet about his work (e.g. Mark 1.44) were later apologetic devices, designed by the author of Mark to account for the failure of Jesus' followers to acclaim him as Messiah. For Wrede, the messianic secret also allowed the early Christians to create a sense of exclusivity about membership of

---

9   Q probably stands for *Quelle*, German for source.

the Church – insiders versus outsiders, special knowledge – and helped it to compete with Gnostic sects, of which there were many in the first centuries after Jesus.

Wrede's theory about the theological status of passages referencing the messianic secret was accepted in the next generation by the developers of form criticism. His attempt to identify the unique perspective and contribution of each individual biblical author later developed into redaction criticism.

In his 1906 book *Paul*, Wrede argued that without Paul's injection of Hellenistic philosophy, Christianity would have fizzled out; he called Paul 'the second founder of Christianity'.[10] Wrede also argued that 2 Thessalonians was inauthentic.

The Quest and the Church

Through the middle decades of the nineteenth century, many faithful Christians felt torn between the compelling arguments of theologians and the requirements of their churches.

Following on from her 1846 translation of Strauss' *Life of Jesus: Critically Examined* (*Das Leben Jesu*), Marian Evans' 1854 translation of Feuerbach's *The Essence of Christianity* raised a storm.

Poems such as Matthew Arnold's 'Dover Beach'[11] and Thomas Hardy's 'God's Funeral'[12] express the feelings many people had as a result of reading Strauss in the second half of the nineteenth century. For many erstwhile Christians it was no longer possible to reconcile their faith with reason, and they were left desperately searching for some other basis for morality, identity, community cohesion and personal hope.

In England the development of biblical criticism and rationalist approaches to theology caused chaos in the Church of England, with periodic attempts to exclude those priests with

---

10   William Wrede, *Paul*, trans. Edward Lummis; Philip Green, 1907, reprint Eugene, OR: Wipf & Stock, 2001, p. 179.

11   Published in 1867, written sometime earlier, maybe in 1849 or 1851.

12   Written between 1908 and 1910.

unorthodox views from ministering religion. The first chapters of *North and South* by Elizabeth Gaskell[13] reflect the mood of the times, with a zealous bishop demanding that all new appointees in his diocese reaffirm their adherence to the Thirty-Nine Articles of the Church of England – and the crisis of conscience that triggered in many learned clergymen who could no longer truthfully say they believed that:

> Holy Scripture containeth all things necessary to salvation: so that whatsoever is not read therein, nor may be proved thereby, is not to be required of any man, that it should be believed as an article of the Faith, or be thought requisite or necessary to salvation.[14]

In the Catholic Church developments in biblical criticism took longer to have an effect on priests and people. Partly this was because the study of the Bible in this way was discouraged in Catholic countries and works of biblical criticism were infrequently translated into the relevant languages. In Great Britain, Catholics were effectively barred from studying at university until the 1870s.[15]

Ernest Renan

Renan was trained for the priesthood in Paris but lost his calling after beginning to study German biblical criticism in the early 1840s. His *La Vie de Jesus* (1863) was primarily a historical work, part of a series of histories of the ancient world aimed at a Catholic audience and far from groundbreaking in its portrayal of Jesus. Nevertheless it was one of the first works to bring the ideas of Reimarus and Strauss to Rome's attention and was consequently highly controversial.

13 Published 1854, www.gutenberg.org/files/4276/4276-h/4276-h.htm.

14 See www.churchofengland.org/prayer-worship/worship/book-of-common-prayer/articles-of-religion.aspx#VI.

15 Alasdair MacIntyre, *God, Philosophy, Universities: A Selective History of the Catholic Philosophical Tradition*, Lanham, MD: Rowman & Littlefield; reprint edition 2011, pp. 138ff.

Schweitzer explained that Renan:

> offered his readers a Jesus who was alive, whom he, with his artistic imagination, had met under the blue heaven of Galilee, and whose lineaments his inspired pencil had seized ... Yet the aesthetic feeling for nature which gave birth to this Life of Jesus was, it must be confessed, neither pure nor profound ... He looks at the landscape with the eye of a decorative painter ... The gentle Jesus, the beautiful Mary, the fair Galileans who formed the retinue of the 'amiable carpenter', might have been taken over in a body from the shop-window of an ecclesiastical art emporium in the Place St. Sulpice. Nevertheless, there is something magical about the work.

He continued:

> For one who writes the life of Jesus on His native soil, the Gospels are not so much sources of information as incentives to revelation. 'I had,' Renan avows, 'a fifth Gospel before my eyes, mutilated in parts, but still legible, and taking it for my guide I saw behind the narratives of Matthew and Mark, instead of an ideal Being of whom it might be maintained that He had never existed, a glorious human countenance full of life and movement.' It is this Jesus of the fifth Gospel that he desires to portray.[16]

Renan was forced out of the Catholic Church and by 1884 his work was seen as sufficiently threatening for Cardinal Newman to leap to the defence of the Church,[17] arguing that Renan was wrong in claiming that it 'insists on its members believing ... a great deal more in pure criticism and pure history than the strictest Protestants exact from their pupils or flocks'.[18]

---

16 See www.earlychristianwritings.com/schweitzer/chapter13.html.

17 *The Nineteenth Century* 15:84 (1884) – www.newmanreader.org/works/miscellaneous/scripture.html.

18 Quoted ibid.

Alfred Loisy

A French Roman Catholic priest, Loisy studied oriental languages under Ernest Renan. Like Renan, he felt stifled by the Church's apparent insistence on members believing in the impossible – the virgin birth, the resurrection, miracles, Moses writing the Pentateuch and so on.

In 1893 Loisy published a lecture in which he summed up his position on biblical criticism; he lost his job. He stated that:

1   the Pentateuch was not the work of Moses;
2   the first five chapters of Genesis were not literal history;
3   the New Testament and the Old Testament did not possess equal historical value;
4   there was a development in scriptural doctrine;
5   biblical writings were subject to the same limitations as those by other authors of the ancient world.

He went on to engage with von Harnack and advance his own theories about Jesus and the origins of Christianity, which he claimed were consistent with Cardinal Newman's writings.

Loisy argued that Jesus could not have understood that he was God or had any idea how his message would catch on or how the Church would change the world. He observed that as Jews, Jesus and his followers would have been appalled by the idea that Jesus and God could be consubstantial; they would only have conceived of Jesus being the Messiah in Old Testament terms. To Loisy, regardless of who Jesus actually was, he could not have claimed to be what the Church taught him to be.

The Church's response was swift and brutal. His works were officially condemned,[19] and in 1907 the Holy Office issued a decree entitled *A Lamentable Departure Indeed*[20] in which it formally condemned so-called modernist (otherwise: liberal) propositions concerning the nature of the Church. This was followed by the

---

19   See archive.org/stream/americancatholic29philuoft#page/550/mode/2up.

20   See www.papalencyclicals.net/Pius10/p10lamen.htm.

encyclical *Feeding the Lord's Flock*,[21] which characterized modernism as the 'synthesis of all heresies'. Loisy realized that there was no hope for reconciliation of his views with the official doctrine of the Church; he was excommunicated in 1908.[22]

George Tyrrell

Following Strauss and Renan, many other scholars made their own attempts to reconstruct the historical Jesus. By the beginning of the twentieth century it was becoming apparent that far from progressing towards the truth about Jesus' identity, life and teaching, historical critics had proposed wildly different, even contradictory visions of Jesus. George Tyrrell, in his *Christianity at the Crossroads*[23] (published in 1910), summarized the position admirably, stating that 'in defiance of history they have shaped Christ to their own image'. Tyrrell first coined what has become a well-used analogy when he wrote: 'The Christ that Harnack sees, looking back through nineteen centuries of "Catholic darkness", is only the reflection of a Liberal Protestant face, seen at the bottom of a deep well.'[24] Like Loisy, Tyrrell had been forced out of the Church as a modernist and was excommunicated in 1908.

The Modernist Controversy

Neither Loisy nor Tyrrell went nearly so far as Protestant or Atheist critics in denying the divinity of Jesus and the value of the Bible, and neither bought into the bigger claims of the biblical critics, yet their relative moderation did them no good in the end. The Church was extremely concerned that their ideas would start down a slippery slope towards atheism and perhaps the collapse of the Church.

---

21 See w2.vatican.va/content/pius-x/en/encyclicals/documents/hf_p-x_enc_ 19070908_pascendi-dominici-gregis.html.

22 For a full account of Loisy's life and conflict with the Catholic Church, see archive.org/stream/harvardtheologic11harvuoft#page/72/mode/2up.

23 See archive.org/details/christianityatc00petrgoog, p. xxi.

24 Ibid., p. 44.

The cartoon below,[25] first published in 1922, sums up the reason why the Catholic Church – and other churches in time – took such strong action against scholars who raised doubts about the Bible. Nevertheless, in 1943 Pope Pius XII gave licence to the new scholarship in his encyclical *Divino afflante spiritu*. He wrote:

> Textual Criticism ... [is] quite rightly employed in the case of the sacred books ... Let the interpreter then, with all care and without neglecting any light derived from recent research, endeavour to determine the peculiar character and circumstances of the sacred writer, the age in which he lived, the sources written or oral to which he had recourse and the forms of expression he employed.

25 'Descent of the Modernists', E. J. Pace, *Christian Cartoons*, 1922; licensed under public domain via Wikimedia Commons.

Two decades later the Second Vatican Council found:

> The books of Scripture must be acknowledged as teaching solidly, faithfully and without error *that truth which God wanted put into sacred writings* for the sake of salvation.[26]

The *Catechism of the Catholic Church* now states:

> In order to discover the sacred authors' intention, the reader must take into account the conditions of their time and culture, the literary genres in use at that time, and the modes of feeling, speaking and narrating then current. For the fact is that truth is differently presented and expressed in the various types of historical writing, in prophetical and poetical texts, and in other forms of literary expression.[27]

In the 1960s, Catholic scholars like Raymond E. Brown, Joseph Fitzmyer and John P. Meier felt liberated; for the first time they were free to apply the techniques of historical criticism to the New Testament without much fear of censure. Given that the Catholic Church never upheld biblical inerrancy, their work has not done much to undermine faith, although some would say that the cautious approach many Catholic biblical scholars still voluntarily adopt has helped to ensure that.

A Crisis in Historical Criticism?

By the beginning of the twentieth century, biblical criticism had begun to lack credibility.

First, the whole enterprise of questioning the historicity of the New Testament had become associated with the liberal, revolutionary thinkers whose attempts to overthrow governments across Europe had been a constant threat since the 1830s. People were suspicious about the political and social motivations of biblical critics in undermining the authority of the Church and threatening the stability of society.

---

26 Second Vatican Council, *Dei Verbum*, Dogmatic Constitution on Divine Revelation, 11 (1965), emphasis added.

27 Article 3, section 110.

Second, biblical criticism generated such diverse claims and suggestions about the character and teachings of Jesus and how the New Testament came to be written that the effect was to cancel each other out. Different scholars offered different, even contradictory interpretations of the same evidence and many people suspected that their interpretations owed more to their own prejudices and concerns than to historical fact.

Textual criticism had shown that the canon was selected from a larger body of work, that the accepted text of the Bible was selected from a range of alternative texts, and that popular translations often failed to convey other plausible meanings for passages. The rise of source criticism suggested that the New Testament was far from the complete, neutral record of historical events that Christians would have liked it to be; early redaction critics suggested that each author had a particular set of political and theological concerns in writing and/or editing as and when they did, and that their work should not be understood as pure history. The effect of applying form criticism to the New Testament was to suggest that the process of the stories and sayings of Jesus being transmitted through the early Church had distorted them to such a degree that the original had been almost or even totally lost.

It is not difficult to understand how believers in and around the First World War felt about biblical criticism. Either it had shown Christianity – nay religion itself – to be a human construct and probably the tool of oppression Marx had said it was, or it had betrayed people of faith, leaving them rudderless when they most needed religion and knew that, despite the evidence, there was more to Christianity than the critics suggested.

Although published as early as 1871, George Eliot's novel *Middlemarch* offers insight into how biblical criticism was received by real people.[28] Reverend Edward Casaubon is a total hypocrite – he occupies the position of a clergyman but fails either to minister effectively to the poor, weak and dispossessed or to live by Christian principles. He is obsessed by obscure and outdated scholarly research, as represented by his unfinished book *The Key*

---

28 The novel is available at www.gutenberg.org/ebooks/145.

to All Mythologies. Would it matter even if Casaubon was right about the origins of Christianity? Should this really be the business of ordained ministers when poor tenants struggle to survive while serving rich absentee landlords?

It did not take long for biblical critics to become the target of criticism themselves.

Albert Schweitzer

Schweitzer's groundbreaking *The Quest of the Historical Jesus* was first published in 1906 (1910 in English). In an engaging style it surveyed multiple attempts to reconstruct the historical Jesus, just a few of which have been outlined above, and concluded that the attempt to identify truth about Jesus by analysing the Bible was bankrupt. Just as Tyrrell would claim (and as Feuerbach had observed decades before in his *The Essence of Christianity*), scholars project themselves, their needs and aspirations on to the shadowy form of Jesus and find 'historical' evidence to suit their own concerns.[29] Following Schweitzer, William Lane Craig has described what is often called the First Quest thus:

> apparently unaware of the personal element they all brought to their research, each writer reconstructed a historical Jesus after his own image. There was Strauss's Hegelian Jesus, Renan's sentimental Jesus, Bauer's non-existent Jesus, Ritschl's liberal Jesus, and so forth.[30]

Albert Schweitzer was a truly amazing man. A gifted musician and native of Alsace, he started his academic career by studying the religious philosophy of Kant in Paris and then at Tübingen. His strong conviction was that Christianity was a call to live an ethical life, to serve the poor and weak and reform the system that oppressed them. Squabbles about points of doctrine and all forms of religious intolerance were, as he saw it, a wicked distraction.

---

29 See www.earlychristianwritings.com/schweitzer.

30 William Lane Craig, *Reasonable Faith: Christian Truth and Apologetics*, 3rd edn, Wheaton, IL: Crossway, 2006.

As a teenager he realized he was called not only to be an academic but also to live out his Christian faith. Because of this he looked to leave his academic position at the height of his powers when he was 30.

To this end he started to study medicine and in 1913 set out for Africa to work as a missionary doctor. He set up a hospital and worked in Lambaréné, Gabon, on and off into the 1950s, by which time he had won the Nobel Peace Prize and had become one of the foremost peace campaigners of his age, working against the threat of nuclear weapons.

It is clear that Schweitzer's approach to his Christian faith influenced his work in biblical criticism. For him, the historical detail of the Gospels is subsumed by their life-affirming message; the Christ of faith is real and works in the world regardless of what the historical Jesus may or may not have been like.

Rudolph Bultmann

A student of Herman Gunkel and Johannes Weiss, Bultmann was as sceptical regarding *what* we can know about the historical Jesus as Schweitzer. He argued that the only thing we can know about Jesus is *that* he existed and was resurrected. For Bultmann, this is the central Gospel proclamation or kerygma, to which the evangelists and Paul responded in their different ways and which is the basis for Christianity. In order to reconstruct how the early Church developed in faith, scholars must attempt to demythologize the texts they study, showing how early phrases, ideas and stories were re-imagined and incorporated into more and more complex works.

As part of this process, and initially working with Martin Dibelius, Bultmann applied form criticism to the Synoptic Gospels[31] and later to the Gospel of John, suggesting that it drew on a (lost) Signs-Gospel source.[32] He argued that they are made up of discrete narrative units of text or pericope, strung or sometimes

31 In his *History of the Synoptic Tradition* (1921).

32 *Das Evangelium des Johannes* (1941). Gerhard Ebeling, one of Bultmann's

woven together to create each Gospel story. As he saw it, identifying each pericope and then reconstructing its original context or *Sitz im Leben* should be the focus of biblical scholarship.

For Bultmann, demythologization is like stripping the layers from an onion: eventually there is nothing left but the layers. He played down the significance of knowing Jesus as a historical figure, focusing instead on the importance of how we respond to the Christ of faith. Like Schweitzer (and Schleiermacher), Bultmann saw religion, and faith, as independent of scholarly opinion about the historical Jesus.

Martin Heidegger

Bultmann worked with Martin Heidegger at Marburg between 1923 and 1928; the two became close friends. Heidegger's main philosophical interest was ontology, the study of being, existence itself.

By way of context, Kant had distinguished between the world as we are conscious of it (the *phenomenal* world) and the world of things in themselves, independent of human consciousness (the *noumenal* world), and Hegel had argued that by studying the phenomenal world we can get an insight into the essence of being. In part under the influence of his teacher Franz Brentano, Edmund Husserl questioned what existence is precisely. He concluded that existence is how we experience things directly, free of intellectualizing. He proposed phenomenology, a new science of consciousness aimed at categorizing direct experience and so explaining the reality of things.

Heidegger was a pupil of Husserl but he did not accept Husserl's conclusion about the nature of existence. In *Being and Time* (1927) he attempted to analyse the phenomenon of human existence (*Dasein*). Heidegger came to see language as the vehicle through which we can come to understand being. He analysed a range of historical texts as part of his attempts to understand

---

students, further developed Bultmann's idea that a lost 'Signs Gospel' had been used in the writing of the Gospel of John.

existence without resorting to traditional metaphysical speculation which, like Husserl, he saw as bankrupt. His relationship with Bultmann reinforced his conviction that analysing text is a good way into the mind and experience of other people in other ages, and assured him of the possibility of entering into the world of the author, understanding the effects of literary form and language, and by sharing in the author's experience, identifying something close to their intended meaning.

In the 1920s Bultmann and Heidegger – somewhat in the tradition of the Young Hegelians of the 1840s – shared a radical political vision in which philosophers would play a part in revitalizing human culture by replacing worn-out traditions, institutions, religions and myths, and building a new world order in which men and women could live authentically, engaging with the essence of their human existence and rejecting the facile answers to human questions offered by the media, technology and popular ideologies. In the 1930s, after leaving Marburg for Freiburg, Heidegger worked with the Nazis and seemed to support their ideology, although he later realized his mistake, stepped back and was even punished for his lack of cooperation during the war. Bultmann lost friends, including Rudolph Otto, over his close relationship with Heidegger,[33] and was quite slow in his own response to Nazism.[34]

During the 1940s Bultmann argued that Christianity must progress and adapt, stripping away all supernaturalism in order to remain relevant to modern, scientifically aware people. As he saw it, language that was proper to the mythological world view of first-century Palestine was an obstacle to contemporary congregations, and Christianity should strive to create a new 'religion without myth' for the modern world if it was going to survive, let alone thrive.

---

33   William D. Dennison, *The Young Bultmann: Context for His Understanding of God*, 1884–1925, New York: Peter Lang, 2008, pp. 133–4.

34   See Shawn Kelley, *Racializing Jesus: Race, Ideology and the Formation of Modern Biblical Scholarship*, London: Routledge, 2002.

Ninian Smart and the Development of Religious Studies

In the 1960s, building on Bultmann's approach and the phenomenological ideas of Edmund Husserl, Ninian Smart attempted to
demythologize religion and describe it as a human phenomenon,
identifying its constituent parts and showing how they are common
to traditions across the world. Smart's seven dimensions of religion
are:

1   Myth – narratives expressing and exploring fundamental
    questions of meaning, being, value and truth.
2   Ritual – patterns of ceremony and worship, devotions
    expressive of the faith and belief characteristic of the religion,
    also re-enactments of mythic elements.
3   Dogma – doctrines, teachings, principles and theories
    constituting the theology and philosophy of the tradition in
    question, which may be expressed in myth and ritual.
4   Ethics – principles for the practice of life, moral values and
    principles for how life is to be fulfilled. Mythic writing may
    explore and present the ethical principles;.Experience – the
    experiential dimension of religion might entail the special or
    distinctive experiences the religion involves or it may denote
    the particularity of engagement with the religion through all
    of the dimensions.
5   Social – the communal aspect of the religion. This may be
    closely linked to experience and ritual.
6   Material – the physical aspects of religion within a historical
    and/or cultural tradition; buildings and shrines, art, artefacts,
    modes of dress.[35]

By this phenomenological description, myth is only a small part
of religion. Within Christianity the Bible is mostly myth. Ritual,
dogma and ethics are largely independent of the Bible. It might
follow that where the Bible has become an obstacle to faith, and its
myths no longer offer believers insight into meaning, being, value

---

35   See Ninian Smart, *The Religious Experience of Mankind*, London: Fontana,
1969.

and truth, it would be better to abandon it and develop new ways of expressing and exploring fundamental questions.

No-quest?

Bultmann was the dominant voice in German theology from the 1920s until the 1950s. His students included the philosophers Hans Jonas and Hannah Arendt and the biblical critics Ernst Käsemann and Günther Bornkamm. Under Bultmann's influence, theologians saw studying the historical origins of the Bible as less and less central to what they were doing, while engaging with philosophy became far more important than it had been since the Reformation.

Bultmann's relationship with Heidegger and the period of Nazi dominance taught his students the potential political significance of biblical criticism; how it could and should be used to subvert biblical and theological interpretations generated by extremists. In the 1940s and 1950s, biblical critics realized how dangerous it could be to give up on being able to claim historical truth; without it, what would make one popular interpretation more or less valid than another?

From the First World War until the 1950s there was a period in which exploring the origins of the New Testament became deeply unfashionable, at least in Germany.

It has become accepted practice to divide the quest for the historical Jesus into three phases: the First Quest until 1910; the Second Quest from the 1950s to 1970s; the Third Quest in the 1980s and 1990s. However, this neat model might not fit the facts and apparently discounts the historical-critical work being done in the English-speaking world and the seamless connection between English-speaking historical critics of the interwar period and the work of their students in the 1970s, 1980s and 1990s.

Throughout the so-called 'period of no-quest' in the first half of the twentieth century, British scholars such as B. H. Streeter in Oxford, C. H. Dodd in Manchester and Cambridge and C. K. Barrett in Durham retained confidence in the possibility of reaching knowledge of the historical personality of Jesus.

Burnett Hillman Streeter

Canon Streeter, Provost of Queen's College, Oxford, was an early adopter of a phenomenological, comparative-religions approach and fully appreciated the political significance of theology. He was an active member of the Oxford Group, which tried to address the growth of Nazism and looming international conflict by advocating a moral reawakening, both in ordinary Christians and leaders of all nations. Streeter died in a plane crash in Switzerland in 1937.[36]

Streeter's most important book was *The Four Gospels: A Study of Origins* (1924). After surveying the evidence, he proposed a development of the old two-source hypothesis developed by Weisse a century before, which would better explain the nature and extent of similarities and differences between Mark, Matthew and Luke, the Synoptic Gospels. According to Streeter's four-source hypothesis, both the author of the Gospel of Matthew and the author of the Gospel of Luke had access to the Gospel of Mark and Q, already widely accepted to be a collection of Aramaic sayings. Each of the authors also had access to a quantity of original material; M-Source was unique to the author of Matthew and L-source to the author of Luke. Streeter's hypothesis went on to become the most widely accepted solution to the synoptic problem through the rest of the twentieth century and is still the basis of most introductory textbook accounts of the authorship and development of the Gospels.

In 1955 Austin Farrar criticized Streeter's hypothesis and argued for a simpler explanation, whereby Matthew used Mark plus his own research and ideas and Luke used both Mark and Matthew plus his own research and ideas. The arguments in and conclusions of Farrar's essay 'On dispensing with Q' were used by Michael Goulder at the University of Birmingham and have since been taken up by Goulder's student Mark Goodacre, currently at Duke University in the USA.

---

36   See www.bricecjones.com/blog/canon-b-streeter-dead-in-air-crash.

Charles Dodd

Dodd worked at Oxford, Manchester and latterly Cambridge Universities, focusing on interpreting the Gospel of John. He started out as a classicist before spending a year in Berlin, where he was taught by Adolf von Harnack. Dodd saw realized eschatology, the idea that the 'kingdom of God' referred to a present reality rather than a future apocalypse (whether imminent or far in the future), as key to understanding passages of the New Testament, particularly in John's Gospel and the writings of Paul.

Dodd taught William Davies, who developed the idea that Paul was not influenced only by Greek thought but more by Pharisaic Judaism. This understanding of the Jewish context for Paul and the development of the Gospels was advanced by Martin Hengel, Professor of New Testament and Early Judaism at the University of Tübingen until his death in 2009. William Davies taught Ed (E. P.) Sanders, whose important book *Jesus and Judaism* (1985) really forced New Testament scholars to engage with the influence of first-century Judaism on Jesus, Paul and the evangelists. Sanders' work on Paul has been taken up by Tom (N. T.) Wright and James (J. D. G) Dunn.

The Second Quest

The effect of Bultmann's dominance was to stifle historical criticism in Germany between the two world wars. As Nazism took hold, the historical vacuum at the heart of Christianity was exploited by fascists, who sought to justify their ideas through the Church. The German Evangelical Church, or *Reichskirche*, developed a revisionist account of Jesus' teaching and the origin of the New Testament, editing out all dependence on Judaism. Mainstream German theologians struggled to respond; not only were they in professional and even personal danger but they lacked the means of arguing that Nazi revisionism was less true to the historical facts than other versions of Christianity because they subscribed to the view that almost nothing can ever be known about the historical Jesus, that faith is based on religious feelings that can be claimed by fascists as much as by anybody else.

Through the 1930s and 1940s Bultmann was a member of the German Confessing Church but a notably quiet opponent of Nazism. His students were rather more outspoken, however, and several of them came to believe that Bultmann was too negative about the possibility of discovering *what* Jesus taught and plain wrong about the need to establish a historical basis for Christian teachings.

Ernst Käsemann

With left-wing sympathies, Käsemann – a student of Bultmann – came into conflict with the Gestapo and spent much of the war as a prisoner. From 1953 he revived the quest for the historical Jesus while acknowledging the real difficulties that exist with trying to uncover anything of the authentic Jesus of history.

Today he is chiefly remembered for developing criteria to support the evaluation of the historicity of passages of the Gospels. For example, Käsemann's double criterion of difference suggests that if material makes no sense in either a Jewish or a first-century Christian context, then it seems likely to refer to the historical Jesus. He also argued that traditions with multiple attestation and that were coherent with other material already found to be reliable historical traditions about Jesus were also more likely to be reliable. Käsemann also returned to the work of Johannes Weiss, suggesting that imminent eschatology and apocalypticism were key to identifying authentic Jesus material.

Günther Bornkamm

Another student of Bultmann who had an uneasy relationship with the Gestapo, in his book *Jesus von Nazareth* (1956), Bornkamm aimed to show that romantic portrayals of Jesus had little basis in history.

During the Nazi period the German Evangelical Church taught that Christianity was perfectly in accord with National Socialism. Using the techniques of biblical criticism and exegesis,

Nazi-sympathizing theologians and priests portrayed Jesus as an Aryan and an active preacher, organizer and fighter who opposed the institutionalized Judaism of his day. In particular, this warped version of Christianity rejected all 'Jewish-written' parts of the Bible, including the entire Old Testament. These ideas were based on the work of a number of leading German biblical critics of the nineteenth century, including Paul de Lagarde (Professor of Oriental Languages at Göttingen 1869–91).

Despite the difficulties of reconstructing the historical Jesus, Bornkamm felt that it was important to try because however familiar it might have seemed, by the 1950s Christianity had in fact become strange and unintelligible to many people. This allowed unscrupulous scholars and priests to make all sorts of wild claims in its name, without people being in a position to challenge them. Bornkamm wrote:

> If the journey into this often misty country is to succeed, then the first requirement is the readiness for free and frank questioning, and the renunciation of an attitude which simply seeks the confirmation of its own judgements arising from a background of belief or of unbelief.[37]

He advocated genuinely open-minded research into the historical origins of Christianity as the remedy for ignorance and the sort of fundamentalism that feeds off it.

Helmut Koester

Koester studied under Bultmann at Marburg and worked for Bornkamm in the 1950s before leaving Germany for the USA. As Professor of Divinity at Harvard Divinity School, he developed the idea that references in the work of the Apostolic Fathers that parallel elements in the Synoptic Gospels need not necessarily suggest a dependence on the Synoptics in the form that they are known to us. This was important as it allowed biblical critics to

---

37   G. Bornkamm, *Jesus of Nazareth*, London: SCM Press, 1960, p. 10.

speculate about later dates for the Synoptic Gospels than had hitherto been plausible.

Koester worked with James M. Robinson, who in 1959 wrote *A New Quest of the Historical Jesus*,[38] which cemented the idea and ideals of the Second Quest in the minds of many people. Robinson later became Professor of Religion at Claremont Graduate University, edited the Nag Hammadi codices and tried to reconstruct Q.

Hans Conzelmann

Conzelmann's *The Theology of St. Luke* (1954) was important for the development of redaction criticism and its application to the New Testament. He challenged Käsemann's view that Jesus should be identified with passages characterized by an imminent eschatology or sense of the apocalyptic. Conzelmann understood Jesus' authentic message to be one of the kingdom of God breaking into the present, and that when the final judgement would happen or how are essentially irrelevant to Jesus' ethical teaching, which is equally as applicable now as then.

According to Conzelmann, the author of Luke's Gospel changed the general expectation that Jesus would soon return to an expectation that Christianity would exist for the foreseeable future and must find ways of enabling people to live their whole lives in Christ's message. So Conzelmann's broader approach to *Heilsgeschichte* or Salvation history involved the reconstruction of how Christians understood their own place in relation to the last judgement over time.

Oscar Cullmann

Oscar Cullmann, the leading ecumenist, worked in a similar way to Conzelmann, combining research in the application of historical criticism with theological exegesis and a particular interest in Salvation History. He is associated with the development of the

---

38 James M. Robinson, *A New Quest of the Historical Jesus*, Studies in Biblical Theology, London: SCM Press, 1959.

concept of inaugurated eschatology – the idea that through Jesus' life, the movement towards the end of time and ultimate judgement had already begun but would not be complete for some time. For Cullmann, there are both 'already' and 'not yet' aspects to the kingdom of God.

In the end, the Second Quest was characterized by its very theological approach to identifying authentic Jesus material and by the political concern that most of its proponents had to find such historical authority for their version of Christianity that would enable it to triumph over the revisionist version of Christianity proposed by Nazi sympathizers.

Historical Criticism in the USA

The USA was established by strict Protestant Christians and has remained a bastion of conservative theology. Even today about a third of Americans are literalists and believe that the Bible is the actual word of God.[39] However, the influence of biblical criticism, the growth of secular liberalism and an influx of people with different faiths all contributed to a slow but steady decline in conservative Christianity and in biblical literalism through the middle decades of the twentieth century.

Despite the decline of historical criticism and rise of postmodernism in Europe, American critics have continued to reconstruct Jesus to speak to contemporary concerns. Robert H. Gundry from Westmont College in Santa Barbara, California and Robert M. Grant from the University of Chicago are quite well-known examples of how rigorous application of historical-critical methods to the New Testament continued pretty much regardless of the quests and so-called periods of no-quest. In 1993 Richard Horsley described his view of the historical Jesus thus:

> The focal concern of the kingdom of God in Jesus' preaching and practice, however, is the liberation and welfare of the people ... he had utter confidence that God was restoring

---

39 See www.gallup.com/poll/148427/say-bible-literally.aspx.

the life of the society, and that this would mean judgment for those who oppressed the people and vindication for those who faithfully adhered to God's will and responded to the kingdom. That is, God was imminently and presently effecting a historical transformation. In modern parlance, that would be labelled a 'revolution'.[40]

It is not difficult to imagine Jesus as a Palestinian Martin Luther King after reading this!

John S. Kloppenborg and Burton L. Mack

Like James M. Robinson, Kloppenborg and Mack have attempted to reconstruct Q. They suggest that it had three parts or layers, which might have been added sequentially: wisdom sayings; details on how the community ought to behave; apocalyptic pronouncements.

It is notable that in the USA, biblical critics face bigger obstacles to their work than they have done in Europe, both because many theological faculties exist within avowedly religious universities and because public opinion was far less tolerant of any question being raised about the inerrancy of Scripture. Possibly because of this, some American scholars use historical criticism within a particular faith perspective, perhaps – like Schleiermacher – by arguing that faith does not depend on historical events or the precise word of Scripture. Examples of this approach can be seen in the biblical work of Gary Habermas and William Lane Craig.

Other American scholars, embracing the big US market for popular books about Christianity, have become minor celebrities.

Bart Ehrman

In popular books including *Jesus, Interrupted* (2009), *Forged* (2012), *Did Jesus Exist?* (2012) and *How Jesus Became God: The Exaltation of a Jewish Preacher from Galilee* (2014), Ehrman

40 Richard A. Horsley, *Jesus and the Spiral of Violence*, San Francisco: Harper & Row, 1993, pp. 207–8.

has skilfully repackaged scholarly arguments from the past 200 years for an interested but untutored American readership. Where scholars have long accepted the existence of pseudepigraphical works in the New Testament, Ehrman draws attention to the existence of *forged* books in the New Testament. Where scholars have always recognized the relatively late origin of doctrines such as that of the Trinity, Ehrman exposes the lack of biblical basis that they have and questions where they came from and why.

Between the 1980s and the present, theological enquiry in the USA has become increasingly politicized. Social conservatives have bankrolled scholars who embraced inerrancy with the intention that they should provide research refuting the more extreme claims of historical critics.[41] Liberals have bankrolled historical critics to demonstrate the flaws in the literalist approach and undermine moral and political arguments that claim biblical authority.[42]

Robert Funk

Funk founded the Jesus Seminar and Westar Institute in Santa Rosa, California to promote research into biblical literacy, using a historical-critical approach to educate the American public about the basis for Christian doctrine and undermine teachings based on literalist interpretations of Scripture. The Westar Institute has employed James M. Robinson alongside other well-known and sympathetic scholars ranging from Karen Armstrong and Don Cupitt to Richard Holloway and Gerd Lüdemann.

Unsurprisingly, Funk's work was highly controversial in the USA – although he rarely says much that has not previously been said by European biblical critics. He is a fellow of the rival Discovery Institute, a conservative evangelical organization that aims to 'support the theistic foundations of the West',[43] most

41 E.g. the Discovery Institute, theology faculties in seminaries, Bible colleges and religious universities.

42 E.g. the Westar Institute.

43 See www.discovery.org/about.

famously by advancing so-called 'intelligent-design' arguments. J. P. Moreland has claimed that the scholars of the Jesus Seminar 'leave people spiritually bankrupt and hopeless'.[44]

The Third Quest?

In *The Interpretation of the New Testament 1861–1986* (1988), Stephen Neill and Tom Wright coined the term 'Third Quest' for a range of different approaches to investigating the historical origins of the New Testament first proposed during the 1970s and 1980s.[45] If anything brought these approaches together it was their use of a better understanding of the Judaism of the inter-testamental period and of archaeological evidence to support their application of techniques in historical criticism to the New Testament. Work on the Dead Sea Scrolls and Nag Hammadi codices, as well as the discovery of a range of other historical sources and parallels, informed the work of scholars engaged in historical criticism in the 1980s and 1990s. Scholars involved in the Third Quest included members of the Jesus Seminar, Ed (E. P.) Sanders, Geza Vermes, James Charlesworth and Tom (N. T.) Wright.

The Third Quest is predominantly a North American phenomenon – with the honourable exception of N. T. Wright. As Mark Goodacre has pointed out, like previous quests it has tended to assume the validity of source-critical insights into the formation of the New Testament – such as the priority of Mark, Streeter's four-document hypothesis, the existence of Q – without proper investigation, as well as to ignore research that is not available in the English language.[46] Since the millennium the quest has struggled on while other approaches to studying the New Testament have become dominant. There are still scholars using

---

44 See articles.latimes.com/2005/sep/07/local/me-funk7.

45 Stephen Neill and N. T. Wright, *The Interpretation of the New Testament 1861–1986*, 2nd edn, Oxford: Oxford University Press, 1988, pp. 379–403.

46 See markgoodacre.org/digest.htm.

historical-critical techniques to uncover Christian origins, but this approach is now very unfashionable!

Conclusion

The quest for the historical Jesus endured through the eighteenth, nineteenth and twentieth centuries. It started with textual criticism, the process of establishing the most authentic text and translation of the Bible, but historical critics soon applied techniques such as source criticism, form criticism and redaction criticism to explore the relationship between the Gospels, their dating and authorship, and to establish an authentic core of Jesus material. It soon became apparent that neither the techniques nor those wielding them were neutral and the core of Jesus material identified varied substantially between scholars and often seemed to reflect their ideas, values and concerns.

The validity of the attempt to reconstruct the historical Jesus was very much in question from the turn of the twentieth century, but the consequences of accepting that it was not possible to establish the actual historical events and teachings on which Christianity is based made scholars try and then try again. After the Second World War, in Germany scholars of the Second Quest worked to show how neither the superficial, romantic claims about Jesus nor the theological interpretations made by Nazi sympathizers had historical foundation. In the 1980s and 1990s, scholars of the Third Quest worked to address and understand the effect of the Jewish context of Jesus and the New Testament that – in part due to anti-Semitism – had been largely ignored before.

Today most scholars accept that historical investigation often tells us more about those doing the investigating than it does about the Bible, Jesus or his teachings, but this does not altogether invalidate the enterprise of investigating the New Testament in terms of historical truth. With qualifications and caveats it could be that the quest will continue for decades – even centuries – to come in some form or other.

9

The Waning of Historical Criticism

Albert Schweitzer began his famous *Quest of the Historical Jesus* thus:

> When, at some future day, our period of civilization shall lie closed and completed, before the eyes of later generations, German theology will stand out as a great, a unique phenomenon in the mental and spiritual life of our time. For nowhere save in the German temperament can there be found in the same perfection the living complex of conditions and factors – of philosophic thought, critical acumen, historical insight, and religious feeling – without which no deep theology is possible. And the greatest achievement of German theology is the critical investigation of the life of Jesus. What it has accomplished here has laid down the conditions and determined the course of the religious thinking of the future. In the history of doctrine, its work has been negative; it has, so to speak, cleared the site for a new edifice of religious thought.[1]

That is one way of looking at it!

For Schweitzer and those Protestant Christians who maintained that faith was not dependent on the historical status of the Gospels, that it does not matter how the historical Jesus lived and died or even precisely what he taught, historical criticism could be seen in terms of clearing the ground, exposing the nature of faith and the need for unconditional commitment. However,

---

1 www.earlychristianwritings.com/schweitzer.

for the majority of Christians and for Jews, German historical criticism could not be such an object of admiration; its work was undoubtedly negative – and not in the sense Schweitzer intended, for it attacked the basis for faith, often fatally weakening it.

Biblical criticism was born from the Enlightenment and founded on the principle that rational analysis could yield objective truth. It soon became clear that so-called neutral, rigorous rational tools yielded different accounts of the truth when wielded by different hands. Further, the truth that the tools revealed mirrored the concerns, ideals and desires of the one applying them. By the beginning of the twentieth century, real doubt as to the possibility of objectivity in biblical criticism were being voiced. As Tyrrell and Schweitzer observed (building on the insights of Feuerbach and Marx), the values and even politics of Europe were being projected into biblical texts so that works of ancient history or scriptural exegesis told readers more about the author than about the subject.

Sadly, Northern Europe was affected by rampant anti-Semitism throughout the Enlightenment period – the anti-Semitic concerns, ideals and desires of scholars shaped their thinking in many different directions and, odd as it might seem, were manifest in biblical criticism.

As we have seen, scholars progressed towards discrediting the historicity of the Hebrew Scriptures more quickly than towards discrediting that of the New Testament. Their first target was the history of the Jewish people, leaving criticism of the law and prophetic works to one side. The covenant between God and God's chosen people, the claim to the promised land, was of little import to Christian scholars, whereas Christian faith relied to some extent on so-called messianic prophecies and a core of laws.

It made little or no difference to Christians if the Pentateuch was written in its present form in the time of Moses, of David or in the post-exilic period, but they preferred to preserve the idea that the Prophet Isaiah foretold the virgin birth and the Prophet Hosea foretold the journey into Egypt, however much the evidence suggests that the Christian interpretation of these passages is based on nothing more than wishful thinking.

In fact as a matter of routine both the Hebrew Scriptures and New Testament were interpreted in such a way as to discredit any idea that Christianity was indebted to Judaism. To give just one example: for centuries the Gospel of John and the letters of Paul were seen to have been influenced by Greek philosophy – the idea that the influence of rabbinic Judaism was more likely was discounted, partly at least because Christian scholars could not credit Jewish thinkers with having the same level of sophistication as the Greeks.

In 1903 Solomon Schechter, the founding father of Conservative Judaism in America, delivered an impassioned address entitled 'Higher Criticism – Higher Anti-Semitism', claiming:

> The Bible is our sole *raison d'être*, and it is just this which the Higher anti-Semitism is seeking to destroy, denying all our claims for the past, and leaving us without hope for the future ... Can any section among us afford to concede to this professorial and imperial anti-Semitism and confess ... we have lived on false pretences and were the worst shams in the world?[2]

For Schechter:

1   The idea was ridiculous that European and North American academics could presume to preach the true meaning of the Hebrew Scriptures when most were relatively ignorant of Hebrew and Aramaic and totally ignorant of the Oral Torah, Haggadah, Mishnah and rabbinic teachings that had been carefully passed down alongside the Scriptures and had always been used to guide its interpretation!

---

2   Quoted in Jon Douglas Levenson, *The Hebrew Bible, the Old Testament, and Historical Criticism: Jews and Christians in Biblical Studies*, Louisville, KY: Westminster John Knox Press, 1993, p. 43.

2   Further, European and North American scholars usually started with the 'Old Testament', the parts of Hebrew Scripture crudely cut up, rearranged and (badly?) translated to suit Christian priorities.

3   Further still, biblical critics' claim to academic objectivity and neutrality was absurd. Their obsession with disputing the Mosaic authorship of the Torah and unbounded confidence in their alternative highly speculative explanations was obviously designed to discredit the Jewish claim to a covenant relationship with YHVH – and to the Land, Israel, which sealed his promise.

Schechter might have had a point.

Other Jewish responses to biblical criticism were more measured but no less critical. Rabbi David Tzvi Hoffmann, a leading Orthodox academic and head of the Berlin Rabbinical Seminary, wrote in 1905: 'We must not presume to set ourselves up as critics of the author of a biblical text or doubt the truth of his statements or question the correctness of his teaching.' His two-volume refutation of the Graf-Wellhausen Hypothesis and entire biblical commentary drew on his vast secular and religious learning significantly devoted to demonstrating the unity of Torah and its essential historicity. In the 1980s Meir Sternberg wrote:

> [We have now seen] two hundred years of frenzied digging into the Bible's genesis ... Rarely has there been such a futile expense of spirit in a noble cause; rarely have such grandiose theories of origination been built and revised and pitted against each other on the evidential equivalent of the head of a pin; rarely have so many worked for so long or so hard with so little to show for their trouble.[3]

By that stage many non-Jewish scholars shared his opinion that historical criticism was a waste of time.

---

3 Meir Sternberg, *The Poetics of Biblical Narrative: Ideological Literature and the Drama of Reading*, South Bend, IN: Indiana University Press, 1985, p. 13.

Following the Second World War, scholars became increasingly aware of the flawed assumptions on which much of their so-called knowledge of the Bible was built. Anti-Semitic assumptions were but one part of the problem – sexist and racist assumptions, theological blinkers, chronological snobbery and the naïve assumptions underpinning the Enlightenment model of truth – that massive elephant in the room – had to be accounted for.

Finally, dispassionate analysis of the state of historical criticism exposed the seemingly contradictory claims that application of the same techniques to the same text generated. The story of the origins and development of the Bible told by historical critics grew ever more complicated and contradictory. Astruc's two sources became Wellhausen's four, and soon enough each of these were sub-divided until diagrams of the sources and stages of redaction of even the Pentateuch resembled extended barcodes! For the informed reader, reading the Bible became a rough and confusing experience, characterized by countless changes in voice, and all sense of the texts – let alone of the Bible as a whole, unified work – was lost.

Radical alternatives were proposed, which highlighted and questioned the basic assumptions made by heroes of historical criticism such as Wellhausen and Streeter.

- Perhaps ideas of literary consistency have been applied to the Pentateuch anachronistically and there were no separate sources (e.g. R. N. Whybray, *The Making of the Pentateuch* (1987)).
- Perhaps Griesbach's old idea that length and complexity equals a later date is mistaken, and arguments for the priority of Mark – and John being the last Gospel to be written – are wrong (e.g. J. A. T. Robinson, *Redating the New Testament* (1976) and *The Priority of John* (1984)).

Students of the Bible were faced with an apparent choice: either accept that the Bible is just a mess and that its exalted position in Judeo-Christian culture is an unaccountable mystery; or accept that techniques in historical criticism, such as source criticism, form criticism and redaction criticism, do not seem to work. These techniques fail to offer a clear account of the historical events recorded by the texts and the development of the texts themselves and, beyond this, fail to address truth in the texts that is in no way historical.

In 1986 James Crenshaw concluded that:

[a] purely historical analysis of the [Hebrew Scriptures] cannot yield satisfactory results. Efforts to specify dates for biblical books and to examine them according to their historical sequence are doomed from the start. It has become increasingly clear that no satisfactory history of the literature can be written ... Thus far no satisfactory criteria exist by which to separate later glosses from early writings.[4]

In 1987 Norman Whybray wrote:

It is difficult to avoid the conclusion that the likelihood of modern scholars succeeding in discovering – except perhaps in very general terms – how the Pentateuch was compiled is small indeed. This does not necessarily mean that it is not worthwhile to make the attempt. But the self-assurance with which many scholars, especially in the last hundred years, have propounded their views on the subject should be regarded with suspicion ... It will be found that often conjecture has been piled on conjecture.[5]

Edward Greenstein said in 1989:

Many contemporary Biblicists are experiencing a crisis in faith ... [We are losing] faith in believing the results of

---

4 James L. Crenshaw, *Story and Faith: A Guide to the Old Testament*, Basingstoke: Macmillan, 1986, p. 2.

5 R. N. Whybray, *The Making of the Pentateuch: A Methodological Study*, London: Bloomsbury, 1987, p. 15.

> our study. The objective truths of the past we increasingly understand as the creations of our own vision ... [M]odern critical approaches are no more or less than our own midrash.[6]

After this, biblical scholars really embraced the postmodern turn, which saw philosophers move away from seeing truth in terms of history, correspondence with particular events, and towards seeing truth in terms of interpretation, meaning and use. They used postmodern philosophy to underpin a different smooth approach to the text, one that did due honour to the unity of the Scriptures, their meaning and use in religious communities today. This enabled scholars to look beyond the claimed multiplicity of sources to themes and ideas apparent throughout books, sections or even the whole Bible.

Perhaps for some scholars this change was also influenced by clarifications of the churches' formal teachings on biblical inerrancy, through the Second Vatican Council in the case of Roman Catholics and the Chicago Statement on Biblical Inerrancy for evangelical Protestants. While biblical inerrancy (the belief that the Bible cannot err or contain a lie) should not be confused with biblical literalism (taking isolated parts of the Bible at face value), it was extremely difficult to reconcile depending on the patronage of a Church that upholds inerrancy (as many biblical scholars did and still do) with taking techniques in historical criticism of the Bible to their logical conclusion.

As John Barton observed in the Introduction to *The Cambridge Companion to Biblical Interpretation*,[7] in a sense this 'new' approach can be seen to be a return to the oldest approach, predating attempts to see the Bible as history and again seeing it as the literary product of more or less inspired minds. To the non-specialist, so long as nobody asks too many questions about how the word 'truth' is used, postmodern interpretations of the Bible

---

6 Edward L. Greenstein, *Essays on Biblical Method and Translation*, Atlanta, GA: Scholars Press, 1989, p. 23.

7 John Barton (ed.), *The Cambridge Companion to Biblical Interpretation*, Cambridge: Cambridge University Press, 1998, pp. 1–6.

and traditional Christian interpretations of the Bible seem similar and compatible.

Nevertheless this was a strange new world for religion. Although apparently tolerant, pluralist and less likely to lead to conflict, the postmodern world turned out to be less tolerant, and even encouraging of extremism and violent fundamentalism. It is relatively easy to ignore or indulge ignorance, even to agree to differ with a fellow searcher after truth, but it is more difficult to ignore or indulge those who question the existence of the truth and pour scorn on the search for it; more difficult to agree to differ with those who reject all reason and seek to impose their crazy fanaticism on others, whether through:

- using mass terror, rape and public acts of barbarism to protest injustice and the abuse of power;
- or using law to marginalize women, homosexuals, the poor, sick and disabled and religious minorities – in the name of he who taught 'love thy neighbour', 'judge not', opened his arms to outcasts and gave his life so that the last might be first and the first last.

The postmodern world has really exposed the difficulties in believing passionately in pluralism, in defending liberalism, in being intolerant of intolerance. Sadly, the strengths of postmodernism (modesty, acceptance of diversity, willingness to listen, collaborate and change) come with significant weaknesses (apathy, unwillingness to seek or take advantage of unity, indecisiveness, obscurity, seeming delight in obfuscation and pointlessness).

Postmodernism is, in the end, a poor match for fundamentalism. Far from being able to compete and persuade fundamentalists of their error, postmodernists are forced to absent themselves from the debate. They could not disagree more with the fundamentalist claim to truth, yet just because of this they have no ground on which to build a persuasive case! Fundamentalists have no such issue.

10

Studying the Bible Today

To take stock, through this part of *Bible Matters* we have explored the historical status of biblical texts in terms of:

- **external evidence** that might corroborate events, dates, people and places referenced in the Bible, including archaeological remains, inscriptions, references in other early works, literary and religious parallels;
- **internal evidence** indicating how the text developed, when elements of it might have been written, by whom and for what purpose, how and why these elements came to be in their current form.

To some people, including some believers (Jewish and Christian) and most atheists, the extent to which the Bible records historical fact is of the highest importance when it comes to validating, supporting and enriching faith. As Paul explained:

> [I]f Christ has not been raised, our preaching is useless and so is your faith. More than that, we are then found to be false witnesses about God, for we have testified about God that he raised Christ from the dead. But he did not raise him if in fact the dead are not raised. For if the dead are not raised, then Christ has not been raised either. And if Christ has not been raised, your faith is futile; you are still in your sins. Then those also who have fallen asleep in Christ are lost. If only for this life we have hope in Christ, we are of all people most to be pitied. (1 Cor. 15.14–19)

In this context the historical status of the Bible is make or break for the religions based on it.

Yet for other believers, Jewish and Christian, the fact that their faith exists is sufficient evidence of God's saving action in history. The Bible might tell us how faithful people received and interpreted God's actions in the distant past, but neither the historical events it refers to, nor the way people understood and responded to them, can completely explain faith today. By this way of thinking, focusing biblical studies, let alone theology, on an investigation of the historical status of the texts misses the point – it is a diversion, of academic interest only and not of any great significance to the life and future of religions today.

Through centuries, historical critics have been drawn from both groups.

- Some historical critics have investigated the Bible historically in order somehow to prove their faith, attune it with the most 'authentic' events and teachings so as to maximize the possibility of salvation.
- Other historical critics have investigated the Bible in order to discredit faith, add evidential support to their atheistic world view by demonstrating how religion develops by human agency.
- Still other historical critics have investigated the Bible to discover and highlight the limits of the historical-critical approach, somehow denying knowledge in order to make room for and vivify faith[1] of a particular non-propositional or even fideist variety.

Historical critics of all these types still do exist, although the decline of historical criticism has now led to a renewed focus on biblical interpretation, part of what Eichhorn called 'lower criticism' – exploring the meaning of the texts assuming their essential unity and place in the biblical canon.

Like historical criticism, biblical interpretation provides insights that might guide believers in reading the Bible and shaping

---

1 Echoing Kant's famous phrase in the *Critique of Pure Reason* (B.xxx): 'So I had to deny knowledge in order to make room for faith.'

their faith. Unlike historical-critical insights though, (post)modern biblical interpretations rarely claim to offer the truth about what a text means, just a perspective that might be more or less useful: one truth – among many – on which like-minded people might agree.

Today biblical scholars might approach the Bible as literature, as a sociological case-study, as a political document; or they might consider how it might be read from an LGBT, black, feminist – or womanist – perspective. Many scholars focus their attention on a particular book or even passage of the Bible rather than dealing with collections of books or testaments, realizing that each author has a unique style and perspective, so what might be said about their work may not apply to the work of other biblical authors. Increasingly scholars specialize and focus on a tiny area of the discipline, be it the relevance of the Synoptic Gospels to disability studies, literary readings of Ecclesiastes or women's role in the religion of pre-exilic Israel.

In effect biblical studies has become a fragmented discipline, extending across and into multiple university departments. Biblical scholars might have one foot in the theology faculty and the other in a department of literature, history, philosophy, sociology, anthropology, oriental studies, classical studies or linguistics. They might even work under the aegis of law, political science, Latin American Studies, LGBT studies or women's studies. Consequently there is little sense of direction or consensus in biblical studies these days.

In some ways this is good – it allows for the development of a whole range of novel approaches to the Bible and offers opportunities for many different types of people within biblical studies who might in the past have felt or been excluded. In another sense, however, it has led to a crisis in both biblical studies and theology as a whole. It can be difficult to communicate the importance and relevance of studying the Bible to young people applying to university at the moment.

PART THREE

The Use and Interpretation
of the Bible

11

The Bible and Christian Theology

Beyond what may or may not have happened in the Middle East two to three thousand years ago, the question of what the Bible really means and how it should be interpreted and used by believers today has always preoccupied Christians. Gerhard Ebeling called Church history the history of the interpretation of Scripture, and this is really not far wrong!

The Use and Interpretation of the Bible

Of course, Jesus' own teaching centred on his reading of the Hebrew Scriptures; like a good rabbi he often gave one or more extracts to support each point. Paul did the same, referencing the Hebrew Scriptures to support his teaching about Jesus' identity, significance and message. The first centuries of the Church saw many different Christian writers using and interpreting the Bible in different ways in support of their arguments. The Bible was quoted and re-quoted to support contradictory positions in the various doctrinal disputes that dominated the period between Paul's death and the Council of Chalcedon in AD 451.

To give just one example: Irenaeus of Lyons rebutted second-century heresies – most of which were based on philosophical speculation and a long way from being biblically grounded – using arguments supported with copious biblical references. He observed:

> Since therefore we have such proofs, it is not necessary to seek the truth among others which it is easy to obtain from the Church; since the apostles, like a rich man [depositing his money] in a bank, lodged in her hands most copiously all

things pertaining to the truth: so that every man, whosoever will, can draw from her the water of life. For she is the entrance to life; all others are thieves and robbers.[1]

Through his *Against Heresies* and *Proof of Apostolic Preaching*, Irenaeus tried to show how what he understood to be orthodox Christian teaching related to Scripture, both in terms of the Old Testament and such widely circulated Christian texts as were later incorporated into the New Testament. He used Scripture as an effective check against heretical speculation and the growth of philosophical cults in part based on Christianity.

In the third century, Origen was one of the first to apply himself to the systematic study of Scripture. He learnt Hebrew, using his Hexapla – a verse-by-verse comparison of Hebrew and Greek versions of the Old Testament – to produce detailed commentaries on almost every book of Hebrew Scripture and a range of Christian texts. Origen was influenced by Philo of Alexandria, who was associated with rules stating that an allegorical interpretation of Scripture is necessary when the text:

1 says something 'unworthy of God';
2 self-contradicts;
3 is actually allegorizing;
4 unnecessarily repeats certain expressions;
5 uses superfluous words;
6 repeats known facts;
7 uses synonyms;
8 uses a play on words;
9 uses an unusual expression;
10 includes grammatical anomalies.

Yet Origen could see that allegorical interpretations could offer licence to any interpreter to foist almost any meaning on a passage of Scripture and so lend their arguments and actions unwarranted authority. In this context Origen chose to explain both the literal

---

1 Irenaeus, *Against Heresies*, Book 3, 4, 1–2.

and the allegorical meanings of texts. He explored the probable date, authorship and origin of each text but assessed its significance in terms of the philosophical truth it offers, rather than just its antiquity.[2] The ideas that resulted became highly controversial.

For example, Origen argued that the Bible, when interpreted allegorically, supports a world view otherwise expressed by Greek philosophers under the influence of Plato and Aristotle and commonly held in Gnostic sects at the time. God first created a host of spiritual intelligences, free to love God or not. Over time some of these beings lost their love for God and became demons, others lost some of their love for God and became human souls, a few remained close to God and became angels, and the one who remained in perfect love with God was the *Logos* who became incarnate in Jesus to save human beings from error. He quoted the Gospel of John, Paul's letters and the Hebrew Scriptures to support this view.

In the fourth century, influenced by Origen, Neoplatonism and Gnosticism, Arius appealed to Scripture to support his argument that Jesus, although *Logos* (the Word of God), was essentially an exalted man, and that God is single, indivisible and primary. Arius quoted verses such as John 14.28: 'the Father is greater than I' and also Colossians 1.15, which described Jesus as 'the firstborn over all creation'.

Bishop Athanasius appealed to Scripture in his denunciation of Arius. He was one of the first to suggest the total sufficiency of Scriptures (*Sola Scriptura*) in the battle against false doctrine – 'the sacred and inspired Scriptures are sufficient to declare the truth'[3] – and does not really appeal to tradition or philosophical arguments in the way his opponents did and indeed most church leaders had before him. Nevertheless Athanasius was careful to prescribe his canon, ensuring that works that might be useful to Arians or others who disagreed with Athanasius' 'orthodoxy' ended up being buried in the desert! This was no coincidence.

---

2 A good introduction to the life and works of Origen by Rowan Williams can be read at people.bu.edu/joeld/ascetic-enthusiasm.pdf.

3 Athanasius, *Against the Heathen*, Part 1, 1, 3.

In a fairly typical passage, Athanasius wrote:

> [O]ur faith is right, and starts from the teaching of the Apostles and tradition of the fathers, being confirmed both by the New Testament and the Old. For the prophets say: 'Send out Thy Word and Thy Truth', and 'Behold the Virgin shall conceive and bear a son, and they shall call His name Emmanuel, which is being interpreted God with us.' But what does that mean, if not that God has come in the Flesh? While the Apostolic tradition teaches ... [he then quotes 1 Peter 4.1; Titus 2.13; Heb. 2.1][4]

In the early fifth century, Bishop Augustine of Hippo explored the right use and interpretation of Scripture in *On Christian Doctrine*. Addressing the use and abuse of Scripture to lend authority to a wild variety of beliefs and practices, as was common in the Church of his time, Augustine suggested some rules for biblical interpretation. In essence, he argued that:

- the biblical interpreter should approach Scripture with humility and avoid claiming truth for their own interpretation;
- they should have knowledge of the whole Bible and not interpret bits out of context;
- they should respect the historical teaching of the Church and accept that if their reading is not consistent with the principles of love and charity, then it is wrong.

Augustine went on to offer seven rules for reading the Bible:

1 Be aware of how language works.
2 Compare translations, or learn Greek and Hebrew.
3 Make selective use of secular learning for background knowledge.
4 Compare difficult passages to clearer ones.
5 Consider the context.

---

4 Athanasius, *To Adelphius*, Letter 60, 6.

6 Don't take literal things figuratively or figurative things literally.

7 Pray for understanding.

For Augustine, a single passage of Scripture may have more than one meaning; this is positive and part of the richness of God's revelation. A biblical author may have realized that his writing could convey further possible meanings or may not have foreseen all that God intended to communicate to later readers.

However, Augustine would not accept that 'anything goes' in terms of biblical interpretation. Any new interpretation must be shown to be consistent with the author's *intended meaning*, which means that it must not stray far from the literal meaning and that which it would have had to historical readers.[5]

Councils, Creeds and the Catholic Church

It seems clear that the foundations for a range of different Christian approaches to using and interpreting the Bible were in place by the time the major principles of doctrine were established through councils and their creeds in the fourth and fifth centuries. The canon was slowly established and with it the parameters of acceptable philosophical and doctrinal discussion. The idea that Scripture could be, at most, full and sufficient justification for a theological argument and, at least, a check on rational speculation was out there, as was the idea that scriptural interpretations had to remain consistent with what had traditionally and literally been understood, even if deeper layers of meaning were mooted.

Both literalism and fully allegorical readings of Scripture were ruled out by ecclesiastical decisions to make a belief in Jesus as BOTH fully God AND fully man, of one substance (Greek *homoousion*), consubstantial with God and an equal part of a pre-existent Trinity (not really mentioned in Scripture) a

---

5 Stephanie L. Black, 'Augustine's Hermeneutics: Back to the Future for "Spiritual" Bible Interpretation?', *Africa Journal of Evangelical Theology* 27:1 (2008); biblicalstudies.org.uk/pdf/ajet/27-1_003.pdf provides a more detailed introduction to Augustine's hermeneutic.

test of orthodoxy. The Council of Nicaea (AD 325) the Council of Constantinople (AD 381) and the Council of Chalcedon (AD 451), along with a host of other smaller councils, documents and decisions, demonstrated the dominance of the Church and its intention to use Scripture but not be led by it.

In effect, after the fifth century, Scripture meant what the Church said it meant and anybody who suggested otherwise was promptly denounced as a heretic! Supported by Augustine's eloquent insistence that all interpretations should be consistent with *traditional understanding*, which was open to definition by those who kept the keys to the archives, Church doctrine became the only acceptable lens through which to read Scripture, however much the meaning of the text seemed to be distorted by this process.[6] Although this principle was only officially established by the Council of Trent in the sixteenth century, it had been accepted for a thousand years before this point.

For example, in AD 418 the teachings of the British monk and opponent of Augustine, Pelagius, who dared to suggest that sin and redemption depended on good works and not on inheritance and the sacramental offices of the Church, were denounced as heresy, despite Matthew 5—7, the Sermon on the Mount, which seems to offer clear support for Pelagius' position – and actively warns against those who will offer an easier way into heaven and claim that they act in Christ's name.

While the limitations of education and copying texts by hand ensured that relatively few people realized the extent to which church doctrine had diverged from Scripture during the Middle Ages, by the thirteenth century the Church was being challenged on this point quite regularly and had to resort to more and more brutal forms of suppression.

• From AD 1208 the Church mounted a crusade against the Cathars in the South of France because they were strict about

---

6 Ormond Rush, *The Eyes of Faith: The Sense of the Faithful and the Church's Reception of Revelation*, Washington, DC: The Catholic University of America Press, 2009.

biblical injunctions on living in poverty, not telling lies, not killing and not swearing oaths, and questioned the scriptural basis of church teachings on a host of issues, from sex to suicide. Thousands were tortured and burned to death in the name of Christ.

- As the Franciscans and Waldensians, who were committed to living in Christ-like poverty and following Gospel teachings, grew more popular, the Church decided to suppress them. In 1323 it declared the idea that Jesus and his apostles were poor to be a heresy, despite Luke 10.4: 'Do not take a purse or bag or sandals; and do not greet anyone on the road.' The Church went on to try to exterminate the Waldensians, killing some 1,700 in 1655 alone. Pope Francis issued a formal apology to the Waldensians on 28 June 2015.[7]

- In 1415 John Wycliffe and Jan Hus were declared heretics and publicly executed – in Wycliffe's case, he was already dead but his corpse was duly desecrated. They had dared to translate the Gospels and advocate reform of the Church to bring it back into line with Jesus' teachings. This signalled the beginning of a series of bloody crusades mounted by the Church against ordinary people who simply wanted to read and follow the Bible.

- In the sixteenth century Luther, Calvin and Zwingli were all denounced for their work in translating the Bible and using it to call for reform of the Catholic Church. The Protestant Reformation and later the Catholic Counter-Reformation caused the deaths of countless ordinary Christians. To give just one example: in the Thirty Years War an estimated 40 per cent of the German population died.

The Bible was at once the most important source of authority for the Church and a constant source of embarrassment in that its teachings simply did not support what the Church taught – let alone did – in its name. This tension has never really been resolved.

---

7   See   www.huffingtonpost.com/2015/06/28/pope-francis-waldensians_n_
7644916.html.

Until relatively recently Catholics were actively discouraged from reading the Bible. Until the 1960s, Catholic Mass was usually said in Latin and did not have to include Bible readings or homilies in the vernacular. Religious instruction in Catholic schools focused on the Catechism, the history and doctrine of the Church and current practice of Catholicism, rather than on Jesus or the Bible. It was quite possible – even a badge of honour in some circles – to be an observant Catholic and know little about what the Bible actually says.

Today, to outsiders, the Catholic Church might seem content to use the Bible when and where it is useful while disregarding its obvious sense when it conflicts with traditional teaching. For example, without any sense of irony the website Catholic Answers appeals to the Bible to explain the existence and prevalence of heresies and to guarantee that the Church will prevail.

> The Bible warned us this would happen. Paul told his young protégé, Timothy, 'For the time is coming when people will not endure sound teaching, but having itching ears they will accumulate for themselves teachers to suit their own likings, and will turn away from listening to the truth and wander into myths' (2 Tim. 4.3–4) ... Fortunately, we have Christ's promise that heresies will never prevail against the Church, for he told Peter, 'You are Peter, and on this rock I will build my Church, and the gates of hell will not prevail against it' (Matt. 16.18). The Church is truly, in Paul's words, 'the pillar and foundation of the truth' (1 Tim. 3.15).[8]

It chooses not to mention either the doubtful authorship and date of both letters to Timothy or Bultmann's widely supported argument that Matthew 16.18 is a later interpolation into the Gospel text (the Roman Catholic Church has embraced biblical criticism since the 1960s), while roundly criticizing the unsophisticated use of the Bible by heretics in the same article.

---

8 See www.catholic.com/tracts/the-great-heresies, which carries the Imprimatur of the Bishop of San Diego.

Officially, the Roman Catholic Church teaches that the Bible is inerrant, although different authorities differ on what that really means.

The First Vatican Council reaffirmed that:

> The books of the Old and New Testament, whole and entire, with all their parts, as enumerated in the decree of the same Council [Trent] and in the ancient Latin Vulgate, are to be received as sacred and canonical. And the Church holds them as sacred and canonical not because, having been composed by human industry, they were afterwards approved by her authority; nor only because they contain revelation without errors, but because, having been written under the inspiration of the Holy Spirit, they have God for their Author.

but the Second Vatican Council, in explaining that:

> Those divinely revealed realities which are contained and presented in Sacred Scripture have been committed to writing under the inspiration of the Holy Spirit ... they have God as their author and have been handed on as such to the Church herself ... However, since God speaks in Sacred Scripture through men in human fashion, the interpreter of Sacred Scripture, in order to see clearly what God wanted to communicate to us, should carefully investigate what meaning the sacred writers really intended, and what God wanted to manifest by means of their words.[9]

seemingly recommends that Catholics employ methods in biblical criticism that had been almost exclusively employed by Protestants and Atheists – and had got Loisy and Tyrrell into so much trouble barely half a century before.

In practice Roman Catholics range between:

---

9 *Dei Verbum* 11–12; www.vatican.va/archive/hist_councils/ii_vatican_council /documents/vat-ii_const_19651118_dei-verbum_en.html.

- a very few literalists who uphold absolute inerrancy (mostly in the USA and Africa);
- a majority who believe that the Bible is divinely inspired but that its meaning must be uncovered through detailed historical research and extensive interpretative work;
- a few who uphold limited inerrancy – that the Bible is inerrant but only in matters relating to faith; it may contain errors of historical and scientific fact;
- a few who reject the idea of biblical inerrancy altogether, seeing it as a repository of myth and a record of the truths upheld by ancient communities, not truth in any way.

Sola Scriptura: Protestantism, the Use and Interpretation of the Bible

Following a series of Catholic biblical scholars who were inspired by their work to call for reform of church doctrine and practice, Martin Luther translated and interpreted the Bible. Both his objections to Catholic doctrine and practice and his own teachings were inspired by his study of the Psalms, and Hebrews, Romans, Galatians and Ephesians. He never missed an opportunity to point out the extent to which church doctrine had departed from the sense of what Jesus taught and did and the teachings of the Early Church Fathers, arguing that the Church should move back to the position most clearly reflected in the New Testament and Nicene Creed.

Following on from Luther's approach, the principle of *Sola Scriptura* is the first and most important of the five *Sola* principles that – officially or unofficially – underpin most forms of Protestant Christianity.

1   *Sola Scriptura* (by Scripture alone).
2   *Sola Fide* (by Faith alone).
3   *Sola Gratia* (by Grace alone).
4   *Solo Christo* (through Christ alone).
5   *Soli Deo Gloria* (Glory to God alone).

The *Apology of the Augsburg Confession* was written by Luther's friend and collaborator Philipp Melanchthon during and after the 1530 Diet of Augsburg and was the basis for much later Protestant thought. It clearly identifies Holy Scripture with the word of God and calls the Holy Spirit the author of the Bible.[10] Nevertheless, as any person reading the Bible will attest, the sense in which this could be true is not clear.

The Bible is most obviously the work of different authors at different times; very little of it even claims to record the words of God. Further, the different theological positions evident in different parts of the Bible make it difficult to see how all could be the result of the same divine inspiration.

German historical criticism developed out of the natural Protestant desire to know and understand what the Bible really said. Built on the assumption that God's revelation took place in and through history, and so the earliest parts of the Bible are most likely to be authentic, it sought to analyse the texts to identify the context in which each unit of biblical text was written, so making it easier to know which passages should be given priority when it comes to getting the sense of biblical teaching.

Liberal Protestant scholars such as Friedrich Schleiermacher argued that the Bible is a historical text like many others, which can be understood only by engaging with its authors in their various contexts. Schleiermacher dismissed the idea that the Bible can be understood literally or be seen to offer a consistent teaching; we have a religious feeling that assures us that God exists – studying how people have responded to their relationship with God is a separate intellectual exercise.

Following Schleiermacher, some liberal Protestants questioned whether the miracles recorded in the Bible – even the incarnation and resurrection – actually occurred as described. Influenced by Spinoza and Kant, Schleiermacher argued that the suggestion that God intervened and broke the laws of nature would be an argument against God's omnipotence and/or goodness and ultimately a point against God's existence. If God needs to break

---

10   Article II, of Original Sin / Preface, 9.

God's own laws for human benefit, it rather suggests there is a defect in creation. Perhaps references to such miracles in the Bible record how human beings understood their experiences rather than what actually happened. As he put it:

> [E]verything – even the most wonderful thing that happens or has happened – is a problem for scientific research; but ... when it in any way stimulates the pious feeling, whether through its purpose or in some other way, that is not in the least prejudiced by the conceivable possibility of its being understood in the future.[11]

Unsurprisingly the liberal questioning of central Christian ideas was highly controversial. Also, the liberals failed to make progress towards identifying a core of early, authentic, authoritative material and a clear understanding of Scripture; like peeling back layers of an onion, in the end all that was left were the disassembled layers and it was nigh on impossible to put them back together and regain a sense of unity and authority in Scripture.

The historical approach caused a crisis within Protestant Christianity.

- How could people base their faith *Sola Scriptura*, when the Bible had been dismantled and trampled underfoot?
- If the historical Jesus remained elusive (or was defined by this scholar or that according to their own preferences), were believers just quixotic?
- If no part of the Bible was the authentic word of God, where was its authority?

Scholars such as Emil Brunner and Karl Barth[12] responded to this

---

11 Friedrich Schleiermacher, *The Christian Faith*, eds H. R. Mackintosh and J. S. Stewart, Berkeley, CA: Apocryphile Press, 2011: Part 1, Section 1, 47:3.

12 Brunner and Barth are associated with dialectical theology, which – in the ashes of the First World War – rejected nineteenth-century liberalism, Catholic natural theology and biblical inerrancy and proposed a new direction for theology

crisis by arguing that the Word of God is not in fact the Bible. John's Gospel begins with the words:

> In the beginning was the Word, and the Word was with God, and the Word was God. He was with God in the beginning ... The Word became flesh and made his dwelling among us. We have seen his glory, the glory of the one and only Son, who came from the Father, full of grace and truth.

For Brunner, Barth and neo-orthodox Protestants, Jesus was and is the Word of God, God incarnate, God's ultimate revelation to humankind – not another historical figure alongside Julius Caesar or Elizabeth I. Christians study the Bible not to identify an authentic kernel of revelation amid accretions (as might be suggested by liberals or modernists), or because it provides a literal record of God's words, but because the *process* of exegesis is of existential significance – it helps them to focus on and in some sense participate in Christ.

Because God is transcendent and because there is an infinite qualitative distinction between God and humankind, human beings cannot fully conceive of, understand or describe God's revelation. Scripture was written by human beings, in human language; it bears witness to how human beings received God's revelation but is not that revelation in itself.

---

in answer to the clear 'no' God had given to all previous attempts to be righteous and attain salvation. Bultmann, Tillich, more recently Reginald H. Fuller and, in a way, Nicky Gumbel can be associated with this movement –

Jesus commanded us to love God, our neighbours and ourselves, not a book written by human beings; it is wrong to worship Scripture and set the Bible, a human production, in place of God as some sort of idol. God's revelation is not a one-off, historical event, but continues in the lives of believers. That is not to say that the Bible is wrong about much (although it does contain errors), but the Bible on its own is not a sufficient basis for or guide to faith.

Nevertheless, and despite Barth's influence, in 1978, evangelical Protestants issued the Chicago Statement on Biblical Inerrancy, signed by more than 200 leading figures including J. P. Moreland, James I. Packer, Norman Geisler, Walter Kaiser, Edwin Yamauchi and the British Anglican scholar – and author of the famous textbook on New Testament Greek – John Wenham. The statement limited the extent to which it would be acceptable for scholars to speculate about the historical status of the Bible while remaining within the Protestant evangelical churches.

This is the wording of the short statement:

1   God, who is Himself Truth and speaks truth only, has inspired Holy Scripture in order thereby to reveal Himself to lost mankind through Jesus Christ as Creator and Lord, Redeemer and Judge. Holy Scripture is God's witness to Himself.

2   Holy Scripture, being God's own Word, written by men prepared and superintended by His Spirit, is of infallible divine authority in all matters upon which it touches: it is to be believed, as God's instruction, in all that it affirms; obeyed, as God's command, in all that it requires; embraced, as God's pledge, in all that it promises.

3   The Holy Spirit, Scripture's divine Author, both authenticates it to us by His inward witness and opens our minds to understand its meaning.

4   Being wholly and verbally God-given, Scripture is without error or fault in all its teaching, no less in what it states about God's acts in creation, about the events of world history, and

about its own literary origins under God, than in its witness to God's saving grace in individual lives.

5   The authority of Scripture is inescapably impaired if this total divine inerrancy is in any way limited or disregarded, or made relative to a view of truth contrary to the Bible's own; and such lapses bring serious loss to both the individual and the Church.[13]

Since 1978 there has been a renewed effort on behalf of conservative Protestant Christians to assert a traditional view of biblical origins and provide holistic readings of the Old and New Testaments. In particular a lot of work has been done to show the truth and meaning in controversial passages, such as the creation narratives in Genesis 1—3.

One of the first applications of historical criticism was to the Pentateuch, and one of its first conclusions was that Genesis was made up of four different source-documents of different dates and origins. This suggested that far from being a revelation of divine truth about the origins of the world and humankind, Genesis 1—3 was an edited together mish-mash of ancient aetiological myths poached from Egypt, Babylon or Canaan bolted on to the History of Israel, with most of the original polytheistic references taken out and replaced with the names of local tribal deities YHVH and EL. The immediate effect of this insight was to undermine the central Christian belief in God as creator, compounding the effect of scientific research into evolution through natural selection and the origins of the universe, which raised major questions about God's goodness and very existence.

Nevertheless, evangelical Protestant scholars have defended biblical inerrancy and the basic tenets of Christian faith in very different ways.

Importantly, *biblical inerrancy is not the same as biblical literalism*. Throughout Christian history, church leaders have accepted that truth in the Bible cannot often be accessed through a literal, superficial reading of the text.

---

13   The full text is available at library.dts.edu/Pages/TL/Special/ICBI_1.pdf.

C. S. Lewis understood the power that stories have to tell the truth without describing it in literal terms. He accepted that the Genesis accounts of creation are composites of ancient Near Eastern myths but did not see that taking away from the essential truth that they teach – that God created the world. In a controversial essay, 'The Funeral of a Great Myth', published in 1970, he pointed out how evolution through natural selection has itself become a myth, a story through which we see ourselves and our world and which seems to explain far more than the bare biological theorem can justify. He concluded:

> The content of the Myth thus knocks from under me the only ground on which I could possibly believe the Myth to be true. If my own mind is a product of the irrational – if what seem my clearest reasonings are only the way in which a creature conditioned as I am is bound to feel – how shall I trust my mind when it tells me about Evolution? They say in effect 'I will prove that what you call a proof is only the result of mental habits which result from heredity which results from biochemistry which results from physics'. But this is the same as saying: 'I will prove that proofs are irrational': more succinctly, 'I will prove that there are no proofs'. The fact that some people of scientific education cannot by any effort be taught to see the difficulty, confirms one's suspicion that we touch here a radical disease in their whole style of thought. But the man who does see it, is compelled to reject as mythical the cosmology in which most of us were brought up. That is has embedded in it many true particulars I do not doubt: but in its entirety, it simply will not do. Whatever the real universe may turn out to be like, it can't be like that.

Today evangelical Protestant scholars such as Alister McGrath – C. S. Lewis' biographer – look to Augustine's guidelines for reading and interpreting the Bible and see that there is no conflict between holding a sincere belief in biblical inerrancy and embracing an allegorical interpretation of Genesis 1–3.[14] There could be deep truth in Genesis – such as that God created the world and saw that it was good, and that mortality and suffering originate in human choices – without anyone having to deny the truth of strictly scientific insights into the origins of the universe and process of evolution.

Alternatively it could be that the Bible is essentially true and science is limited or in error.

Since the 1990s, advocates of intelligent-design theory have sought to highlight both the limitations of the theory of evolution through natural selection and the need for a supernatural explanation for the Big Bang and for its resulting in a universe like this. Many, although not all scholars advocating intelligent design are evangelical Protestants and many receive funding from the Discovery Institute's Centre for Science and Culture, which has the stated aim to:

> advance the understanding that human beings and nature are the result of intelligent design rather than a blind and undirected process. We seek long-term scientific and cultural change through cutting-edge scientific research and scholarship; education and training of young leaders; communication to the general public; and advocacy of academic freedom and free speech for scientists, teachers, and students.[15]

Importantly, no intelligent-design argument suggests that Genesis creation accounts are true; they just point out the shortcomings of scientific accounts and sometimes propose that an intelligence is a more probable explanation than mere chance. The extent to which intelligent design is actually a form of creationism is still a source of heated debate.

Of course, some evangelical Protestant Christians want to go far further than intelligent design will allow, arguing that God must be the source of all creation and even that the process by

---

14 See www.dts.edu/read/an-interview-with-alister-mcgraith-mcgill-jenny.

15 See www.discovery.org/id/about.

which God created is accurately recorded in Genesis, in some interpretations at least. Different varieties of creationism include:

1   **Young-earth creationism**: Genesis is literally true, and the earth and all forms of life were created by God in six days, around 10,000 years ago. Scientists are almost unanimous in saying that the earth is four billion years old, and that the young-earth theory is false.

2   **Old-earth creationism**: the earth is around four billion years old but was created by processes in which God played an active part. Further, God continues to act through special creation – including miracles and religious experiences – throughout history.

3   **Gap creationism**: there were two creations – one four billion years ago and a second one, the creation of Adam and Eve in Eden, which began biblical history around 10,000 years ago.

4   **Day-age creationism**: each 'day' in the biblical 'six days' of creation wasn't really a day but a period of millions of years. There are other biblical references that show that a day for God is an age for human beings, such as Psalm 90.4 and 2 Peter 3.8.

5   **Progressive creationism**: God created the various 'kinds' of plant and animal one after another, as is shown in the fossil record. Evolution can explain changes within kinds but not one kind changing to another. God created each kind as it is – and created some kinds with the intention that they would become extinct.

Today the polling organization Gallup calculates that some 42 per cent of Americans uphold young-earth creationism, 31 per cent believe that God guided evolution in some way and only 19 per cent deny God's role in creation. The number of young-earth creationists has not changed much in a quarter of a century, although the number of atheists has doubled.[16] Gallup notes how:

16   See www.gallup.com/poll/170822/believe-creationist-view-human-origins.
aspx.

Religiousness relates most strongly to [creationism] ... The percentage of Americans who accept the creationist viewpoint ranges from 69 per cent among those who attend religious services weekly to 23 per cent among those who seldom or never attend. Educational attainment is also related to these attitudes, with belief in the creationist perspective dropping from 57 per cent among Americans with no more than a high school education to less than half that (27 per cent) among those with a college degree. Those with college degrees are, accordingly, much more likely to choose one of the two evolutionary explanations. Younger Americans – who are typically less religious than their elders – are less likely to choose the creationist perspective than are older Americans. Americans aged 65 and older – the most religious of any age group – are most likely to choose the creationist perspective.

Elsewhere far fewer people hold young-earth creationist views (around 10 per cent of Britons[17] and 23 per cent of Australians[18]), although numbers embracing science and excluding God from the process of creation altogether are low as well (around 25 per cent of Britons and 12 per cent of Australians).

Where Do the Anglicans Fit In?

It's complicated! The Anglican Communion is very broad and includes those whose views match any and all of the theological positions outlined above.

- **Anglo-Catholics** – sometimes described as High-Church Anglicans – might look back to Augustine, embracing biblical criticism and the existence of different interpretations of each passage and holding on to the idea that interpretations must be consistent with tradition.

17 See www.theguardian.com/science/2009/feb/01/evolution-darwin-survey-creationism.

18 See www.smh.com.au/national/faith-what-australians-believe-in-20091218-l5qy.html.

- **Episcopalians** and those who lean towards the **Reformed** tradition – sometimes described as 'low-Church' Anglicans – might uphold *Sola Scriptura*, biblical inerrancy and even, in some cases, biblical literalism. On the other hand, some members of the Episcopal Churches are very liberal.
- **Liberal Anglicans** might be willing to question almost any aspect of tradition and follow historical research where it leads, holding on to religious feeling (see Schleiermacher) to sustain their faith throughout.
- **Evangelical Anglicans** might embrace a more **Charismatic**, **Pietistic** or even **Pentecostal** approach that focuses on personal revelation and experience rather than tradition, rational exegesis or historical research. Alternatively, some within the evangelical tradition are closer to **neo-orthodox** Protestant Christianity (e.g. Barth, Moltmann).

Methodism started off as a movement within the Church of England and holds a mainstream position on the place and use of the Bible in theology today, a position that has been described as *Prima Scriptura* and is shared by many Anglicans, Roman Catholics and members of the **Eastern Orthodox Churches**:

> Scripture is considered the primary source and standard for Christian doctrine. Tradition is experience and the witness of development and growth of the faith through the past centuries and in many nations and cultures. Experience is the individual's understanding and appropriating of the faith in the light of his or her own life. Through reason the individual Christian brings to bear on the Christian faith discerning and cogent thought. These four elements taken together bring the individual Christian to a mature and fulfilling understanding of the Christian faith and the required response of worship and service.[19]

---

19 'The Wesleyan Quadrilateral', in *A Dictionary for United Methodists*, ed. Alan K. Waltz, Nashville, TN: Abingdon Press, 1991.

Given this level of diversity, the fact that Anglicans struggle to agree on issues such as the ordination of women and homosexuality is no surprise; in fact it should be more of a surprise that Anglicans manage to agree about so much!

Post-liberal Theology and Radical Orthodoxy

Alternative approaches adopted by some Anglicans and Methodists (as well as some members of other Protestant Churches) can be found in the post-liberal theology (sometimes called narrative theology or the theology of the Yale School), in the work of scholars such as Hans Frei, George Lindbeck, Alasdair MacIntyre, Stanley Hauerwas and James Childress, and later in Radical Orthodoxy, a movement associated with John Milbank, Catherine Pickstock and Graham Ward in the UK.

For post-liberal theologians the weakness of earlier work (e.g. Schleiermacher, Barth) is its epistemological naïvety. Following Kant, theologians of the Enlightenment suggest that they are describing and advancing towards truth and that reason and experience are somehow universal and neutral. Post-liberal theology recognizes the advances made by postmodernism in philosophy and accepts that reason and experience only make sense within the form of life and language game in which they arise or occur.

Building on his readings of Søren Kierkegaard, Ludwig Wittgenstein's thinking in *Philosophical Investigations* and C. S. Lewis, Paul L. Holmer at Yale developed his concept of theology as a 'grammar of faith': meaningful theological statements depend not on correspondence with some external point of reference but on the extent to which they cohere with and enrich the religious form of life within which they are made. By this logic the Bible provides the basis for a particular religious language game played out through theology and worship. The process of reading the Bible enriches peoples' worship and develops their faith; perhaps as reading *Wisden* develops peoples' ability to play and appreciate a game of cricket.

Just as post-liberal theology responded to Enlightenment liberalism/modernism in theology, Radical Orthodoxy responded to postmodernism, aiming to establish Christianity in its traditional sense – as articulated by Augustine, complete with belief in incarnation, resurrection, miracles and Trinity – for a twenty-first-century world. As James Smith quipped:

> The news of modernity's death has been greatly exaggerated. The Enlightenment project is alive and well, dominating Europe and increasingly North America, particularly in the political drive to carve out the secular ... the religious response to this has been ... confused.[1]

Radical Orthodoxy denounces the response of most Protestant and Catholic thinkers to the Enlightenment – they tried to defeat it on its own terms and this attempt ended in most abject failure. As is reflected in Kantian epistemology, the Enlightenment started from worldly experience and worked through logic built on this experience towards what it claimed is objective truth.

In response, as part of some sort of Christian apologetic, Catholic natural theology tried to prove God's existence and provide a metaphysical foundation for Christian moral teaching but failed on both accounts. As Kant succinctly observed, there is simply no way that any system that limits possible knowledge to experience and what can be understood of it by human beings can claim any knowledge of God, who is by definition outside experience and understanding.

In response, Protestant thinkers such as Barth and Bultmann positively affirm the impossibility of basing faith on argument or evidence and in so doing undermine the traditional basis for belief – the Bible – and all possible appeal to the historical fact of Jesus' incarnation, miracles, teaching, death and resurrection.

For Milbank and followers of Radical Orthodoxy, both responses are deeply mistaken; both accept the flawed

---

1 James K. A. Smith, *Introducing Radical Orthodoxy: Mapping a Post-secular Theology, Grand Rapids*, MI: Baker, 2004, p. 31.

Enlightenment world view and its anthropocentric epistemology uncritically. Instead they advocate a new world view drawn from Plato and Augustine, one that sees ultimate reality in terms of God, not human experience or some ill-defined independent entity. In this context Christian belief can be confidently reasserted – and the Bible read as containing deep truth – despite, and in some ways as an antidote to, post-Enlightenment nihilism and social collapse.

It is clear that the question of what we mean by truth really matters for any reading of the Bible, and is not going away any time soon!

12

The Bible and Ethics

Christians have at least seven different positions on the relationship between the Bible and ethics – how Scripture could and should be used and applied to life:

1   The Bible *is* Christian Ethics; it can be read and taken literally as a guide for decisions and life. This position is mostly held by evangelical Protestant theologians such as Carl Henry.[1]
2   The Bible demonstrates that God is free to and does command. This position was held by Karl Barth.
3   Christian Ethics should be consistent with the Bible but are not sourced from it. This position is held by advocates of Natural Law, for example Aquinas, Germain Grisez.
4   The Bible, when taken as a whole, provides and explains the principles of Christian Ethics, for example agape; all actions should be consistent with these principles, if not with the letter of the laws in the Bible (William Temple, Joseph Fletcher).
5   Reading the Bible forms, identifies and develops virtuous character traits. This position is held by Stanley Hauerwas and also by J. L. Houlden[2] and Bruce Birch and Larry Rasmussen.[3]
6   Reading the Bible provides a good opportunity to reflect on right and wrong and develop ethical principles. This is a position held by Paul Ramsey, Brevard Childs and James Childress.

---

1   Carl Henry, *Christian Personal Ethics*, Grand Rapids, MI: Baker, 1957.

2   J. L. Houlden, *Ethics and the New Testament*, Edinburgh: T. & T. Clark, 1973.

3   Bruce C. Birch and Larry L. Rasmussen, *Bible and Ethics in the Christian Life*, Minneapolis, MN: Augsburg, 1976.

7   The Bible is in truth irrelevant for Christian ethics. This is a position held by some historical critics and some postmodernists, even those who profess Christianity.

Ethics Matters[4] explores numbers 3 (Christian Natural Law) and 4 (situation ethics) in far more detail, so here we will focus on numbers 1 (biblical literalism), 2 (divine command ethics) and 5/6 (Christian forms of virtue ethics).

Biblical Literalism and Ethics

For those Christians who choose to take the Bible as a direct guide to decision-making, choices have to be made about which commands in the Old Testament remain authoritative and which have been countermanded in the New Testament. This is not straightforward.

- In Matthew's Gospel, Jesus is recorded as saying that he had not come to alter one jot or iota – the smallest Greek letters – of the Law, yet in Mark's Gospel he is recorded teaching that the commands to love God and love neighbour are the most important.
- In Mark's Gospel, Jesus holds Christians to higher standards than the Jewish Law demanded, such as in not allowing divorce at all. Nevertheless, in Matthew's Gospel and in Paul's writings, certain divorces are allowed, such as when a husband finds his wife sexually displeasing (Greek *porneia* – Matthew) or when one partner is not a Christian (Paul).
- While in Matthew's Gospel Jesus teaches forgiveness and warns against judging others, in John's Gospel he demands that his followers be 'perfect as your Father God is perfect' and is not shy of judging the Jews!
- Although twice in Acts Christians are enjoined to refrain from blood (keep kosher), in the same book Peter received a vision that seemingly released Christians from food laws.

---

4   Peter and Charlotte Vardy, *Ethics Matters*, London: SCM Press, 2012.

- While early Christian leaders in Jerusalem required non-Jewish Christian converts to be circumcised and to comply with the Torah, Paul taught that circumcision was not necessary for non-Jewish converts.

As Simon Blackburn observed at the end of his admirably clear summary of the problems with biblical literalism: '[T]he Bible can be read as giving us a carte blanche for harsh attitudes to children, the mentally handicapped, animals, the environment, the divorced, unbelievers, people with various sexual habits, and elderly women.'[5]

Confusion about which laws to follow and which to ignore extended through the Early Church and bubbled to the surface again after the Reformation. In practice those who claim to take the Bible as a direct guide differ in their decision-making depending on which bits of the Bible they reference and whose interpretation they rely on. This point was made quite clearly in the television series *The West Wing* Season 2, when President Bartlett (a devout Catholic) argues with a talk-show host (a strict evangelical Protestant) over her views about homosexuality.[6]

Divine Command Ethics

In *Church Dogmatics* Volume II, Part 2 (1957), Karl Barth suggested that human reason is inadequate to form a complete understanding of the moral order of the universe; Christians must rely on God's direct, personal commands to guide them towards a form of behaviour that makes them worthy of salvation.

For Barth, God's commands are presented to Christians through the person of Jesus, but rather than rationally inferring what to do from knowledge of what Jesus said or did, they must make moral decisions out of a sort of instant understanding or *intuition*, the result of God commanding them directly in the

---

5 Simon Blackburn, *Being Good: A Short Introduction to Ethics*, Oxford: Oxford University Press, 2001, pp. 10–13.

6 See www.youtube.com/watch?v=eD52OlkKfNs.

specific situation they face.[7] Barth argued that each moral situation is a distinct, separate occasion requiring a distinct command; this emphasizes human dependence on God's will and removes the possibility of applying commandments to multiple situations through reason. Every individual good action is the result of God's grace – no genuinely good action can be performed without it. It seems to follow that only Christians and specifically the recipients of God's grace (quite possibly not all Christians) can do what is right in God's sight and attain salvation – even the most moral non-believer will be damned.[8]

To be clear: Barth's ethics draws on the ideas of Paul, Augustine and John Calvin, all of whom stressed the necessity of grace and questioned any idea that human beings could do what is good, let alone achieve salvation, through reason and will alone.

How then does Barth's ethics relate to the Bible?

For Barth, the Bible provides the essential context for any divine command, without which neither the command nor the choice to follow it would make sense. As he wrote, God's 'command is an event which performs a particular step in the nexus of the history of divine grace, and, which in fact, can only be understood in this context'.[9] Understanding one's own place within the narrative of Scripture is the first step, which makes each individual receptive to God's command. Commands never contradict the Bible, they just direct believers to do what the Bible suggests in general terms in the specific situation they face. It is probably fair to say that from the outside there would be no difference between a Christian following Barth's divine command ethic and a Christian following a standard, Protestant interpretation of biblical ethics; the difference exists in the *justification* for what they do, not *what* they do.

Unsurprisingly, Barth's ethics have been controversial. Major

---

7 Yes, ethics students: Barth does advocate a form of intuitionism.

8 See William Werperhowski, *Karl Barth and Christian Ethics: Living in Truth*, Farnham: Ashgate, 2014; 'Command and History in the Ethics of Karl Barth', *Journal of Religious Ethics* 9:2 (1981), pp. 298–320.

9 Karl Barth, *Church Dogmatics* II:2, Edinburgh: T. & T. Clark, 1957, p. 681.

critics of this part of his theology have included James Gustafson and Stanley Hauerwas, both writing in 1975. Gustafson claimed that Barth's ethic 'short-cuts the rational processes' and encourages 'passive conformity'; Hauerwas criticized Barth for undermining any idea of freedom, self-determination and growth in Christianity and for ignoring the idea of developing a moral character. How can a good God punish people who have no opportunity to be good or reward those who had almost no real choice but to do what God commanded?

Christianity, the Bible and Virtue Ethics

Christians have always been interested in virtue – how cultivating it can help build character and support a good life. Drawing on Aristotle, Thomas Aquinas saw virtue ethics – efforts to develop an excellent character – as the essential corollary of Natural Law. Much more recently, Alasdair MacIntyre came to recognize the close relationship between Christianity and virtue ethics. As Hauerwas explained:

> MacIntyre notes that when he wrote *After Virtue* he was already an Aristotelian but not yet a Thomist. His Thomism came when he became convinced that in some respects Aquinas was a better Aristotelian than Aristotle. Indeed, MacIntyre reports, he learnt that his attempt to provide an account of the human good in social terms was inadequate without a metaphysical grounding. 'It is only because human beings have an end toward which they are directed by reason of their specific nature', he writes, 'that practices, traditions, and the like are able to function as they do'.[10]

While Natural Law explores the metaphysical foundations of ethical principles, virtue ethics explores the way people come to realize what is right and wrong in practical terms, through and

---

10   Stanley Hauerwas, 'The Virtues of Alasdair MacIntyre', *First Things* October 2007.

in real life. Theism, Christianity, provides an explanation for the existence of a common human nature, moral purpose and freedom as well as, for some, a promise that living well will have a reward beyond this life.

In books such as *The Peaceable Kingdom: A Primer in Christian Ethics*,[11] Stanley Hauerwas has proposed his own Christian ethic, which has much in common with MacIntyre's virtue ethics. He rejects both solely utilitarian and solely deontological approaches to decision-making because they focus on dilemmas, extreme, atypical situations. He proposes instead a combination of a virtue approach, which develops character traits, and a broad biblically based code of principles. As William Frankena quipped, '[P]rinciples without traits are impotent, and traits without principles are blind.'[12]

As Hauerwas sees it, exploring what Christian virtues consist in and how they relate to the experiences most people really have is a more fruitful approach to moral philosophy. Hauerwas discusses Christian virtues such as patience and courage, and draws on them in considering how to respond to aging, sickness and disability, how to face death and the question of suicide. He questions the usefulness of ideas that often feature in discussions of applied ethics, including rights and informed consent.

James Childress, also part of the Yale School of post-liberal narrative theology, considers the part the Bible could play in shaping decisions relating to bioethics.[13] He suggests that the Bible can provide an overarching legal (normative) framework within which Christians have to reflect and make appropriate decisions. Reading the Bible gives people a good opportunity to reflect on the principles that underpin their choices and the extent to which these are coherent and compatible with what they believe and want.

---

11 Stanley Hauerwas, *The Peaceable Kingdom*, London: SCM Press, 1984.

12 William Frankena, *Ethics*, 2nd edn, Englewood Cliffs, NJ: Prentice Hall, 1973, p. 65.

13 James Childress, 'Scripture and Christian Ethics', *Interpretation* 34:4 (1980), pp. 371–80; see also his *Principles of Biomedical Ethics*, Oxford: Oxford University Press, 2001.

13

Women and the Bible

'If God is male then the male is God.'[1]

So said Mary Daly in 1973, voicing the frustration of generations of women with an unfair, patriarchal society and the ongoing oppression of women. Religion was and is at the heart of the problem: it shapes, reflects and reinforces misogynistic attitudes through myths and narratives, rituals, doctrines and ethics – in fact the whole experience – but discredits itself in the process. God is perfect, wholly simple, beyond time and space and bodiless – so how can God be male? If we suggest that God has characteristics of one gender and not the other, we offer support to Feuerbach, Freud and Marx, who saw God as a mere projection of human ideals, a psychological idol and political device. For Daly, it is necessary to 'castrate God' in order to liberate religious language and religious belief from being employed as a tool of oppression and give it the chance of engaging with its true object.

That the Bible supports a patriarchal world view is hard to dispute. While the Bible contains hints that the Hebrews once worshipped the goddess Asherah alongside their God YHVH,[2] this practice seems to have been systematically suppressed, the maleness of God asserted and the validity of all other forms of worship and ways of expressing religious ideas denigrated. In the existing text God is most definitely Lord and Father. Adam was created first and directly; Eve was taken out of Adam as an

1 Mary Daly, *Beyond God the Father: Toward a Philosophy of Women's Liberation*, Boston: Beacon, 1973, p. 19.

2 See Francesca Stavrakopoulou, *Baal and Asherah: Image, Sex, Power, and the Other*, Oxford: Oxford University Press, forthcoming, 2015; Francesca Stavrakopoulou with John Barton, *Religious Diversity in Ancient Israel and Judah*, London: T. & T. Clark, 2010.

afterthought, to be Adam's companion. She was the cause of the fall and humankind's constant struggle to survive.

There were almost no wholly positive female role models in Scripture before Mary, and arguably she was made into an impossible ideal by successive generations of men. Although certainly open-minded for his time, Jesus is described as the Son of God and the Son of Man, and all his Apostles were men. Paul seems to have been a confirmed misogynist, even when oft-quoted references in the letters to Timothy and Titus – which Paul might not have written – are ignored:

- 'Women should remain silent in the churches. They are not allowed to speak, but must be in submission, as the law says.' (1 Cor. 14.34)
- '[E]very woman who prays or prophesies with her head uncovered dishonours her head – it is the same as having her head shaved.' (1 Cor. 11.5)
- 'Wives, submit yourselves to your own husbands as you do to the Lord. For the husband is the head of the wife as Christ is the head of the church ... as the church submits to Christ, so also wives should submit to their husbands in everything.' (Eph. 5.22)

In the Hebrew Scriptures, biblical women either ensnare men with their charms, manipulating them to do what they should not, or are ignored and submit to a life of unimaginative domestic drudgery. The choice offered to any rare woman educated and able to read the Bible seems to have been: be bad or be boring – and either way be damned.

- Abraham's wife Sarah, though beautiful, was acquisitive, jealous, callous, a liar and lacked her husband's faith.
- Lot's wife disobeyed her husband, regretted the loss of home and possessions and was promptly turned into a pillar of salt.
- Isaac's wife Rebekah cosseted her favourite son and conspired with him to trick her husband.

- Jacob's wives Rachel and Leah were sisters and opposites. Rachel was beautiful, manipulative, a liar and thief – Leah was ugly and boring, though dutiful.
- Tamar, Judah's daughter-in-law, tricked him into sleeping with her by pretending to be a prostitute – shortly before the land is plunged into famine and Judah held ransom for his brother.
- For all his strength, Samson was destroyed by his weakness for unscrupulous prostitutes like Delilah.
- Esther and Ruth used trickery and female charms to get what they wanted, albeit their interests were the same as those of the country.
- King David was led into error by Bathsheba's beauty, conspiring to kill her husband and being exposed by Nathan the Prophet.
- John the Baptist was put to death at a woman's whim because of her charms.

It is little wonder that women found the Bible rather off-putting and focused on more ways of engaging with God.

Female Mystics

Through the Middle Ages, female mystics struggled to express their religious experience in inclusive terms that reflected their own experience of God and that other women could relate to, when the structures of the Church, their lack of education and the framing of language itself threatened to exclude them from consideration.

In the twelfth century, Hildegard of Bingen – made a Doctor of the Church only in 2012 – received a steady stream of multi-sensory revelations. She wrote:

But I, though I saw and heard these things, refused to write for a long time through doubt and bad opinion and the diversity of human words, not with stubbornness but in the exercise of humility, until, laid low by the scourge of God,

I fell upon a bed of sickness ... I set my hand to the writing. While I was doing it, I sensed, as I mentioned before, the deep profundity of scriptural exposition; and, raising myself from illness by the strength I received, I brought this work to a close – though just barely – in ten years. [...] And I spoke and wrote these things not by the invention of my heart or that of any other person, but as by the secret mysteries of God I heard and received them in the heavenly places. And again I heard a voice from Heaven saying to me, 'Cry out therefore, and write thus!'[3]

The better to describe her experiences, she invented a private language or *Lingua Ignota*, a new form of 'unheard music', and employed an artist to try to communicate her insights in visual terms. She used the term *veriditas* to express a quality of God and describe the close relationship between truth (*veritas*) and greenness (*viriditas*), implying that what is true is what exists in nature, as it is.[4] In this, Hildegard was an inspiration for a new generation of postmodernist eco-feminists.

In the fourteenth century the anchoress Julian of Norwich had a series of revelations in which she discovered a God of love and compassion who, she hoped, would save everybody from their sufferings. She described God as both mother and father; she spoke of Jesus as mother, wise, loving and merciful, and God's creative act as feminine – motherhood at work. She used the metaphor of the mother and child to describe the relationship between God and human beings.[5]

In the sixteenth century Teresa of Avila had visions of God's love. She is reputed to have written the prayer:

---

3 *Hildegard von Bingen's Mystical Visions*, trans. Bruce Hozeski. See for example Vision 9 – self.gutenberg.org/articles/hildegard_of_bingen#cite_note-21.

4 The word had been used by Augustine, by Gregory the Great and perhaps by Heloise in her love letters to Peter Abelard.

5 Grace Jantzen, *Julian of Norwich: Mystic and Theologian*, London: SPCK, 1987.

Christ has no body now, but yours.
No hands, no feet on earth, but yours.
Yours are the eyes through which he looks
With compassion on this world.[6]

Feminism and Biblical Studies Today

Feminist approaches to theology were not new in the 1970s, when
Mary Daly called for God to be castrated.

- From its origins in the 1650s, the **Religious Society of
  Friends** (Quakers) asserted the equality of men and women
  before God. They had no priests or ministers and centred
  down in silence to listen for God's guidance, but – extremely
  unusually for the time – allowed women to travel, publish and
  preach like any man. Early feminist campaigners in the USA
  were influenced by the Quaker example.
- Out of the early **US Civil Rights Movement**, *The Woman's
  Bible* was published in sections between 1895 and 1898; it
  encouraged people to reconsider how they spoke and thought
  of God, suggesting that the Trinity was composed of 'a
  Heavenly Mother, Father, and Son', and that prayers could be
  addressed to an 'ideal Heavenly Mother'.

Nevertheless it was in the last quarter of the twentieth century that
the effect of feminism on biblical studies was really felt.

In 1983 Rosemary Radford Ruether summed up the three
major directions in feminism:

1 **Liberal feminism** works for political reform within the
   existing system. In religious terms this might take the form
   of campaigning for women to become priests or bishops,
   to have the right to participate fully in services or to study
   theology. Liberals would retain the Bible as the centre of
   worship, stating that the problem has been with inadequate
   interpretation, not with the texts themselves.

---

6 See www.spck.org.uk/classic-prayers/st-theresa-of-avila.

2   **Socialist feminism** aims to restructure society completely so as to integrate women into the workforce and relieve them of the burden of childcare. By Marxist ideals, religion would be dispensed with: at worst it is a tool of social oppression; at best a personal obstacle to understanding the truth and wanting to change. For feminist theologians of this type, the only honest response to the oppression woven through Christianity is to abandon it and look elsewhere for philosophical and/or spiritual sustenance.

3   **Romantic feminism** revels in the differences between men and women and upholds the feminine as superior. In religious terms this would suggest casting God as mother, Gaia, using all-female metaphors and re-imagining rituals and practices to suit women. It might even mean abandoning mainstream monotheistic religions and embracing goddess worship or some form of pantheism.[7]

Recent changes in the Church of England that allowed women to be ordained and – much later – progress to become bishops, demonstrated the existence of many liberal-feminist Christians, male as well as female, but also the difficulty of advancing women's rights in religion and the limitations women face even when barriers are removed.

The 1960s and 1970s saw many women exploring socialist feminism. Although the difficulties in changing the world order soon became apparent, many feminists still feel that embracing liberal social ideals entails dispensing with religion entirely.

Mary Daly is a good example of a romantic feminist. She pointed out that addressing the problems in religion and the society it reflects cannot be effected just by a change in the way we use language, although that should be one element of our approach. Daly suggests that the first thing must be to educate people out of diminishing the transcendence of God by referring to God in human

---

7   Rosemary Radford Ruether, *Sexism and God-Talk: Toward a Feminist Theology*, Boston: Beacon, 1983, pp. 41–5, 216–32.

terms, of either gender; the second thing must be to recognize and correct existing flawed terminology; and the third thing must be to draw attention to sexism as a form of injustice that theology must try to address constantly because failure to acknowledge the problem simply perpetuates it. Language is inherently male and inadequate for theological purposes; it remains to invent new, better and fairer ways of expressing our understanding and experience of the transcendent. This suggests that the Bible, at least in its current form, should cease to be the focus of religion and that mainstream Judaism and Christianity are finished, bankrupt and not fit for any woman to be a part of.[8]

Women's Liberation Theology

More recently, Radford Ruether and Elisabeth Schüssler Fiorenza have proposed different approaches to feminism that build on postmodernism and liberation theology.

Schüssler Fiorenza argues that Christianity must change, transitioning from a Kyriarchy (rule of the lord/master) to a genuine Ekklesia (gathering) of wo/man. She sees a major problem in all post-Enlightenment philosophy, centred in the epistemological naïvety and crude model of language it assumes. For Schüssler Fiorenza, postmodernism has shown us that truth is not simple but always determined by perspective, form of life and language game. Language does not refer to some external reality but in some sense creates its own reality. In the first instance readers should not take the Bible literally but should appreciate that it deals in metaphor, which speaks about one thing (God) in terms of another (humankind). Moving on from this, the metaphor of an other provides us with a fruitful insight into the relationship between God and human beings that draws out the existence of marginalized people and suffering as part of the human condition.

For Schüssler Fiorenza, the biggest contrast between God and

---

8   Mary Daly, *Beyond God the Father: Toward a Philosophy of Women's Liberation*, Boston: Beacon, 1973, ch. 1.

humanity is between God and the most other of the other: poor, despised women. She insists that because wo/men have both the authority and the right to interpret experience, tradition and religion from their own perspective and in their own interests, the biblical struggle for freedom, justice and well-being for all cannot be realized if wo/men's voices are silenced or ignored.[9] The Bible's promise can only be fulfilled if human beings move forward from a Kyriarchy that oppresses many people and towards a democratic Ekklesia in which everybody is valued and able to participate in religion on an equal footing. As Johannes Metz remarks: 'God-talk is either the talk of the vision and the promise of a great justice, which also touches on past suffering, or it is empty and without promise.'[10]

In her study of the Bible, Schüssler Fiorenza proposes a new approach to interpretation that speaks to women. She focuses on texts of the New Testament that transcend androcentric-patriarchal structures to express a new vision of redeemed humanity, just as other feminist interpreters choose to work with passages that speak to women's concerns and avoid those that are overtly sexist. The presumption behind the liberation feminism approach to biblical interpretation is summed up thus:

> Whatever diminishes or denies the full humanity of women must be presumed not to reflect the divine ... or to be the message or work of an authentic redeemer or a community of redemption and, what does promote the full humanity of women is of the Holy, it does reflect true relation to the divine ... the authentic message of redemption and the mission of redemptive community.[11]

---

9 Anne Tuohy, 'Rhetoric and Transformation: The Feminist Theology of Elisabeth Schüssler Fiorenza', *Australian eJournal of Theology* 5 (August 2005). See also Elisabeth Schüssler Fiorenza, *Sharing Her Word: Feminist Biblical Interpretation in Context*, Edinburgh: T. & T. Clark, 1998, pp. 76–87.

10 Johannes Metz, 'Suffering from God: Theology as Theodicy', *Pacifica* 5:3 (1992), p. 275.

11 Radford Ruether, *Sexism and God-Talk*, p. 19.

Biblical revelation and truth are given only in those texts and interpretative models that transcend critically their patriarchal frameworks and allow for a vision of Christian women as historical and theological subjects and actors.[12]

We will explore liberation theology further in the next chapter.

---

12 Elisabeth Schüssler Fiorenza, *In Memory of Her: A Feminist Theological Reconstruction of Christian Origins*, London: SCM Press, 1983, p. 30.

14

Political Readings of the Bible

In the first instance, Christianity was a political movement.

The Gospels describe Jesus leading the poor and oppressed with promises of a revolution, reform of institutions and a new world order. For Jesus, faith was no mere private matter, was not about participating in rituals, conforming to tradition or submitting to authority, rather it was about sacrificing everything – even one's life – to change the world.

The Church reached a settlement with the political masters of Europe at the waning of the Roman Empire. Although this was at the price of stepping away from Jesus' core revolutionary message, 'So the last will be first, and the first will be last' (Matt. 20.16), that message remained plain for anyone to read in the Bible. Is it any wonder that reading the Bible has been, throughout the history of the Church, a controversial matter?

Wealth and Poverty

In particular, Jesus praised the poor; reversing popular attitudes, he saw them as far closer to God than the rich. Luke 4.16–20 describes Jesus announcing the beginning of his mission:

> He went to Nazareth, where he had been brought up, and on the Sabbath day he went into the synagogue, as was his custom. He stood up to read, and the scroll of the prophet Isaiah was handed to him. Unrolling it, he found the place where it is written: 'The Spirit of the Lord is on me, because he has anointed me to proclaim good news to the poor. He has sent me to proclaim freedom for the prisoners and recovery of

sight for the blind, to set the oppressed free, to proclaim the year of the Lord's favour.' Then he rolled up the scroll, gave it back to the attendant and sat down. The eyes of everyone in the synagogue were fastened on him.

Jesus acted very much like a revolutionary leader: 'In the same way, those of you who do not give up everything you have cannot be my disciples' (Luke 14.33). Matthew 19.21 affirms that: 'Jesus answered, "If you want to be perfect, go, sell your possessions and give to the poor, and you will have treasure in heaven. Then come, follow me."' Jesus demanded total commitment from his followers, in terms of worldly possessions as well as professions of faith. In Luke 16.19–25 he teaches by means of a parable:

There was a rich man who was dressed in purple and fine linen and lived in luxury every day. At his gate was laid a beggar named Lazarus, covered with sores and longing to eat what fell from the rich man's table. Even the dogs came and licked his sores. The time came when the beggar died and the angels carried him to Abraham's side. The rich man also died and was buried. In Hades, where he was in torment, he looked up and saw Abraham far away, with Lazarus by his side.

Elaborating on the blunt teaching in Mark 10.24–31:

The disciples were amazed at his words. But Jesus said again, 'Children, how hard it is to enter the kingdom of God! It is easier for a camel to go through the eye of a needle than for someone who is rich to enter the kingdom of God.' The disciples were even more amazed, and said to each other, 'Who then can be saved?' Jesus looked at them and said, 'With man this is impossible, but not with God; all things are possible with God.' Then Peter spoke up, 'We have left everything to follow you!' 'Truly I tell you,' Jesus replied, 'no one who has left home or brothers or sisters or mother or father or children or fields for me and the gospel will fail to receive a hundred times as much in this present age: homes, brothers, sisters, mothers, children and fields – along with persecutions – and in the age to come eternal life. But many who are first will be last, and the last first.'

Jesus saw wealth as at worst an obstacle to salvation and at best a test for those who possess it. To have and remain open-handed and generous, not become acquisitive and jealous, is difficult indeed.

Following Jesus' teaching, in Acts 2.44–45 we read about the disciples disavowing private property, even punishing those who hold back assets from being shared according to need (Ananias and Sapphira for example): 'All the believers were together and had everything in common. They sold property and possessions to give to anyone who had need.' Acts 4.32–35 confirms:

> All the believers were one in heart and mind. No one claimed that any of their possessions was their own, but they shared everything they had. With great power the apostles continued to testify to the resurrection of the Lord Jesus. And God's grace was so powerfully at work in them all that there was no needy person among them. For from time to time those who owned land or houses sold them, brought the money from the sales and put it at the apostles' feet, and it was distributed to anyone who had need.

Acts 20.35 explains: 'In everything I did, I showed you that by this kind of hard work we must help the weak, remembering the words the Lord Jesus himself said: "It is more blessed to give than to receive."' The apostle Paul taught the churches he founded to behave in the same way and reminded members: 'The one who is unwilling to work shall not eat' (2 Thess. 3.10). That uncompromising teaching about wealth would be an obstacle to Christianity being adopted by those with wealth is no surprise. The Church had to compromise in order to expand in influence, if not in numbers, but this compromise came at the price of unity.

- After the destruction of the Temple in AD 70 and through the first centuries of the Church, the Ebionites (from the Hebrew for 'poor') upheld Jewish laws and customs, did not accept the more philosophical claims about Jesus' identity (such as divinity, pre-existence), embraced poverty and vegetarianism. They were denounced as heretics by St Irenaeus among other Church Fathers.

- In the tenth century the Bogomils upheld a dualist world view, with the forces of evil working through the rich and powerful and the forces of good working through the poor. They were subject to multiple persecutions into the nineteenth century. The Cathars had similar dualist views and ideas about poverty; they were the target of a full-blown military crusade from 1208.

- By the fourteenth century a split had developed between the Papacy and mendicant orders (including the Franciscans, Waldensians and Humiliati), whose members tried to live by Jesus' teachings on wealth and poverty. In 1323 Pope John XXII issued a Bull *Cum inter nonnullos*, which declared 'erroneous and heretical' the belief that Christ and his apostles had no possessions. Shortly thereafter the followers of John Wycliffe (Lollards) and Jan Hus (Hussites) were persecuted for teaching the virtue of poverty. During the Peasants' Revolt of 1381 the rebels chanted 'When Adam delved and Eve span / who was then the gentleman?', echoing the unofficial teaching of John Ball, which pointed out what Jesus would probably have made of their feudal society and the part the Church played in propping it up.

- Of course, one of the issues that ultimately started the Protestant Reformation was the profiteering of some officials within the Church, yet neither the abuse of the poor nor the Church's defence of the abusers stopped. In 1834 the Tolpuddle Martyrs kick-started the Trades Union movement by drawing attention to the inconsistency between basic Christian beliefs and the behaviour of those calling themselves Christians: 'God is our guide! from field, from wave / From plough, from anvil, and from loom / We come, our country's rights to save / And speak a tyrant faction's doom / We raise the watch-word liberty / We will, we will, we will be free!'[1]

- Through the nineteenth century the Church was split between supporting the establishment and calling for radical social reform. Prominent figures including John Ruskin (the Art critic), William Morris (the designer), Charles Kingsley (the author of *The Water Babies*) called for Christians to support socialism and stand up for the rights of the poor. Many Christians were involved in the labour movement, from Beatrice Webb to Gordon Brown and the late Tony Benn. In 2014 the celebrity Russell Brand claimed that socialism is 'Christianity politicized'.[2]

The political significance of Christianity ensured that the twentieth century was particularly difficult for the Church. The extension of the franchise (right to vote) and rise of extremist politics, whether in the form of communist totalitarianism, fascism or free-market capitalism, made it more important than ever for Christians to apply their beliefs to contemporary political decision-making. Different Christians interpreted the political application of their beliefs in different ways.

Christianity and Communism

In 1848, the year of revolution across Europe, Karl Marx and Friedrich Engels put forward the *Communist Manifesto*. They wrote:

The history of all hitherto existing society is the history of class struggles ... Society as a whole is more and more splitting up into two great hostile camps, into two great classes

---

1 For a good summary of heresies through the history of the Church, see sites. google.com/site/transcendingproof/heresies.

2 See www.truthdig.com/avbooth/item/russell_brand_socialism_is_christianity _politicized_20140120.

directly facing each other – Bourgeoisie and Proletariat ... The bourgeoisie, historically, has played a most revolutionary part ... It has resolved personal worth into exchange value, and in place of the numberless indefeasible chartered freedoms, has set up that single, unconscionable freedom – Free Trade. In one word, for exploitation, veiled by religious and political illusions, it has substituted naked, shameless, direct, brutal exploitation ... It has converted the physician, the lawyer, the priest, the poet, the man of science, into its paid wage labourers ... Of all the classes that stand face to face with the bourgeoisie today, the proletariat alone is a really revolutionary class ... Communism abolishes eternal truths, it abolishes all religion, and all morality, instead of constituting them on a new basis; it therefore acts in contradiction to all past historical experience ... In place of the old bourgeois society, with its classes and class antagonisms, we shall have an association, in which the free development of each is the condition for the free development of all.[3]

Marx denounced religion because it is an irrational delusion, because it makes people servile and amenable to the status quo and because it is hypocritical and, while preaching help for the poor, collaborates in oppression. Famously, he wrote:

Religious distress is at the same time the expression of real distress and the protest against real distress. Religion is the sigh of the oppressed creature, the heart of a heartless world, just as it is the spirit of a spiritless situation. It is the opium of the people.[4]

Nevertheless some Christians saw similarity between Marxism and Christian teaching, while stopping well short of supporting what was done by despotic powers in the name of communism, whether in Russia, China or North Korea. As James Cone

---

3 See www.marxists.org/archive/marx/works/1848/communist-manifesto.

4 See www.marxists.org/archive/marx/works/1843/critique-hpr/intro.htm.

observed, Christians manage to reconcile atheistic Marxism with their faith position by 'distinguishing between Marxism as world view (Weltanschauung) and Marxism as an instrument of social analysis, rejecting the former and enthusiastically taking up the latter'.[5]

Thomas J. Haggerty was a Catholic priest and one of the founders of Industrial Workers of the World, whose later members included Helen Keller. Keller, who was both deaf and blind but still managed to get an education and career, was one of the founders of the ACLU, which worked to promote civil liberties and combat all forms of discrimination in American society, including sexism, homophobia, racism and discrimination against disabled people. Many other Christians came to support the ACLU, including Martin Luther King. King was a fierce critic of capitalism but could not voice support for socialism or communism because of the mood of the time.[6] As Obery M. Hendricks observes:

> King's ethics are firmly in the tradition of radical biblical prophets like Amos, Micah, and Isaiah, who together proclaimed that everyone, including the rich and the powerful, were to be governed by ethical principles that included *mishpat* (foundational egalitarian justice), *sadiqah* (justice put into action), *hesed* (steadfast love; in politics, civility at the least) and *emet* (truthfulness, in public and in private). The political implications of this ethical constellation are reflected in this proclamation by the Prophet Isaiah: 'A throne shall be established in *hesed* (steadfast love) ... and on it shall sit in *emet* (truthfulness) a ruler who seeks *mishpat* (egalitarian justice) and is swift to do *sadiqah* (put justice into action).' (Isa. 16.5)[7]

5   See   archive.org/stream/TheBlackChurchAndMarxismWhatDoTheyHave ToSayToEachOther/BCM_djvu.txt.

6   See www.huffingtonpost.com/obery-m-hendricks-jr-phd/the-uncompromising -anti-capitalism-of-martin-luther-king-jr_b_4629609.html.

7   See www.huffingtonpost.com/obery-m-hendricks-jr-phd/the-uncompromising -anti-capitalism-of-martin-luther-king-jr_b_4629609.html.

Black Liberation Theology

More recently, African American theologians such as James Cone have developed a form of black liberation theology, building on the work of Martin Luther King and postmodernist philosophy to provide a distinctive form of Christianity that speaks to people of God's power to free individuals and whole nations from the toils of injustice. Cone wrote that Marxism could be a useful part of that Christianity and serve the cause of civil rights and black liberation:

> I think that blacks can overcome the problem of Marxism being white and racist the same way we overcame the problem of Christianity being white and racist. We can indigenize Marxism, that is, reinterpret it for our situation. We do not refuse to ride in cars or airplanes, nor do we reject any other useful instrument just because they were invented by whites. Why then should we reject Marxism if it proves to be of use in our struggle for freedom?[8]

Cone also wrote: 'God is a God that makes liberation meaningful to those who are marginalized no matter where they are. God takes on that identity of the oppressed.'[9]

In this way he has suggested that Jesus is black. He is not making a historical or metaphysical claim, he is using a powerful metaphor that speaks to African Americans, just as feminists speak of God as mother. Metaphors speak of one thing in terms of another. God doesn't have a body yet Christians have always used the metaphors of father and shepherd.

Why are some metaphors valid and others not?

For the postmodernist, the validity of the metaphor relates to its coherence within a particular form of life and the power it has to illuminate a language game and add meaning. There is no doubt that within black communities the metaphor of God as black is

---

8   See   archive.org/stream/TheBlackChurchAndMarxismWhatDoTheyHave ToSayToEachOther/BCM_djvu.txt 6.2.

9   See   www.huffingtonpost.com/2015/01/16/god-is-black-james-cone_n_ 6487012.html.

coherent and meaningful, just as the metaphor of God as mother is coherent and meaningful for many women. Nevertheless for many Christians, doing theology according to what is acceptable to some group of people is not really what it is about.[10]

Liberation Theology

The Catholic author Graham Greene wrote about the hypocrisy of both the Church and politicians who claimed to be communists. *The Power and the Glory* (1940), set in Mexico, is Greene's best known exposé of the gulf that exists between those who talk the talk and those who walk the walk in terms of compassion. In 1969 Greene was more explicit in identifying practical Catholic ethics with communism. He identified the martyred South American priests Camilo Torres and Father Pro with the revolutionary communist leader Che Guevara[11] and described the 'benevolent communist rule of the Jesuit missions'. Of course, it was Pedro Arrupe, Superior General of the Society of Jesus, who coined the phrase 'preferential option for the poor' in a letter to the Jesuits of South America in 1968. This idea became the foundation of a powerful movement that shook the Catholic Church and caused it to re-evaluate its stance on issues of social justice.

Gustavo Gutiérrez, a Peruvian Dominican priest, confronted injustice and spoke out for the Church to work in the interests of the poor, actively putting their interests ahead of those of others as Jesus did in the Gospels. Returning to the Gospels, he suggested that Jesus came to liberate the poor, maybe even through revolution: 'Do not suppose that I have come to bring peace to the earth. I did not come to bring peace, but a sword' (Matt. 10.34). For Gutiérrez, Christianity must be practical, not theoretical, and demands that believers act in history to make God's words a reality.

In this vein, Gutiérrez and other local, South American

---

10   See www.bbc.co.uk/newsbeat/article/32958213/god-is-neither-she-nor-he-say-anglican-priests.

11   Michael G. Brennan, *Graham Greene: Fiction, Faith and Authorship*, London: Bloomsbury, 2010, p. 127.

Catholic priests supported people in setting up base communities, often where there was/is no formal church to attend. In these, groups of people meet to read and discuss the Bible and consider what it means in practice for their lives and their politics. This is bottom-up Christianity rather than the more familiar top-down form, driven by the needs and passion of ordinary people and seeking to shape the practice of faith and Christian doctrine to serve the poor majority rather than institutions or an elite. Unsurprisingly, base communities were and are seen as a threat by some in the church hierarchy. Highly political, base communities often embrace Marxist ideas and bring Christianity into unwelcome conflict with civil authorities. Nevertheless priests and people on the ground cannot accept the idea that the Church should ignore the causes of poverty while it seeks to address and relieve it in other ways. As the Archbishop of Recife, Dom Hélder Pessoa Câmara (who died in 1999) said: 'When I give food to the poor, they call me a saint. When I ask why they are poor, they call me a communist',[12] drawing attention to the real difficulty of priests' positions in the developing world and the basic hypocrisy of those who suggest that the Church should not get involved in politics. What is Christianity about if it is not political? Jesus came to serve the poor and oppressed, to change the world so that the last would be first and the first last in the kingdom of God, and he died a revolutionary's death. He did not spend his time cuddling baby lambs and wearing white flowing robes in wildflower meadows, whatever the manufacturers of religious tat might imply! Reading the Bible makes it hard to miss or ignore that fact.

Gustavo Gutiérrez was a highly controversial figure within the Church for decades, but recently Pope Francis has moved towards reconciliation. In May 2015 Gutiérrez was invited to speak as a guest of the Vatican and, in June 2015, the new Encyclical *Laudato Si* contained several passages that echo the liberation theologians' demand that the poor be given a preferential option and their belief

---

12   Cited (in the original Portuguese) in Zildo Rocha, *Helder, O Dom: uma vida que marcou os rumos da Igreja no Brasil* (Helder, the Gift: A Life that Marked the Course of the Church in Brazil), Petrópolis: Editora Vozes, 2000, p. 53.

that the rich owe a debt to the poor for exploiting their labour and natural resources.

Following Gutiérrez, liberation theologians included some who remained firmly within the mainstream Catholic Church and others who became its outspoken critics, embracing radical politics.

Óscar Romero, who was appointed Archbishop of San Salvador in 1977, became the moderate face of liberation theology. While he was a faithful Catholic and opponent of Marxist elements, Romero spoke out fearlessly against the persecution of those in the Church who worked with and for the poor. He said:

> In less than three years, more than 50 priests have been attacked, threatened, calumniated. Six are already martyrs – they were murdered ... If all this has happened to persons who are the most evident representatives of the Church, you can guess what has happened to ordinary Christians ... But it is important to note why [the Church] has been persecuted. Not any and every priest has been persecuted, not any and every institution has been attacked. That part of the church has been attacked and persecuted that put itself on the side of the people and went to the people's defence. Here again we find the same key to understanding the persecution of the church: the poor.[13]

Romero was shot in 1980 while celebrating Mass; he had just called for soldiers, as Christians, to obey God's higher order and to stop carrying out the government's repression and violations of human rights. While several conservative cardinals blocked his beatification for years (they were concerned his death was prompted by politics, not faith), he was beatified in May 2015.

At the other end of the spectrum, the Brazilian Franciscan Leonardo Boff has been sharply critical of free-market capitalism and of the US foreign policy used to further it. Controversially, he also criticized the power structures and corruption within the

---

13 Speech at the Université catholique de Louvain, Belgium, 2 February 1980.

Church and offered a measure of critical support to communist regimes. He was silenced by the Vatican in 1985 and again in 1992 (which drove him to leave the priesthood), but he has remained an influential figure, respected by many ordinary Catholics for the sincerity of his beliefs.

Cardinal Joseph Ratzinger led the Catholic Church in rejecting liberation theology through the 1980s and 1990s before taking the papal crown in 2005. Having grown up in Nazi Germany, he had a deep understanding of the relationship between the Church and politics and what could happen if it grew too close. He saw liberation theology as a form of Marxism, likely to bring the Church into conflict with the USA and to offer encouragement to the many so-called communist regimes who abused their power and went against every principle the Church held dear. Further, he recognized the deep contradiction in Catholics voicing support for an atheistic anti-religious world view that places a low value on individual human lives. Nevertheless the strained relationship between the church hierarchy and those doing most to reach out and serve the interests of the poor added to the impression that it was out of touch or even corrupt.

Pope Francis – Pope Benedict's successor, a Jesuit, previously Archbishop of Buenos Aires – understands better than most the need for the church hierarchy to re-engage with Jesus' mission to the poor. He was immediately embroiled in controversy for acknowledging the close relationship between Christian and communist ideals. An outspoken critic of free-market capitalism, he recently said: 'The Gospel does not condemn the rich but idolatry of wealth, that idolatry that renders [us] insensitive to the cries of the poor.'[14] In 2014 he said: 'I can only say that the communists have stolen our flag. The flag of the poor is Christian. Poverty is at the centre of the Gospel.'[15]

While Pope Francis would not offer the slightest support to

14   See ncronline.org/news/vatican/new-interview-francis-strongly-defends-criticisms-capitalism.

15   See www.independent.co.uk/news/world/europe/pope-francis-says-communists-are-really-closet-christians-9572324.html.

brutal totalitarian manifestations of communism, his politics do seem to have something in common with idealistic Marxism.[16] This has brought him into conflict with Christians in the USA who, following decades of anti-communist propaganda, see any left-wing sympathy as evidence that somebody is an enemy.

It should be borne in mind how communist leaders – and leading opponents of the USA – have claimed to be acting out Jesus' teaching. Hugo Chavez explained:

> I am a Marxist to the same degree as the followers of the ideas of Jesus Christ ... Who can imagine Christ as a capitalist? Christ was more radical than any of us. It was He who said – 'it is easier for a camel to go through the eye of a needle than for a rich man to enter into the kingdom of heaven.'[17]

Fidel Castro said: 'If people call me Christian, not from the standpoint of religion but from the standpoint of social vision, I declare that I am a Christian.'[18]

In this context it might be easier to understand why Christians in the USA find Pope Francis' ideas disturbing.

Prosperity Theology

In the USA, prosperity theology has been very influential. It enables many Christians to reconcile their beliefs with right-wing politics, wholehearted support for free-market capitalism and identifying communism, socialism and even liberalism with metaphysical evil.

After the Second World War, popular Protestant preachers, including Oral Roberts and A. A. Allen, drew huge crowds to revival meetings across the United States. Taking a worship style

---

16 See philosophersforchange.org/2013/07/30/taking-notes-24-why-i-am-a-christian-communist. This offers some reasons why a Christian might also be a Communist.

17 See sputniknews.com/world/20100116/157569985.html.

18 Fidel Castro, *My Life: A Spoken Autobiography*, London: Allen Lane, 2007, p. 156.

from Pentecostal churches, offering faith healing, Bible study and plenty of singing, they drew on theological themes that spoke to the American dream and so appealed to the public.

The Old Testament in particular teaches that wealth is a gift from God, recognizing righteousness, whereas poverty is a sign of sin and divine disfavour. Wealth must be gained honestly and used in God's service.

> There need be no poor people among you, for in the land the LORD your God is giving you to possess as your inheritance, he will richly bless you, if only you fully obey the LORD your God and are careful to follow all these commands I am giving you today. (Deut. 15.4–5)

> Be careful that you do not forget the LORD your God, failing to observe his commands, his laws and his decrees that I am giving you this day. Otherwise, when you eat and are satisfied, when you build fine houses and settle down, and when your herds and flocks grow large and your silver and gold increase and all you have is multiplied, then your heart will become proud and you will forget the LORD your God, who brought you out of Egypt, out of the land of slavery ... You may say to yourself, 'My power and the strength of my hands have produced this wealth for me.' But remember the Lord your God, for it is he who gives you the ability to produce wealth, and so confirms his covenant, which he swore to your ancestors, as it is today. (Deut. 8.11–19)

Soon preachers such as Benny Hinn, Kenneth Copeland, Joyce Meyer and Paula White took to radio and television, using this sort of reference to connect peoples' prosperity with their social conservatism and teaching them that the more righteous they were – and the more they gave to the Church – the more wealth God would reward them with.

As the US economy boomed through the 1950s, 1960s, 1980s and 1990s, people did grow wealthier and wealthier – and so did their churches. Such wealth attracted attention, and scandals came to light, including those relating to fraud and financial mismanagement. To take just one recent example: Pastor Creflo Dollar – yes, really! – has been investigated by the Senate Finance Committee for dealings that have resulted in his owning two Rolls-Royces, houses worth some $10 million and a brand new $65 million Gulfstream G650 private jet – to replace the one he crashed in November 2014.

Conclusion

Liberation theology and prosperity theology represent two very different ways of tackling poverty, both rooted in the Bible. Whereas liberation theology – like left-wing politics – sees poverty as a systematic, societal problem and uses the Bible to describe and agitate for a new world order that offers a preferential option for the poor. Prosperity theology – like right-wing politics – sees poverty as a personal problem and uses the Bible to teach people the virtues of hard work, honest living and philanthropy as a means of each individual overcoming it in their own lives by their own will.

It is clear that the Bible is a powerful source of political authority, but also that it can be read and interpreted to support quite different positions and policies. Real care must be taken to avoid eisegesis, 'reading in' to the Bible, which ends up with readers seeing their pre-existing ideals reflected back from the page. On the traditional, historical model that identified the true meaning of biblical texts with what their authors intended or with what original audiences would have understood, there is a standard – however difficult it might be to identify – against which to measure the plausibility of a reading of the Bible. However, if the truth or meaning of a passage is accepted to lie with the modern interpreter or even each individual reader, it becomes much more difficult to say if and when the Bible is being used inappropriately and its authority co-opted to support positions and policies that would probably have been abhorrent to its authors and their audiences.

As this chapter shows, the Bible matters: what might seem like obscure debates about hermeneutics, meaning and truth, and what might seem like petty in-fighting between modernist advocates of historical criticism and postmodernist interpreters, affect the world we all live in in real and important ways.

15

Another Perspective

In the fifth century, Jerome studied the Hebrew Scriptures in preparing his Vulgate Latin translation of the Bible. He came to realize that the Septuagint version of the Old Testament that most Christian scholars had been using was far from inspired. He used the third-century Hexapla of Origen – which placed the Hebrew and Greek texts side by side – but went on to spend time learning techniques in scriptural interpretation as well as language from Jewish rabbis, to develop his philological understanding and ensure that he caught the real and complex meaning of the texts in his translations.[1] However, apart from Origen and Jerome, few of the Early Church Fathers had much knowledge either of the Hebrew text of the Bible or its Jewish interpretation.[2]

In the thirteenth century Thomas Aquinas was heavily influenced by the great 'Rabbi Moses' (Maimonides) in developing his approach to biblical interpretation,[3] an approach that went on to become foundational to Roman Catholic doctrine. And yet again few other Christian scholastic philosophers or major theologians bothered to engage with Jewish scholarship, despite the fact that they were engaged in a similar task and that their work would have been enriched through a proper understanding of the context in which Jesus taught and Paul's letters and the Gospels were

---

1   See Andrew Cain and Josef Lössl (eds), *Jerome of Stridon: His Life, Writings and Legacy*, Farnham: Ashgate, 2009.

2   See G. McLarney, *St. Augustine's Interpretation of the Psalms of Ascent*, Washington, DC: Catholic University of America Press, 2014, p. 45.

3   See Warren Zev Harvey, 'Maimonides and Aquinas on Interpreting the Bible', *Proceedings of the American Academy for Jewish Research* 55 (1988), pp. 59–77.

written. John Duns Scotus dismissed the credibility of Jewish scholarship on the grounds that it rejects the New Testament when it is promised in the Old Testament; he could not conceive of an alternative interpretation of Hebrew Scripture.[4]

Martin Luther had appalling anti-Semitic views, which arguably did much to influence attitudes in Lutheran Northern Europe, justify discrimination, segregation, pogroms and even the Holocaust. In 1543 Luther recommended that Christians should:

1   burn down Jewish synagogues and schools;
2   refuse to let Jews own houses among Christians;
3   take Jewish religious writings away;
4   forbid rabbis to preach;
5   offer no protection to Jews on highways;
6   prohibit usury – lending money at interest – and seize Jews' money and assets unless they truly convert;
7   force Jews to earn their living through manual labour.[5]

In the seventeenth century the work of Baruch Spinoza forced Christian scholars to take notice of Jewish scriptural interpretation – albeit an extreme of Jewish scriptural interpretation that was disowned by most Jews.[6] Spinoza was unusually placed to contribute to a Protestant Christian discussion about the meaning, use and authority of the Bible and argue for intellectual freedom as compatible with both religion and social stability. In the twelfth century, Maimonides argued that the highest form of prophecy was pure and clear rational insight, which can be understood without imagination. To Spinoza this suggested:

•   that philosophy had the potential to provide a better route to truth than theology or most forms of direct religious experience;

---

4   See franciscan-archive.org/scotus/opera/dun01059.html, pp. 72–3.

5   *On the Jews and Their Lies*, Section XI.

6   See J. Samuel Preus, *Spinoza and the Irrelevance of Biblical Authority*, New York: Cambridge University Press, 2001.

- that the Bible should be interpreted in the light of reason as having multiple possible layers of meaning and offering no support to literalism;
- that the Bible's authority should not be greater than is reasonable – as Spinoza saw it, than any other ancient text.

Spinoza drew on his reading of Maimonides and on his study of Enlightenment philosophers such as Thomas Hobbes, but obviously enough, his argument was just as much anathema to Orthodox Jews as it was to most Protestant Christians, who based their faith on the plain word of Scripture.[7] Spinoza was excommunicated by the Jewish community of Amsterdam and had to leave the city as a young man; and his *Theological-Political Treatise*, anonymously published, was condemned and then banned by the Dutch Reformed Church in 1673.

Spinoza became one of the most controversial thinkers in Europe – he was threatened with prosecution, one of his friends was executed and another died in prison. Gottfried Leibniz, who was fascinated by his philosophical ideas, dared not write to or meet Spinoza – who had been called 'the most dangerous man of the century' – in public.[8] Nevertheless, many philosophers, both Jewish and Christian, saw genius in his writings. They included Leibniz, Moses Mendelssohn and later Gotthold Lessing.

Moses Mendelssohn was a major figure in the development of Enlightenment thought in Germany, although today he is chiefly remembered for beating Kant into second place in an essay competition! Like Spinoza, Mendelssohn accepted Maimonides' high view of reason and did not see it as conflicting with faith. He developed the arguments for God's existence and put forward several new ones, including:

---

7 See www.biblicalstudies.org.uk/article_luther_s-wood.html.

8 Matthew Stewart, *The Courtier and the Heretic: Leibniz, Spinoza, and the Fate of God in the Modern World*, New Haven, CT: Yale University Press, 2006, p. 11.

1   an argument based on René Descartes that he summarized
    as 'I am, therefore there is a God.'[9] I exist; my knowledge of
    this depends on my existence so this existence is contingent.
    The fact of contingent existence presupposes the existence of
    a necessarily existing being or else nothing would exist at all
    – God is that necessarily existing being.

2   a version of the ontological argument that pre-empts and
    avoids Kant's famous criticism that it uses existence as a
    predicate. Mendelssohn suggested that if an atheist said that
    God does not exist they could only mean that God is impossible
    or contingent. Since the concept of God is coherent, God is
    possible, and since it is God's nature to necessarily exist, God
    cannot be contingent – hence God cannot not exist.

Mendelssohn spent a lot of time reflecting on language and criticized
Rousseau's view that language is a tool for socialization. As he
saw it, language is the very manifestation of rational capabilities
– the ability to name concepts is key to recognizing and defining
them; the use of signs or labels to categorize experiences is the first
step in understanding the relationships between concepts, natural
laws and logic. For Mendelssohn, language is inextricably bound
up with reason and is part of what makes human beings created
in God's image. Judaism is in a sense a language as much as a
religion; as rational animals, human beings talk and sometimes
write as a way of understanding their situation. Judaism, religion,
is not about eternal rules, static dogmas or revealed truth, it is a
living tradition, an ongoing discussion that supports people in
understanding their lot. Mendelssohn worried about the literal
interpretation of Scripture; as Dahlstrom suggests: 'Frozen in
time, the written word can become an idol itself, obscuring the
distinction between itself and what it is meant to signify.'[10]

Mendelssohn is sometimes called the Jewish Luther, but his
approach to reforming his religion was far more sophisticated than

---

9   *Philosophical Writings*, p. 289; *Gesammelte Schriften* 3/2, pp. 78, 83f.

10 Daniel Dahlstrom, 'Moses Mendelssohn', *The Stanford Encyclopedia of Philosophy*, ed. Edward N. Zalta; http://plato.stanford.edu/entries/mendelssohn.

Luther's ever was! Unlike Spinoza, he managed to work within the bounds of mainstream scholarship and avoided causing major offence to the Protestant Christian authorities, despite Johann Lavater challenging him in 1769 to refute Pietist arguments or convert to Christianity. He was a driving force in the Jewish Enlightenment, the *Haskalah* (1770s to the 1880s), which was inspired by the European Enlightenment but ran in parallel to it.

The Hebrew word *Haskalah* comes from *sekhel*, meaning 'reason'; it was a movement that encouraged Jews to learn European languages, study secular subjects, enter professions and otherwise assimilate in terms of dress, manners and loyalty to secular authorities. While many Jews prospered as a result and a good degree of mixing between Christian and Jewish communities occurred in cities across Europe, this caused tension as much – or more – than it relieved the tension that had always existed as a result of non-assimilated Jewish communities existing in ghettos.

Through the rest of the eighteenth and the nineteenth centuries, as part of their attempt to diffuse the authority of the Church and progress intellectually, technologically and economically, Enlightenment scholars put the accomplishments of Greek and Roman culture on a pedestal. Faithful Christians – and the many who dared not attract the wrath of the Church – sought a means of reconciling essential Christian ideas with classical philosophy and saw a way forward in focusing on those elements of Christianity that were most Greek and associating all that was ignorant, regressive and frankly embarrassing with the Jewish roots of the religion – Jewish roots that could gradually be disowned. This was highly unfair, but few Europeans needed much encouragement to believe bad things about Judaism; anti-Semitism had been endemic since Roman times.

Wilhelm von Humboldt, the Prussian Minister of Education and designer of what has become the model for research universities around the world, idolized the Greeks and put the Classics and (Aristotelian natural) philosophy at the heart of education for generations of Europeans to come, deposing Christian theology from the syllabus, so that[11] 'in Germany especially, it was common to speak of the classical Greeks almost as a kind of super-race, and to hold them up as the sole example of a segment of humanity worth serving as an ideal'.[12]

Immanuel Kant had suggested that Judaism and the Hebrew Scriptures have nothing to add to Western thought and can be bypassed in any survey of the history of ideas! He even claimed that Judaism was not a religion at all until it benefited from Greek wisdom.[13] Georg Friedrich Hegel – who became rector of von Humboldt's flagship university in Berlin in 1830 – described Judaism as characterized by absolute nothingness, so that the birth of Christianity could be seen as a second creation *ex nihilo*![14] After 1850, things degenerated towards the blatant and aggressive racism of the composer Richard Wagner.

The flower of European philosophy, supposedly motivated by truth, seems to have been uncritically infatuated with Greece and unreasonably prejudiced against Israel, willing to rewrite history to suit itself!

- How could Kant dismiss Judaism as legalistic and pragmatic when his own ethic promoted the rules 'do not murder', 'do not lie', 'do not steal', even though following a law mindlessly or out of deference to authority would be wrong according to Kant's own principles?

- How could Hegel, whose own writing suggested the dialectical advancement of history, fail to see his perspective on Judaism as a reflection of his cultural circumstances and fail to see the plausibility of the antithetical view?

---

11 E.g. *Decline and Fall of the Greek Republics*, 1808.

12 Yoram Hazony, *The Philosophy of Hebrew Scripture*, Cambridge: Cambridge University Press, 2012, p. 13.

13 *Religion within the Bounds of Reason Alone*, pp. 116, 118. See also Michael Mack, *German Idealism and the Jew*, Chicago: University of Chicago Press, 2003. How much Kant's pronouncements on Judaism were influenced by his jealousy of Mendelssohn is an interesting question!

14 *Lectures on the History of Philosophy*, trans. E. S. Haldane, Lincoln: Nebraska University Press, 1995, Vol. 1, p. 101.

In this sense the so-called Enlightenment was a long way from being rational, liberal or progressive.

Judaism and Biblical Criticism

Biblical criticism, first in Germany and then elsewhere, took its cue from Enlightenment philosophy and usually absorbed its anti-Semitic assumptions without question. By the turn of the twentieth century, Conservative Judaism, with reason, had started to see biblical criticism as an attack on Judaism, aimed at undermining the Jewish claim to being a chosen people with a promised land. Zionists took the lead in refuting biblical criticism, claiming it was far from objective and riddled with methodological holes. However, some Reform thinkers, like Abraham Geiger and Leopold Zunz, accepted German biblical criticism and its conclusions, seeing that the rational analysis of the texts was a necessary step in understanding them properly and forming a sensible view on how to use and apply them in the modern world.

Today, Rabbi David Steinberg, former outreach rabbi for the ultra-Orthodox organization Aish HaTorah, as well as Professor Marc Brettler, also an Orthodox Jew, have set out to challenge the idea that Judaism depends on the historicity of Torah by developing www.TheTorah.com. This website is an attempt to reconcile the findings of modern biblical scholarship with traditional Jewish beliefs.

Jewish Approaches to Interpreting Scripture

The ancient rabbis spoke of the Torah as 'black fire on white fire' – the black fire being the printed letters and white fire being the spaces around and between. Both kinds of fire must be read and interpreted if anything close to a full understanding is to be reached. God gave the Torah without the vowel marks or punctuation that would enable us to pin down a single, literal translation. So even the act of reading Scripture requires a degree of creative interpretation. Since God does not make mistakes, Jewish scholars have argued that God must intend for them to bring creativity and imagination to the task of reading and interpreting Scripture.

Today rabbis teach young people preparing for their Bar Mitzvah – or Bat Mitzvah in some synagogues – this mnemonic to remember four basic layers of meaning that exist in all passages of Scripture:

PaRDeS (literally 'Paradise')

- **Peshat** (Simple): this refers to the literal meaning of the text. If the Torah says God spoke to Moses through a burning bush, you cannot say God spoke to Moses through a smoking cigar.
- **Remez** (Hint): the Peshat reading often reveals what appear to be textual errors or inconsistencies. These are taken to be hints of deeper meaning to be explored rather than explained away.
- **Drash** (Investigation): this is the imaginal act of exploring the possible meanings hinted at in Remez.
- **Sod** (Secret): this refers to the mysteries revealed when Drash is allowed to imagine freely.

They say: 'When all four levels are operative you are in PaRDeS, Paradise.'

In their scriptural exegesis, rabbis often use the similarity between Hebrew words to open up multiple possible meanings. For example, Rabbi Rami Shapiro points to Leviticus 19.18. The most common reading of this passage is '*Ve'ahavta et, rayecha k'mocha*' ('Love your neighbour as yourself'). However, it can also be vocalized as '*Ve'ahavta et, rahecha k'mocha*' ('Love your evil as yourself'). Both are legitimate readings. Both must be considered to fully understand the text.

Midrash – the process of rabbinic interpretation – recognizes that each person who reads the Torah does so from his/her own perspective; consequently each person has a slightly different understanding of the text, all of which are legitimate. For example, ancient rabbis calculated that given the number of people who witnessed Moses coming down from Mount Sinai and heard the original Torah, there must be at least 345,600,000 different legitimate interpretations of any letter, word or verse of the commandments.

Most rabbis would argue that the more perspectives a textual commentary takes into account, the more complete its understanding. Midrash recognizes that any passage of Scripture has multiple levels of meaning and that superficial readings of Scripture are likely to misunderstand it and lead to error. Scholars should have the ability to entertain seemingly contradictory ideas without choosing between them; through wrestling with paradox, people are able to move towards broader and deeper understandings that are closer to a 'God's eye view'. As Rabbi Rami Shapiro points out, the governing principle in Midrash is '*Elu v'elu divrei Elohim, Chayyim*', which means 'These words and those words (no matter how contradictory) are both the words of the Living God.'[15]

Throughout history the majority of rabbis have resisted taking Scriptures literally; they had developed a range of techniques and even rules for their interpretation well before the first century AD. However, at the time of Jesus there was tension between literalists (such as Rabbi Shamai) and those who saw that Scripture had to be interpreted in the light of its spirit (such as Rabbi Hillel). Jesus seems to have contributed to the debate on numerous occasions, for example when he was challenged about his disciples picking corn or healing on the Sabbath (Mark 2.23; 3.1–6), and seems to have sided with Hillel, despite famously claiming that he had not come to alter one jot or iota of the law (Matt. 5.18).

Rabbi Hillel is credited for writing down the seven rules that came to be the basis for rabbinic readings of Scripture:

1   **Kal vahomer** (light and heavy): what applies in a less important case will certainly apply in a more important case. Such an argument is often, but not always, signalled by a phrase such as 'how much more ...'.

---

15   See bethaverim.files.wordpress.com/2009/05/black-fire-on-white-fire.pdf; see also Jen Howard, 'Christians Need a Deeper Kind of Bible Study', *OnFaith Voices*, 19 May 2015.

2   **G'zerah shavah** (equivalence of expressions): two separate
    texts are related because they use a similar phrase, word or
    root. Where the same words are applied to two separate cases,
    it could follow that the interpretation of one should apply to
    the other.
3   **Binyan ab mikathub echad** (providing a single parallel
    text): a principle is found in several passages – a consideration
    found in one of them applies to all.
4   **Binyab ab mishene kethubim** (building up a 'family' from
    two or more texts): a principle is established by relating two
    texts together – the principle can then be applied to other
    passages.
5   **Kelal uferat** (the general and the particular): general rules are
    connected to particular instances, which then inform how the
    rule should be interpreted.
6   **Kayotze bo mimekom akhar** (analogy made from another
    passage): two passages may seem to conflict until compared
    with a third, which has points of general similarity.
7   **Davar hilmad me'anino** (explanation obtained from
    context): the total context, not just the isolated statement,
    must be considered for an accurate interpretation.[16]

These rules or techniques for interpreting Scripture seem to have
been used by Jesus – who was frequently called 'rabbi' by his
disciples – and even more by Paul and by the author of the Epistle
to the Hebrews.

1   Matt. 6.26, 30 = Luke 12.24, 28; Matt. 7.11 = Luke 11.13;
    Matt. 10.25 and John 15.18–20; Matt. 12.12 and John 7.23 are
    all examples of Jesus using *kal vahomer*. Pauline examples
    include Rom. 5.8–9, 10, 15, 17; 11.12, 24; 1 Cor. 9.11–12;
    12.22; 2 Cor. 3.7–9, 11; Phil. 2.12; Philem. 1.16. Examples
    in the Epistle to the Hebrews include Heb. 2.2–3; 9.13–14;
    10.28–29; 12.9, 25.

16   For a useful introduction, see www.yashanet.com/studies/revstudy/hillel.htm.

2   The author of Heb. 3.6—4.13 compares Ps. 95.7–11 with Gen. 2.2 and highlights the *equivalence* of the words 'works' and 'day'/'today', concluding that there will be 6,000 years of this world followed by a 1,000-year Shabbat.

3   Similarly Heb. 9.11–22 applies 'blood' from Exod. 24.8 to Jer. 31.31–34, providing *a single parallel text* to explain the meaning of a particular passage.

4   In Heb. 1.5–14 the author cites the family of texts Ps. 2.7; 2 Sam. 7.14; Deut. 32.43/Ps. 97.7/Neh. 9.6; Ps. 104.4; Ps. 45.6–7; Ps. 102.25–27; Ps. 110.1 to support his claim that the Messiah is higher than the angels.

5   In the Gospels (Matt. 5.31–32), Jesus particularizes the general rule of divorce being allowed for 'uncleanliness', and suggests that it should mean for sexual immorality only.

6   In Romans, Paul shows that the following scriptural passages *seem* to conflict: 'The just shall live by faith' (Hab. 2.4) and 'There is none righteous, no, not one ...' (Ps. 14.1–3; Ps. 53.1–3; Eccles. 7.20) also '[G-d] will render to each one according to his deeds' (Ps. 62.12; Prov. 24.12) and 'Blessed are those whose lawless deeds are forgiven, and whose sins are covered; Blessed is the man whom YHVH shall not impute sin' (Ps. 32.1–2) by citing the *analogy* of Genesis 15.6 (in Rom. 4.3, 22) to show that under certain circumstances, belief/faith/trust (same word in Hebrew) can act as a substitute for righteousness/being just (same word in Hebrew).

7   In Romans 14.1, 'I know and am convinced by the Lord Jesus that nothing is unclean of itself; but to him who considers anything to be unclean, to him it is unclean', Paul's meaning should be understood in relation to the *context* of his mission to the Gentiles and the difficulty that non-Jews would have had with keeping kosher in Rome.

Scholars associated with the Third Quest for the historical Jesus, including E. P. Sanders, Geza Vermes, Tom (N. T.) Wright and Henry Wansbrough, were particularly interested in the Jewish context within which Jesus and Paul taught. Although most of these scholars come from wholly or mostly Christian backgrounds, they did explore the significance of rabbinic techniques and debates within first-century Judaism for the dating, authorship and meaning of the New Testament.

Judaism, the Hebrew Scriptures and Ethics

Like Christianity, Judaism includes a range of different opinions about how the Scriptures relate to ethics, from legalistic literalism through to Torah-based virtue ethics.

- While many Orthodox Jews will not drive to synagogue on the Sabbath (because starting a car engine lights a fire), most Reform and Liberal Jews have no problem with this.
- While Hasidic Jews do not cut the hair at the sides of their heads and wear clothes made of single fibres, most Jews shave, have regular haircuts and embrace fashion.
- While some traditional congregations follow tradition in reserving the religious adulthood ceremony – the Bar Mitzvah – to boys, many other synagogues now offer a Bat Mitzvah ceremony to girls.

Throughout history different rabbis have advanced different arguments about how Torah or other aspects of Hebrew Scripture and tradition should be interpreted and applied and – most of the time – this diversity has been celebrated and seen as a sign of strength rather than as a sign of weakness or a cause for conflict.

There has always been a spiritual, pietistic tradition within Jewish ethics. The many works of Musar literature suggest that Torah and rabbinic interpretation provides a complete code of ethics without any recourse to philosophy. A good example is the eleventh-century 'The Gates of the Heart'[17] by Bahya ibn Paquda, which quotes liberally from the Scriptures, Mishnah and Talmud to provide a complete Jewish guide to living well. Some works of Musar literature are more mystical, such as the sixteenth-century 'The Palm Tree of Deborah' by Moses ben Jacob Cordovero, which

---

17 See dafyomireview.com/article.php?docid=384.

suggests that ethical insights might be gained through spiritual practices focusing on central ethical principles drawn from the Torah, such as loving kindness.

Yet some rabbis have always used reason to ground their ethical teaching, in some cases partly drawn from the philosophy of Aristotle and his Muslim and Christian commentators.[18] In the twelfth century, Maimonides taught that the ultimate purpose 'of the Law as a whole is to put an end to idolatry'.[19] Most rabbis distinguished between *mishpatim* and *hukkim*, between those commandments that appear rational and those whose justifications are more opaque. Against rabbis such as Saadia Gaon who saw elements of the law that seemed contrary to reason as evidence that the law was divinely revealed, Maimonides argued that every bit of Torah has a rational justification, although it might not be immediately apparent. Seeking the rational justification for the law is the point. The practice of following the law helps us to understand the reason for it and deepen our rational appreciation of the world, human beings' place within it and God.[20]

Following the *Haskalah*, in the nineteenth and twentieth centuries this tradition of philosophical Jewish ethics came to the fore.

Hermann Cohen, who worked at the University of Marburg for more than half a century until his retirement in 1912, was one of the most important developers of neo-Kantian philosophy. He argued that Jewish monotheism was the source of the idea that there are universal ethical laws and that they emerge from and relate to a systematic world view that can be understood through reason without recourse to revelation. Cohen criticized the foundations of Kant's ethics, recognizing the difficulty with the idea that the moral law appeals directly to reason and the difficulty with trying to establish it on the basis of experience. He proposed instead basing a Kantian form of ethics on law, pure jurisprudence, thus

---

18 David Novak, *Natural Law in Judaism*, Cambridge: Cambridge University Press, 2008.

19 *The Guide for the Perplexed*, III, 29, p. 517.

20 *Guide*, III, 31, p. 524 ; *Guide*, III, 27, p. 510.

taking a step towards modern human-rights theory. For Cohen, the Torah tells us a lot about pure law – law based on reason that transcends time and place.

In Cohen's view Kant was right in proposing a religion within the bounds of reason in order to help society advance towards the *summum bonum* – but he was wrong in dismissing the importance of Judaism in accomplishing this. Perhaps Cohen's most important book, *Religion of Reason Out of the Sources of Judaism* (1919), explained the debt European civilization owed to its Jewish roots and the possibility of using those roots as the basis of a more rational, ethical religion, which would avoid the supernaturalism inherent in Christianity and support progress towards a fairer society.

Influenced by existentialism, Martin Buber developed a powerful and influential, philosophical but definitely Jewish, form of ethics. For Buber, how we relate to the world is central to how we choose to act. Most of human existence is dominated by individuals relating to other people as well as other things on a superficial level – as objects or things without appreciating their deeper existence or empathizing in any way. 'I–it' relationships foster selfishness, isolation, materialism and all forms of unethical and brutal behaviour. Human beings are, however, capable of relating beyond themselves on a deeper level, which he described as 'I–thou'. This is an ongoing experience that has no boundaries and no content but changes how we feel about everything, including ourselves. In some sense it is a religious experience but it is not the one-off experience described by, say, William James, rather it is a shift in a person's whole manner of existence and a recognition that God is not other but the very *ground of our being*.[21] This recalls Moses' experience before the burning bush and Elijah's experience of the still small voice.

Building Jewish ethics on central principles drawn from Torah, rather than on following the letter of the law, has long been part of the Jewish tradition. In the first century Rabbi Hillel taught

---

21   Paul Tillich's phrase. Phil Huston, *Martin Buber's Journey to Presence*, New York: Fordham University Press, 2007, p. 96.

that the basis of all right is 'What is hateful to you, do not do unto others.'[22]

In the second century Rabbi Akiva taught:

> Whatever you hate to have done unto you, do not do to your neighbour; wherefore do not hurt him; do not speak ill of him; do not reveal his secrets to others; let his honour and his property be as dear to thee as thine own.[23]

He also explained that the most important commandment is 'thou shalt love thy neighbour as thyself' (Lev. 19.18).

Rabbi Simeon ben Gamaliel taught that the central principles of Jewish ethics are *justice*, *peace* and *truth*.[24] He quoted Torah to suggest that the central purpose of the law is to promote these principles, and it follows that Jewish decision-making should always have the aim of being just, truthful and bringing peace.

Today scholars such as Yoram Hazony – Provost of the Shalem Centre in Jerusalem – see the Hebrew Scriptures advancing a definite philosophical argument about how people should live and behave, but in an idiosyncratic form. Hazony notes that in Ancient Greece, wisdom was often characterized in terms of being a blessing from the Gods.

- Father Parmenides[25] refers to visions, miraculous experiences and revelations[26] from a Goddess.[27]
- Empedocles described his philosophical insights as being sent to him by Calliopeia as an answer to his prayers.[28]

---

22 Talmud, tractate Shabbat 31a; Midrash Avot de Rabbi Natan.

23 Midrash Avot de Rabbi Natan.

24 Avot 1.18.

25 Plato, Sophist 241d.

26 A. H. Coxon, *The Fragments of Parmenides*, Assen: Van Gorcum, 1986.

27 See Sarah Broadie, 'Rational Theology', in *Cambridge Companion to Early Greek Philosophy*, ed. A. A. Long, Cambridge: Cambridge University Press, 1999, pp. 205–24.

28 B. Inwood, *The Poem of Empedocles*, Toronto: University of Toronto Press, 2001.

- Socrates is described by Plato as receiving dreams, revelations and commands from a divine voice, having a prophetic power and receiving spiritual guidance from the gods.[29]

When Greek philosophers refer to dreams, visions, revelations, prayers, miracles, voices and so on, scholars have been content to keep reading their work as philosophy, a product of reason, an argument fit for rational analysis, whereas as soon as prophets in the Jewish tradition use the same ancient conventions their work is consigned to the philosophical scrapheap, relevant only for those willing to suspend mental acuity and accept the value of their work unquestioningly on faith grounds![30] Is it not strange, Hazony asks, that the Bible is usually characterized as revelation *opposed to* reason, when it shares so many characteristics with works *of* reason from Ancient Greece?

What would happen if we tried to look at biblical texts again, free of prejudice? What might the philosophy of the Bible look like?

Hazony suggests that the Hebrew Scriptures can be treated as a philosophical work that advances an argument. Just as philosophers have to understand the stylistic conventions of Ancient Greek, Chinese or Indian philosophy in order to understand the arguments being advanced, philosophers have to understand the stylistic approach of the authors and compilers of the Hebrew Scriptures in order to understand the philosophy they contain. In particular, the potential role of narrative in advancing a philosophical argument should be considered. Long passages of history might *seem* to serve no function at all in terms of providing wisdom, except perhaps to

---

29 References in Plato's *Apology*, *Theatetus*, *Philebus*, *Symposium*, *Republic*, *Laws*, *Timaeus* and *Phaedrus*. See also Mark McPherran, *The Religion of Socrates*, Philadelphia, PA: Pennsylvania State University Press, 1999.

30 Biblical translators continue to render the Hebrew word *lev* as heart when it is quite obvious to the attentive reader that it refers to the faculty of thought and reasoning. That translators carry on using the word 'heart' without qualification perpetuates the idea that the Scriptures are all about emotions and supra-rational revelations rather than reason. See Hazony, *Philosophy of Hebrew Scripture*, p. 194.

provide context and a sense of authority for the laws and works of prophecy, yet that perception might cause readers to miss a wealth of subtle ethical teaching.

Remember, it is not *what* the narrative history says that is significant so much as *how* it is said. The structure of the History of Israel, a single unbroken narrative of some 150,000 words in Hebrew, is carefully crafted and positioned to form the basis for the teachings of the Prophets and for the Writings.[31] It includes the Torah *and* the books of history Joshua, Judges, Samuel and Kings, which Hazony sees as a unified whole – maybe not written, edited or even compiled by the same hand, but brought together by an overarching intention.

THE HISTORY OF ISRAEL		
Genesis– Numbers	Deuteronomy	Joshua– Kings

ORATIONS OF THE PROPHETS		
Isaiah	Jeremiah	Ezekiel
Minor Prophets		

WRITINGS					
Psalms		Proverbs			Job
Daniel	Ruth	Esther	Song of Songs	Lamentations	Ecclesiastes
Minor Histories					

---

31 Diagram based on Hazony, *Philosophy of Hebrew Scripture*, p. 35.

Hazony gives multiple examples of how the Torah seems intimately connected to the historical works, with literary motifs playing across the whole, including:

- The exile of Adam and Eve from Eden in Genesis is mirrored in the exile of the chosen people from their promised land in Kings.
- The Tower of Babylon, whose purpose was to reach the heavens, is destroyed as a punishment for pride in Genesis – the Temple is destroyed by the Babylonians in Kings for much the same reason.
- Abraham sets out from cosmopolitan Babylonia in Genesis – his descendants are sent back in Kings.
- Moses went to face pharaoh with a shepherd's staff – David went to face Goliath with a shepherd's staff.
- The Israelites stole Egyptian gold when they fled into the desert – it was that gold that attracted the jealousy and ambition of the Babylonians.
- Aaron made a golden calf to appease the Israelites in the desert – Jeroboam, King of Israel, makes two golden calves to appease his people in the face of invasion.
- Moses sought God on mount Horeb and God went by, showing his back – Elijah sought God on mount Horeb and God went by leaving only a small voice.
- There are recurrent references to violence between settled farmers and nomadic shepherds – starting with Cain and Abel and returning again in the story of Abraham, again in the story of Moses, again in the story of David.

He concludes that:

the biblical History of Israel is a work with a strong internal coherence and, to the extent that we are concerned to understand the ideas of this History, we should refrain from studying certain parts of it in isolation from the rest of the text, unless we have a good reason for doing so.[32]

---

32 Hazony, *Philosophy of Hebrew Scripture*, pp. 44–5.

Perhaps part of the reason why modern readers find it difficult to understand the meaning of the narrative sections of the Hebrew Scriptures is that we labour under a different conception of history from that which was common in the ancient world. As Michael Mendelson has observed, Augustine was significant in changing the way people understood history in the West:

> In the Greco-Roman world in general and in Neoplatonism in particular, the importance of history is largely in the cyclical patterns that forge the past, present, and future into a continuous whole, emphasizing what is repeated and common over what is idiosyncratic and unique. In Augustine, we find a conception of human history that in effect reverses this schema by providing a linear account which presents history as the dramatic unfolding of a morally decisive set of non-repeatable events.[33]

For Hazony, quite apart from the law and explicit moral teaching of the prophets, the very History of Israel explores the human condition and the complexities of the moral choices we all face, setting out a sophisticated ethical argument. Importantly, reading Scripture invites quite ordinary people to reflect on, discuss and appraise characters and their actions, to compare one with another and consider the different choices that could have been made. In the process they develop in moral *wisdom* – they come to know what is right and what is wrong and become able to apply that knowledge and live well.

In essence the authors of Scripture did what modern virtue ethicists do – they explored character, virtue and vice with reference to heroes and villains real and imagined, past and present. As Kierkegaard and later Ricoeur came to understand, story has a greater potential for communicating truth in all its complexity than more direct forms of communication. We will return to Hazony's argument in the Conclusion of *Bible Matters*.

---

33 Michael Mendelson, 'Saint Augustine', *The Stanford Encyclopedia of Philosophy* (Winter 2012 Edition), ed. Edward N. Zalta; http://plato.stanford.edu/archives/win2012/entries/augustine.

A Note on Anti-Semitism and Biblical Studies

As Edward Greenstein observes, 'so many categories in the study of Biblical literature, and its religion in particular, derive from patently Christian doctrines.'[34] The fact that mainstream academic biblical studies has for so long excluded Jewish scholars suggests that it is content to describe what is true within a Christian faith-community, rather than what is true in a wider or deeper sense. Clearly this has not been the aim of many biblical scholars – but it is a perception with the potential to do much damage to the credibility and future sustainability of the discipline.

If biblical studies is not content to serve faith-communities by generating such truths as affirm pre-existing beliefs, at the very least, as Stefan Reif suggests, it must start to 'distinguish between those who are aware of the bias in at least part of their Old Testament work and those who make a virtue out of it'.[35] As J. D. Levenson suggests, it must 'differentiate scholars who strive after not fully realizable objectivity from those who openly acknowledge their transcendent commitments and approach their work in the vivid hope of deepening and advancing them'.[36] Biblical studies must start to encourage a more inclusive approach that requires students to engage with the Hebrew Scriptures as independent to, not just part of, 'The Old Testament', and to learn about Jewish approaches to interpreting biblical texts as well as Christian approaches, if it is to remain credible.

To use an analogy, how could Japanese-speaking scholars of English literature defend refusing to read, research or engage with English-speaking scholars of English literature, only deigning to use them to teach EFL at summer schools? Would Japanese papers, books and dissertations on Shakespeare be credible, let alone

---

34 Edward Greenstein, *Essays on Biblical Method and Translation*, Atlanta, GA: Scholars Press, 1989, pp. 24–6.

35 Stefan Reif, 'The Jewish Contribution to Biblical Interpretation', in *The Cambridge Companion to Biblical Interpretation*, ed. John Barton, Cambridge: Cambridge University Press, 1998, p. 146.

36 J. D. Levenson, *The Hebrew Bible, the Old Testament and Historical Criticism*, Louisville, KY: John Knox Press, 1993, pp. 37–8.

ground-breaking, if they were produced by scholars with only a rudimentary grasp of the English language and only engaged with East Asian scholarship? What would we think of conferences and seminars in Osaka inviting no English scholars to present, while describing their topic in terms of advancing towards the truth about how, when and where the plays were written, by whom and why?

What Might Christian Scholars be Missing by Not Engaging with the Jewish Perspective?

Apart from the obvious interpretative points that any reader will miss if they have no Hebrew and don't recognize rabbinic techniques in action, basic confusion over the purposes of the New Testament and Hebrew Scriptures is likely to distort how the Bible is read, studied and understood.

The New *Testament* is appropriately named. Like a collection of documents in a court case, it seems concerned to bear witness that certain historical events happened, including the direct revelation of knowledge that could not have been obtained otherwise.[37] Paul wrote that 'If only for this life we have hope in Christ, we are of all people most to be pitied' (1 Cor. 15.19). His intention, and that of the other New Testament authors and later compilers, editors, translators and scholars of the Bible, has been to bear witness to the truth of Jesus' incarnation, death and resurrection – events that confirmed the divine authenticity of Jesus' teaching.

- The New Testament is called a *testament*, a legal document witnessing to facts as in 'The last will and testament of ...', 'the witnesses' testimony suggests ...'. Testament derives from the Latin *testari*, 'to serve as a witness'.
- The Gospels (Greek *evangelion*) contain Good *News*, almost journalistic accounts of the events of Jesus' life, apparently drawing on eye-witnesses and well-known collection(s) of Jesus' sayings.

---

37 E.g. 1 Cor. 2.6–10; 4.1; Rom. 16.25–27; Col. 1.25–27; 2.2–3; Eph. 1.8–10; 3.2–9; Matt. 13.11; Mark 4.11; Luke 8.10.

- The Gospels are keen to list the witnesses to each event or saying, to show when and why a witness might be unreliable.
- John the Baptist is said to *bear witness* to the truth.
- Paul describes himself as *witnessing* for Jesus and calls down doom on anybody who misrepresents the facts, any *lying or false witness*.
- It is as if the New Testament is designed to convert its readers by persuading them of the truth of Jesus' existence and message. Readers are invited to sit on the jury as the witnesses give their accounts and a range of other evidence is submitted before the importance of making – the right? – decision is emphasized in colourful terms in *Revelation*!

The evangelists, Paul and the church leaders, who sifted through early texts and picked the most credible witnesses to the events and teachings on grounds of date, provenance and coherence, all acted to make a case for Christianity, building evidence as in a court of law.

It could seem that the so-called Old *Testament* is inappropriately named, unless one has a very limited purpose in including it in the Bible, namely to provide the source for the messianic prophecies the evangelists claimed Jesus fulfilled. This ignores Jesus own teaching:

Do not think that I have come to abolish the Law or the Prophets; I have not come to abolish them but to fulfil them. For truly I tell you, until heaven and earth disappear, not the smallest letter, not the least stroke of a pen, will by any means disappear from the Law until everything is accomplished. Therefore anyone who sets aside one of the least of these commands and teaches others accordingly will be called least in the kingdom of heaven, but whoever practises and teaches these commands will be called great in the kingdom of heaven. For I tell you that unless your righteousness surpasses that of the Pharisees and the teachers of the law, you will certainly not enter the kingdom of heaven. (Matt. 5.17–20)

Whereas the authors of the New Testament are at pains to say who they are and what they saw, the authors of the Hebrew Scriptures remain in the background and make no personal claims to witnessing anything. Far from trying to convince or convert, they more were concerned to provide an explanation of *how to understand history* and how to live in the light of it for readers whose own history it was, than to provide an accurate record of what had happened and when for outside scrutiny or posterity.

The two parts of the Bible were never intended to fulfil the same purpose; the New Testament is a testament, the Hebrew Scriptures were not. Unless, that is, one accepts Paul Ricoeur's interpretation of Matthew 5.17–20, his contention that:

> [o]riginally ... there was one Scripture [i.e. the Old Testament] and one event [i.e. Jesus' coming] ... [T]here is a hermeneutic problem because this novelty [i.e. Jesus' coming] is not purely and simply substituted for the ancient letter; rather, it remains ambiguously related to it. The novelty abolishes Scripture and fulfils it. It changes the letter into spirit like water into wine. Hence the Christian fact itself is understood by effecting a mutation of meaning inside the ancient Scripture. The first Christian hermeneutic is this mutation itself.[38]

Exploring the Hebrew Scriptures through the lens of Christian faith as the 'Old Testament' makes little sense. Clearly other interpretations of Matthew 5.17–20 are possible and plausible; even if one does accept Ricoeur's interpretation, surely *only* exploring the Hebrew Scriptures in this way will lead to a narrow and impoverished understanding of Jesus' teaching? Also, either way, reading the History of Israel, the writings of the prophets, the Psalms or other writings of Hebrew Scripture as if they were intended to testify to historical events and describe things as they happened misses the point and ends up unfairly presenting

---

38 In *Essays on Biblical Interpretation*, ed. Lewis S. Mudge, Mudge, Minneapolis, MN: Fortress Press, 1980, p. 50.

the Hebrew Scriptures as primitive, unreliable documents.[39] To use an analogy: would it be reasonable to approach and assess Shakespeare's history plays only as witnesses to the events of the reigns of England's kings? Would it be reasonable to dismiss or denigrate them because they contain a few historical inaccuracies or omissions or present a confusing chronology? Are Froissart's Chronicles necessarily more valuable than Shakespeare's *Richard II* – or are the two works actually fulfilling very different purposes although both reference some of the same events and characters?

---

39 For a detailed presentation of this argument, see Hazony, *Philosophy of Hebrew Scripture*, ch. 2.

Conclusion
What Does it all Mean – And Why
Does it *Really* Matter?

There is little doubt that the Bible story refers to historical events, but it is unclear, even unlikely, that the story was written even close to the time, and just impossible to establish whether events were the result of divine action or not using historical methods. Because of this, the extent to which the Bible should be understood or investigated in historical terms is questionable and an emphasis on this approach is not helpful. Following the postmodern turn, scholars increasingly hold the view that the truth of the Bible does not depend on the extent to which details in it are true but on the extent to which the story as a whole speaks to readers today, makes a difference in their lives or is strategically useful. Nevertheless, to return to the question we posed in Chapter 4, few believers are really satisfied with the answer: 'Well, it is true for us.'

- Why bother to get up early to worship, refrain from immorality, forgive others and give what we have to the poor for the sake of a culturally important fairy story?
- How can anybody stake their lives on the saving power of a text whose truth depends on what is popular or useful?
- Wasn't Mao's *Little Red Book* extremely popular and useful to the authorities during the Cultural Revolution in China? Was that sufficient grounds to justify people accepting its teaching unquestioningly and doing what it said?

Consequently it seems that neither a purely historical nor a purely sociological approach to the truth of the Bible is sufficient to answer the obvious question we posed in Chapter 4: 'So is the Bible story true?'

To us it seems that truth, ultimate reality, is what the Bible is about. Truth is not just historical, about what happened in the past, and it is not just sociological, about what people think today, rather it is absolute and, though ultimately largely unknowable, gives meaning to religion, to Scripture and to a life lived in faith. At the climax of the story of the Exodus, God appears to Moses in a burning bush.

> But Moses said to God, 'Who am I that I should go to pharaoh and bring the Israelites out of Egypt?' And God said, 'I will be with you. And this will be the sign to you that it is I who have sent you: When you have brought the people out of Egypt, you will worship God on this mountain.' Moses said to God, 'Suppose I go to the Israelites and say to them, "The God of your fathers has sent me to you," and they ask me, "What is his name?" Then what shall I tell them?' God said to Moses, 'I AM WHO I AM. This is what you are to say to the Israelites: "I AM has sent me to you."' (Exod. 3.11–14)

God in the Bible is 'the ancient of days' – unchanging, eternal. Like time or existence itself, God is the very 'ground of our being' and what makes reality possible. At the climax of the gospel story, Jesus is on trial for his life.

> Pilate then went back inside the palace, summoned Jesus and asked him, 'Are you the king of the Jews?' 'Is that your own idea,' Jesus asked, 'or did others talk to you about me?' 'Am I a Jew?' Pilate replied. 'Your own people and chief priests handed you over to me. What is it you have done?' Jesus said, 'My kingdom is not of this world. If it were, my servants would fight to prevent my arrest by the Jewish leaders. But now my kingdom is from another place.' 'You are a king, then!' said Pilate. Jesus answered, 'You say that I am a king. In fact, the reason I was born and came into the world is to testify to the truth. Everyone on the side of truth listens to me.' 'What is truth?' retorted Pilate. (John 18.33–38)

Jesus testified to the truth, which is not of any particular place or time but endures and speaks to all times and all places. The central Christian claim is that Jesus embodies truth in a way that Pilate cannot comprehend. Pilate's question is *both* a throwaway comment, a brush-off, *and* an eternal testament to the corruption and futility of politics and a limited view of philosophy. Pilate is *both* right – because in practice might is usually right and what is popular is usually what is accepted as truth – *and* profoundly wrong, both in terms of the verdict of history and in terms of the verdict of reason. The question 'What is truth?' is true in at least two different senses – one literal, one ironic. The truth that the Bible testifies to is not external and independent but neither is it the creation of a community, ever-changing between times, places and individuals. It is *both* eternal *and* rooted in this reality we experience.

We cannot and do not agree with Richard Dawkins that the Bible is a 'cobbled-together anthology'.[1] We can't even accept that it is a mere a collection of ancient works, albeit touched by literary genius. The Bible has a strong unified identity for all the plurality of its contents; the whole is much more than the sum of the parts. It is more than a key to understanding the identity of a people or some indication of why they think and behave as they do. The Bible has been preserved and venerated by a whole people over millennia because they sincerely believe it is truthful and contains enduring wisdom.

Although this is not a popular position today – and we recognize that postmodernists will be sharpening stakes at this point, seeing the spirit of the Enlightenment rising from the grave – we both believe that the Bible is in some sense a work of philosophy, a record of the enduring wisdom discovered by some of the greatest thinkers across more than a thousand years in a tradition that rivals that of ancient Greece for its potential significance in uncovering truth.

To be sure, it is not immediately clear or easy to explain *what* truth the Bible points towards.

---

1   Richard Dawkins, *The God Delusion*, London: Black Swan, 2007, p. 268.

- Of the characters in the Bible, none seems a perfect, realistic model for human behaviour. Abraham's behaviour towards Sarah in Egypt was more than a little suspect, without considering his treatment of Hagar, Ishmael – or Isaac. Moses was a murderer, Jacob a thief, Joseph a braggart, David a philanderer, Peter a coward and Paul held the coats while an innocent man was stoned to death! What are people to take from all this about how to live well, in relation to the truth?
- When we turn to the existence and nature of God, a fundamental part of the wisdom that any reader would assume the Bible contains, the evidence provided for God's existence is anecdotal and it is unclear what God's name, let alone nature, is. In the Torah God is referred to as ELOHIM (literally 'the Gods' in plural) and given the personal name YHVH – but other names are used of God as well, such as EL SHADDAI. Leaving aside the confusion over God's name, God's nature is unclear as well.

  o In Genesis 3.8 Adam and Eve hide from God in the Garden and have to tell God where they are and what they have done. In Genesis 4.9 God asks Abel where his brother Cain is. Yet in Jeremiah 16.17 God reveals that 'My eyes are on all their ways; they are not hidden from me, nor is their sin concealed from my eyes.' Can God be both omniscient and not know about Cain's murder, or Adam's betrayal?

  o There is an obvious tension between God as a personal God of love (e.g. 2 Cor. 13.11) or even as morally good, and the source of law and texts such as Exodus 4.11 ('Who makes them deaf or mute? Who gives them sight or makes them blind? Is it not I, the LORD?') and Deuteronomy 20.16–17 ('in the cities of the nations the LORD your God is giving you as an inheritance, do not leave alive anything that breathes. Completely destroy them – the Hittites, Amorites, Canaanites, Perizzites, Hivites and Jebusites – as the LORD your God has commanded you').

o   In the New Testament, when Jesus claims 'I and the Father are one' (John 10.30), how can the creator, who said 'Let there be light' in Genesis 1.3, also die on the cross? How can the God who declares 'the end from the beginning' in Isaiah 46.10 pray '*Abba*, Father ... everything is possible for you. Take this cup from me. Yet not what I will, but what you will' in Mark 14.36? Can God be omnipotent and incarnate in Mary's son, all powerful and a corpse? Of course, we recognize that this challenges a central part of Christian doctrine, but it is difficult to deny the problem with a literal reading of Scripture that does not take account of different layers of meaning or theological exegesis.

- The writings of the prophets might seem like a good place to look for wisdom, yet these books are crammed with political and social commentary on long-dead rulers, long-past situations; their idiosyncratic style and heavy use of symbolism and metaphor makes it difficult for anybody to be sure that their understanding of what is being said could match what the author intended.
- The Ten Commandments and Jesus' teaching about love and forgiveness – 'love your neighbour as yourself' and 'turn the other cheek' (both of which are foreshadowed in the Hebrew Scriptures) – are both important and close to the Bible's core truth, but neither is unique to the Bible. A survey of other historical, religious and philosophical texts – Hammurabi's Code, Confucius' Analects, the Ramayana – would suggest many places human beings could have found those insights if not in the Bible.

To repeat, it is not immediately clear *what* special wisdom the Bible contains. What really are readers supposed to understand about God's existence and nature? How are people supposed to apply these insights and use them to shape how they live?

But, of course, this misses the point.

Wisdom in the Bible is not offered up superficially, it is

revealed through careful reading and reflection because its truth is not simple, accessible, easy to know or describe. The Bible does not communicate directly in the manner of a low-level textbook because it is dealing with truth on a rather larger scale.

The postmodernists are right about the inescapability of the human and even individual perspective, the limits of language in conveying meaning, but it does not follow that objective truth does not exist. We think that the biblical authors and compositors were well aware of the difficulty of knowing and describing the truth in any human language, and sought to communicate their experience of living in the face of it *indirectly*, actually avoiding straightforward statements about God's existence, nature, the moral law, the possibility or nature of the afterlife. They did so because direct communication would lead to more widespread misunderstanding.

In this way the complexity of the Bible and its obscurity in itself advances an argument about the nature of truth. The Bible neither signifies nor directly corresponds with an external reality, nor does it simply record the internally coherent beliefs of a long-dead people. Rather the *process* of reading the Bible in a spirit of humility points people towards a truth that is beyond words, the synthesis of the world we perceive and the reality we conceive of. Verily – and to borrow a means of expression from the prophetic genius and poet R. S. Thomas – the poem in the rock and the poem in the mind are not one, but in writing the biblical authors point towards how they are really so.

The Bible is not truth in itself and does not contain truth in itself. It points towards truth and facilitates the individual search for it. The fact that the Bible does not try to communicate truth in simple, direct terms makes the point about the nature of truth powerfully, if people apply their brains to the process of reading the Bible and don't switch off their critical faculties as many within the Christian tradition have been trained to, in part for reasons of church politics.

For us, the search for truth can never be passive, whether in religion or otherwise. It is not a case of reading and studying the

Bible and waiting for God's grace to impart a special revelation. We agree with Maimonides that reason has the potential to take people a long way towards truth, and maintain that resigning reason, even in the sense of accepting a post-critical naïvety, can be highly dangerous and leave a door open to fundamentalism, whether Christian, Jewish or of another sort. However, reason does not have the final word and must be coupled with insight, judgement and discernment.

As we see it, a respectful and humble dialogue in which people search for truth for its own sake – not in order to impress, play academic games or otherwise use it for their own advantage – is the most important human enterprise there is.

Without truth religion is folk-custom and without truth Scripture is nothing more than a collection of myths and legends. People who are 'on the side of truth' can listen to and begin to understand the Bible story, while those who ask 'What is truth?' can only ever hear it; they will never really understand. In Mark's Gospel, Jesus tells a parable:

> 'Listen! A farmer went out to sow his seed. As he was scattering the seed, some fell along the path, and the birds came and ate it up. Some fell on rocky places, where it did not have much soil. It sprang up quickly, because the soil was shallow. But when the sun came up, the plants were scorched, and they withered because they had no root. Other seed fell among thorns, which grew up and choked the plants, so that they did not bear grain. Still other seed fell on good soil. It came up, grew and produced a crop, some multiplying thirty, some sixty, some a hundred times.'
>
> Then Jesus said, 'Whoever has ears to hear, let them hear.'
>
> When he was alone, the Twelve and the others around him asked him about the parables. He told them, 'The secret of the kingdom of God has been given to you. But to those on the outside everything is said in parables so that,
>
> "they may be ever seeing but never perceiving,

and ever hearing but never understanding;
otherwise they might turn and be forgiven!'"
(Mark 4.3–12)

Believing in God is about living in truth, recognizing the absolute value of living according to God's law and not confusing being religious with having faith in God. It means rejecting all that is transient – including money, power, sex, reputation and appearance – in favour of what is ultimate, what endures.

In John's Gospel, Jesus says:

If you love me, keep my commands and I will ask the Father, and he will give you another advocate to help you and be with you forever – the Spirit of truth. The world cannot accept him, because it neither sees him nor knows him. But you know him, for he lives with you and will be in you. (John 14.15–17)

The trappings of religion, whether in the form of doctrine and theology, authorities, liturgies, festivals or rituals – or Scriptures – are only useful insofar as they help people to appreciate the truth. When people confuse them for the truth – or start to think that truth is relative and they are as valid as any other expression of beliefs – then humanity is in trouble. In the book of Amos, God says:

'I hate, I despise your religious festivals;
your assemblies are a stench to me.
Even though you bring me burnt offerings and grain offerings,
I will not accept them.
Though you bring choice fellowship offerings,
I will have no regard for them.
Away with the noise of your songs!
I will not listen to the music of your harps.
But let justice roll on like a river,
righteousness like a never-failing stream!
Did you bring me sacrifices and offerings
forty years in the wilderness, people of Israel?

You have lifted up the shrine of your king,
the pedestal of your idols,
the star of your god –
which you made for yourselves.
Therefore I will send you into exile beyond Damascus,'
says the LORD, whose name is God Almighty. (Amos 5.21–27)

How sad that religion is often more about binding people together – tying them up, constraining them, shutting down difference and excluding outsiders – than about working together towards truth.

In the Hebrew Scriptures, Jacob wrestled with God (Gen. 32.22–32) – by some accounts the very name *Israel*, which went on to name the people, means 'he who wrestles with God'. The tradition of wrestling with and not meekly submitting to truth goes back a long way. Even the righteous Job questioned God – and God gave him an answer and restored him, despite Elihu's attempts to belittle Job and deny his right to do anything but accept a situation that made no sense (Job 32–34).

At its best, religion can celebrate diversity and difference while affirming that it exists in the face of truth and relates to an ultimate standard that we must all approach with humility. At its worst, religion can give succour to the arrogant, encourage the use of power to establish a unity that denies truth and take people much further from God than they were ever likely to be without it.

Reason and Revelation

Sadly, Christian – and Muslim – scholars' obsession with novel Neoplatonic and then Aristotelian philosophies caused them to overlook the wisdom evident in the Hebrew Scriptures and New Testament. Perhaps this was partly down to anti-Semitism as well. Intoxicated with classical philosophy, philosophers developed unbounded confidence in reason, the human ability to describe and understand the world without recourse to supernatural revelation.

Sadly the early politicization of Christianity sometimes led to wilfully or naturally ignorant men assuming positions of religious authority. They felt threatened by philosophers and immediately questioned whether their activities were compatible with piety and orthodoxy.[2]

Conceivably, some of those in positions of religious authority resented the ideas that people might be able to access truth without deferring to them, that the secret of salvation could not be concealed from non-believers, that there was no absolute need to submit to religion in order to enter heaven. Søren Kierkegaard said 'As you have lived, so have you believed', and perhaps one's life gives a better indication of one's beliefs than mere words, official membership or rank. Jesus himself said something similar in Matthew 25, the parable of the Sheep and the Goats.

Perhaps the common Christian understanding of the relationship between reason and revelation and the resulting tendency to identify the Bible (particularly the Hebrew Scriptures) with supra-rational revelation has caused Christians (and those educated in a framework influenced by a Christian paradigm) to misunderstand and misuse it and so to miss out on the opportunity to explore truth through the Bible in a different way.

In his important book *The Philosophy of Hebrew Scripture*, the Jewish scholar Yoram Hazony argues[3] that the dichotomy and particularly the opposition between revelation and reason has done much to distort peoples' understanding of the Scriptures and has obscured their ability to function in the way that they were intended to – by provoking deep thought and rational, philosophical discussion, pointing towards truth beyond any literal interpretation.

For Hazony, the dichotomy between reason and revelation was in the first place a creation of Christianity, stemming from the new religion's desire to mark itself out from the philosophical cults of the ancient world and necessary for humble Christian leaders to maintain authority. He suggests that the tradition of

---

2 Christianity was not alone in this; Islam followed a similar pattern in the centuries after the death of the prophet.

3 Yoram Hazony, *The Philosophy of Hebrew Scripture*, Cambridge: Cambridge University Press, 2012, pp. 1–27.

opposing reason and revelation was later exploited by Renaissance humanist and Enlightenment scholars seeking to distinguish their approach from that of the Church, and that the claimed opposition of revelation and reason is relatively unknown outside the sphere of Christian influence.[4]

While it is beyond the scope of an introductory book such as *Bible Matters*, it is worth briefly considering what deep philosophical truth the Bible might offer up through rational analysis, if the Hebrew Scriptures were explored in much the same manner as the works of later Greek philosophers have long been.

Perhaps the most important truth suggested by Hazony is *an alternative way of looking at truth itself*. Whereas Enlightenment thinkers (drawing on the classical philosophy of Plato and Aristotle) understood truth as monolithic and in terms of correspondence with an external reality, and postmodern thinkers (reacting against Enlightenment thinking) understand truth in terms of plurality and in terms of coherence with human systems of thought, the Bible understands truth in terms of endurance, reliability, steadfastness; *truth is what remains the case through the ages and withstands the test of time*.

Hazony argues that the writers of the Hebrew Scriptures at least never adopted the dualist idea of reality that has so dominated philosophical thinking since Roman times. In the Hebrew tradition, reality is what people experience, encompassing sense experiences *and* concepts. True experiences, true concepts, are those that endure and illuminate. As Kant remarked:

> Thoughts without content are empty, intuitions without concepts are blind. The understanding can intuit nothing, the senses can think nothing. Only through their union can knowledge arise.[5]

---

4 Where a distinction is made by, for example, Sa'adia Gaon, the great Jewish scholar, writing in Baghdad in the tenth century (*The Book of Beliefs and Opinions*, New Haven, CT: Yale University Press, 1948), Hazony suggests that it is made in the sense that although distinct ways of knowing, reason and revelation provide the same knowledge.

5 *Critique of Pure Reason* A51 / B75.

In the Hebrew Scriptures, Jeremiah 23 recounts God's words:

> [A]mong the prophets of Jerusalem I have seen something
> horrible: They commit adultery and live a lie ... Do not listen
> to what the prophets are prophesying to you; they fill you
> with false hopes. They speak visions from their own minds,
> not from the mouth of the LORD. (Jer. 23.14, 16)

Hebrew is a language that employs earthy metaphors a lot! God
breathes life into Adam, walks in the Garden of Eden at the cool
of the day, has a judgement seat and yet is still EL OLAM, the
everlasting or eternal God, the Ancient of Days (Gen. 21.33; Jer.
10.10; Isa. 26.4) who is called peace and completeness (Judg.
6.24). Even the Hebrew root of the word translated as 'minds'
in Jeremiah 23 is *lev*, elsewhere translated as 'heart'. Looking
beyond the metaphorical language[6] and prophetic style, might not
Jeremiah be saying what Kant is saying, that 'visions from their
own minds' or 'thoughts without content' are false?

Human beings cannot rely on 'visions from their own minds'
and cannot rely on experience without any sense of overarching,
enduring vision – else they become like the prisoners in Plato's
cave or like Pontius Pilate, blind to what they refuse to see. Truth
is a complete, enduring vision that fills empty concepts, makes
sense of limited experience and breathes life into what is otherwise
a mechanical existence. Isaiah wrote:

> A voice said 'Cry out!' and I said what I shall cry out: All
> flesh is grass and all its loyalty is as the flower of the field.
> The grass withers and the flower fades because the breath of
> the LORD blows it out. (Isa. 40.6–7)[7]

As understood in the Bible, truth lightens our darkness and lets us
see a way forward. As we see it, the Bible contains hope for *a new*

---

6 To find out more about the philosophy of metaphorical language, read the
Postscript that comes after this chapter.

7 Our inelegant close-to-literal translation from the Hebrew.

Enlightenment based not on post-critical naïvety but on a properly critical engagement with reality. It is time to revisit Kant's project, to bring together the divided roads philosophers have trodden since he failed to recognize the falseness of the faith/reason, reason/revelation and concept/perception dichotomies that have brought humanity down – and to get over the very stupid idea that Athens and Jerusalem have nothing to do with each other![8] Both Greek philosophy and Hebrew philosophy are journeys towards truth. Both have huge wisdom to offer those who choose to listen.

It is possible that this biblical model of truth could avoid both the pitfalls of Enlightenment thinking and the pitfalls of postmodernism – truth is universal and stays the same over time but also speaks to real human experience.[9] Of course, there are possible problems as well – this approach to truth is potentially extremely conservative and likely to hold back social change – but it might just offer a way forward out of what has become a crisis in philosophy, and also the whole of Western culture which depends on it.

---

8 Tertullian, *De praescriptione haereticorum*, ch. 7.

9 Compare with Kant's concept of the Law being manifest in every aspect of experience (synthetic) but appealing directly to reason as well (analytic).

Postscript
Language and Truth in the Bible

For those who want to find out more about the philosophy of reading the Bible, philosophical understandings of language and how it relates to meaning and truth are of huge importance in shaping interpreters' approach to the text and showing if and how readings such as those we included in the Conclusion are plausible:

Religious Language is Univocal

Augustine saw language as a system of signs, pointing towards a true metaphysical meaning,[1] although he appreciated the difficulties of understanding the true meaning of a text. Augustine believed that every biblical word and passage contained four distinct levels of meaning. This influenced medieval theologians to explore levels of meaning in each discrete biblical term. Take for example *Zion*:

1 literal meaning, e.g. city of Jerusalem;
2 allegorical meaning, e.g. God's ideal state/Church of Christ;
3 moral meaning, e.g. the human soul;
4 eschatological meaning, e.g. the kingdom of God/heaven.

On Christian Doctrine[2] – written between AD 397 and 426 – and *Confessions* Book XII and XIII are good places to start an

---

1 It was Augustine's conception of the relationship between language and meaning in the *Confessions* that Wittgenstein criticized in his *Philosophical Investigations*. See Gerard Watson, 'St. Augustine's Theory of Language', *Maynooth Review* 6:2 (1982), pp. 4–20; see also Patrick Bearsley, 'Augustine and Wittgenstein on Language', *Philosophy* 58:224 (1983), pp. 229–36.

2 See faculty.georgetown.edu/jod/augustine/ddc.html.

exploration of Augustine's theory of language and its application to reading the Bible;[3] his work had a huge impact on Christian biblical scholarship through the Middle Ages and well into the modern period.

Later, in the eleventh century, Anselm explored the relationship between language and meaning through his dialogue *De grammatico*, through parts of *De veritate*, *Philosophical Fragments* and the *Monologion*. Like Augustine, Anselm saw words as *signs* pointing towards concepts that could be based on direct experience, reason or the very essence of things. Anselm saw that most peoples' understanding of things is limited to what they directly experience, although rational conception is possible with effort.

He wrote 'Truth is rightness, perceptible by the mind alone',[4] but by this he did not mean that human beings can conceive of the essence of things, what Kant later called the *Ding an Sich*; that can only be the preserve of God. The word of God signifies and so somehow creates the very essence of things.[5]

Anselm followed what he knew of Aristotle's theory of language from the *Categories* and particularly *De interpretatione* (which had been translated and expounded by Boethius in the sixth century and so survived in the Western tradition), and otherwise drew on the work of Augustine.

For Anselm, there is only one truth and the Bible attests to it. When we read the Bible it is important to eliminate misconceptions based on the everyday misuse of language, but beyond that the meaning is apparent to the ordinary reader.[6] Having said that, although most readers can interpret Scripture, it is always possible that interpretations are mistaken – even when they are put forward

---

3 See www.newadvent.org/fathers/110112.htm.

4 Quoted by Aquinas in *De Veritate*, q. 1. A.1 AD. 1.

5 Peter King, 'Anselm's Philosophy of Language', in Brian Davies and Brian Leftow (eds), *The Cambridge Companion to Anselm*, Cambridge: Cambridge University Press, 2004, pp. 84–110; see individual.utoronto.ca/pking/articles/Anselm_on_Language.CC.pdf.

6 See Anselm, *Three Philosophical Dialogues*, trans. and ed. Thomas Williams, Indianapolis, IN: Hackett, 2002.

by figures in authority, have been accepted for a long time or have passed into doctrine.[7]

Anselm reasons that because language refers to God-created things, and because human beings and our rational capacity are created in the image of God, it is reasonable to suppose that the meaning of words and texts is relatively straightforward, even when they describe God or God's actions, which are beyond ordinary experience.

This is at the root of Anselm's so-called ontological argument for God's existence. If God may be said to be *that than which nothing greater can be conceived of* then God must *really exist* because it follows that things that really exist are greater than things that only imaginarily exist. Further, God must *necessarily exist* – exist in such a way that God cannot not exist – because this is greater than the contingent existence that all normal things have.

Anselm applies a definition to God and then unpacks that definition using logical relationships derived from things he has experienced in this, created, world to uncover the way things must be beyond it. His argument depends on the assumption that God created the world and therefore has a sufficient, ordered relationship with God's creation such as to provide content to Anselm's definition and the notion of real, necessary existence.

Later Franciscan writers such as Bonaventure were happy to assume the philosophical basis for their work on the meaning and interpretation of Scripture and so went along with the traditional understanding of Aristotle's philosophy of language, drawn from their study of Augustine, Boethius and Anselm. In the thirteenth century John Duns Scotus developed and defended this approach to language, holding that '[t]he difference between God and creatures, at least with regard to God's possession of the pure perfections, is ultimately one of degree.'[8]

Whereas earthly things are limited by their physical existence, God is infinite and has no limitations. When we say God is good,

---

7 See Marilyn McCord Adams, 'Anselm on Faith and Reason', in *The Cambridge Companion to Anselm*, pp. 45–6.

8 Richard Cross, *Duns Scotus*, Oxford: Oxford University Press, 1999, p. 39.

the concept of goodness is the same as when we say 'Peter is good', but *to a much greater degree*. As Thomas Williams explains,

> [f]or Scotus infinity is not only what's ontologically central about God, it's the key component of our best available concept of God and a guarantor of the success of theological language. That is, our best ontology, far from fighting with our theological semantics, both supports and is supported by our theological semantics.[9]

In other words, if we believe that we can define and understand God at all, then this guarantees that the reason and language with which we define God is a reliable means of defining and understanding God. Denying the *univocity* of language would, for Scotus, deny the possibility of meaningful philosophy and religion. The basic concept of 'being' (Latin *ens*) cannot mean anything other than what it means; for something to exist must mean the same in any situation, and in this at least we can have direct understanding of what God is – being itself.

The Rediscovery of Aristotle

The relationship between language, meaning and truth were ongoing philosophical preoccupations during the height of the medieval renaissance, between the eleventh and thirteenth centuries AD. Islam had expanded across North Africa and into Spain and, despite violent and largely unsuccessful Christian efforts to regain territory (the Crusades), cultural exchange between Islam, Judaism and Christianity led to a flowering of academic study, the development of universities with some small degree of independence from normal religious and civil authorities.

The first major achievement of the universities was the recovery and exploration of Aristotelian philosophy. While a few of Aristotle's works had always been available in Europe, many

---

9 Thomas Williams, 'Duns Scotus' – see http://plato.stanford.edu/entries/duns-scotus/#DivInfDocUni.

had been lost and were only rediscovered when Christian – and Jewish – scholars gained access to translations, commentaries and textbooks made and used in the Muslim world. The work of Muslim philosophers such as Ibn Sina (Avicenna), Al Ghazali (Algazel) and Ibn Rushd (Averroes) explained the significance of Aristotle and raised significant questions about the traditional approach to language – among many other things.

For Aristotle, knowledge starts with sense experience. Concepts are created out of experiences and have no metaphysical reality. For the vast majority of thinkers in the classical and medieval worlds, 'A judgment is said to be true when it conforms to the external reality.'[10] If words are *signs* pointing towards an external reality, and reality is defined in terms of what human beings can experience through the senses, then there is an obvious difficulty in assessing the meaning of any words that point to anything *beyond* possible sense experience!

Following Aristotle, at the very least it seemed that – as Wittgenstein famously said – 'of what we cannot know we must remain silent'. While compelling, this philosophy was – rightly – perceived as an immense threat to traditional religious belief. As it became better known and understood it caused huge arguments within Islam, Christianity and Judaism.

Religious Language is Equivocal

In the second half of the twelfth century, building on the work of his predecessors at Cordoba such as Abraham Ibn Daud, the great Jewish philosopher Maimonides argued that because God exists beyond our possible experience, nothing positive can be said about God.

He reasoned that the meaning of a word like 'good' when applied to God would share no meaning with 'good' applied to a human being – or an apple pie. God is timeless, spaceless, immutable – things in the world are the very opposite. For a human

---

10 *De Veritate* Q.1, A.1 and 3 – www.corpusthomisticum.org/qdv01.html provides the Latin; Google provides a functional translation service!

being to be good implies choice, comparison, action or separate qualities, whereas all these are impossible for God. The words good (God) and good (human being) share as little meaning as bat (cricket) and bat (flying rodent) – they are *equivocal* terms.

A similar *via negativa* was being trodden by Christian theologians such as Gilbert of Poitiers and Alan of Lille. They concluded that because God is wholly simple, totally other, using any positive terms to describe God's nature or attributes would be folly. This was a dangerous position to adopt in a Europe dominated by the Church, not least because it implied that the Bible was meaningless and even dangerously misleading.

For Maimonides, although using language univocally of God is impossible, it is possible to use God-created logic to work out and articulate what God is not. This approach is sometimes known as the apophatic way – literally the way of denial.

The Deeper Meaning of Scripture

For Maimonides, it was still possible for the Scriptures to contain real meaning, but that meaning had to be teased out with proper techniques and should not be taken at face value. In the Introduction to *The Guide for the Perplexed*, Maimonides explains how the key to understanding the Bible is to realize that the prophets spoke in metaphors and similitudes – the language of dream and vision, imagination. He refers to Hosea 12.10: 'I have also spoken by the prophets, and I have multiplied visions, and used similitudes, by the ministry of the prophets' (KJV).

The Hebrew word *adammeh* could be translated either 'I used similitudes' or 'I imagined', and you can hear the poetic connection with the word for the 'man' (*haadam*) God originally fashioned from the 'ground' (*haadamah*) and gave the breath of life.

In *The Guide for the Perplexed*, Maimonides considered the meaning of scriptural references to angels.[11] He pointed out that the word 'angel' (*mal'akh*) otherwise means 'messenger', and is also used to signify 'intellect' or a 'physical force', so it

---

11 *Guide for the Perplexed*, II, 6, [7].

is possible to read Scripture as using a metaphor to describe amazing, natural occurrences, parts of God's wondrous creation, in imaginative language that 'ignorant pietists' can appreciate but that still contains truth for the educated to uncover through reason. Unsurprisingly, few people – Jewish or Christian – were willing to accept Maimonides' suggestion; even Aquinas thought this went too far and said that it was 'alien to the custom of Scripture' to use metaphor in this way.[12]

Interestingly, both Maimonides and Aquinas use Psalm 104.4 to support their arguments.

- Maimonides has verse 4, 'Who makes winds his angels', which is faithful to the Hebrew. In the context of Psalm 104.3 this then reads 'He makes the clouds his chariot and rides on the wings of the wind.' Psalm 104.4 seems likely to mean 'He makes winds his messengers, flames of fire his servants.'[13] In other contexts the Hebrew word *ruchot* could mean 'spirits', or even 'breaths' as well as 'winds'.
- Aquinas uses Jerome's Latin Vulgate translation of Psalm 104.4, *qui facis angelos tuos spiritus*, which means 'Who makes his angels spirits'; this supports his argument that angels are definite spiritual beings and not natural forces under God's control.

This illustrates the significance of translation and philological understanding in interpreting the Bible quite nicely.

Maimonides also sought to grade the prophecy contained within Scripture, preferring prophecy where the meaning is clear to prophecy where the language is confusing.[14] He saw Judges as an example of the lowest grade of prophecy, Proverbs as an example of the second lowest grade. Prophecies that originate in dreams are accounted as lower than those received through visions. Parables

---

12 Summa 1, Ar.50, Q.3.

13 This is from the NIV, which gets the sense of the Hebrew much better than the traditional KJV.

14 *Guide for the Perplexed*, II, 45.

are seen as the lowest form of revelation whereas being addressed directly by God is seen as the highest.

Controversially, Maimonides argued that prophecies that are purely rational, not dependent on any aspect of imagination and described in straightforward language (such as the law of Moses), are the highest form of prophecy of all. He saw that such prophecy is *natural* to some human beings and, contrary to the teachings of Rabbi Yehuda Halevi, it requires no specific divine action to liberate the insights of pure reason. Human beings can cultivate their reason in order to increase the likelihood that they would be able to speak truth, either in terms of new philosophical insight or right interpretation of prophecy. As we saw in Chapter 15, this line of thought inspired Baruch Spinoza and Moses Mendelssohn to develop a very liberal, rationalistic approach to Hebrew Scripture in later centuries.

It is important to understand that in most respects Maimonides was not departing from rabbinic tradition, although he represented one extreme of it. Some rabbis had always tended to see descriptions of God or God's actions in Scripture as metaphorical – containing multiple layers of meaning and requiring a good deal of sophisticated exegesis. The rabbinic approach to reading Scripture included a broad spectrum of opinion, and in most cases rabbis celebrated this diversity, seeing it as a source of strength rather than a sign of weakness.

Religious Language is Analogical

Refusing the *via negativa*, Aquinas took the *via analogiae* instead (from *analogia*, the Greek for 'proportion'). Saying 'Mary is good' and 'God is good' shares some meaning, a proportion of the meaning, but not all the meaning. Aquinas read and agreed with much of Maimonides' work, but in Part 1 of the *Summa Theologica* he explicitly rejected his claim that *nothing* positive could be said about God. He developed the idea that terms applied to God share a proportion of their meaning with the same terms rightly applied to other things:

These names signify the divine substance, and are predicated substantially of God, although they fall short of a full representation of Him ... We cannot know the essence of God in this life, as He really is in Himself; but we know Him accordingly as He is represented in the perfections of creatures; and thus the names imposed by us signify Him in that manner only.[15]

He tried to explain exactly what the proportion and nature of shared meaning would be when a quality is predicated of God and to an earthly thing. For Aquinas, God created the world and therefore the world must tell us something about God; but God is other, different from the world of time and space and potentiality that God caused to be. Language tends to imply a worldly framework. If I say that Peter acts, then we can imagine what that might mean – but how can God act in the same way? God is beyond time and space; God doesn't have a body so what can God's action really mean?

Aquinas used a common medieval example to explain: a good bull has a sleek coat, big muscles and a strong interest in cows; a good God would scarcely have these attributes! Nevertheless a good bull also produces good things – healthy urine and manure, high-quality semen and prize-winning calves – and does what good bulls are supposed to do, conforms to the ideal. Some *attributes* of the meaning and a *proportion* of the meaning of 'good' could be shared between a good bull and a good God; both God and the bull could be said to produce good things and fulfil their natures, not falling short in any respect, although many things could be said of the good bull that could not be inferred of God, however good.

- God being good in that God produces good things is known as **analogy of attribution**.
- God being God in that God perfectly fulfils God's nature is known as **analogy of proportion**.

Altogether this is known as Aquinas' doctrine of analogy.[16] The

---

15   See www.newadvent.org/summa/1013.htm#article2.

16   You should read Aquinas' full statement of his position online at www. newadvent.org/summa/1013.htm#article5.

idea that the meaning of some terms can only be analogical when applied to God had its roots in Aristotle, but was discussed extensively by Arabic philosophers in the heyday of Islamic philosophy – including Al Farabi (870–950), Ibn Sina (980–1037, sometimes called Avicenna) and Al Ghazali (1058–1111) – and by Christian thinkers such as Aquinas' tutor, Alexander of Hales, in the early thirteenth century. Originally the term 'analogical' was used interchangeably with 'ambiguous', stressing the uncertainty over the degree of meaning that could be shared by the same word used in different senses, but Aquinas was clear that by 'analogical' he did not mean 'ambiguous'; he had a clear logical system for defining the precise proportion of meaning concerned.

What then does 'analogy' mean for the meaning of Scripture? For Aquinas, the Bible should not be seen as containing literal (univocal) truth but nor should it be seen as containing no truth (being equivocal). The meaning of the Bible is substantial, if slim and fragile, and has to be teased out by those who have been properly trained to do so. Aquinas disagrees with Maimonides that nothing in the Bible can be understood straightforwardly but also disagrees with literalists who take everything at face value. God is, in two particular senses, good. Angels are real, if spiritual, beings that can be encountered and act in the world to effect miracles that are more than natural occurrences.

In the end, most Jewish thinkers ended up following Aquinas' *via analogiae* rather than Maimonides' *via negativa*. In the fourteenth century both Gersonides (a follower of Maimonides) and Hasdai Crecas (a critic of him) both adopted positions closer to Aquinas. While Maimonides' argument is more logically persuasive, from a faith perspective the consequences of accepting it are enormous and will probably lead to the destruction of religion in the way that we know it.

Religious Terms are Not Signs

Since the dawn of the Enlightenment, philosophers had been dissatisfied with the traditional idea that language is composed of signs that refer to an external, static point of reference.

Thomas Hobbes questioned the traditional idea that any universal form or concept of anything exists, whether in the mind or independent reality, for words to sign towards. As he saw it, words are arbitrary labels or names that people give as shorthand for groups of experiences they see as similar, for whatever reason. Words do not signify any metaphysical *Ding an Sich* or even formal classes of things; they just gather together similar experiences and thus might have slightly different content depending on the different experiences or different rationales different individuals have in using them. John Locke also saw understanding as the product of multiple sense experiences; the mind starts as a *tabula rasa* ('blank slate'), and is filled over time through experience. As he saw it, 'Language itself is ... an instrument for carrying out the mainly prosaic purposes and practices of everyday life. Ordinary people are the chief makers of language.'[17]

Opening up the concept of meaning a hundred years later, Jean-Jacques Rousseau agreed that language had its roots in individuals expressing their unique experience of the world. He went further than Hobbes or Locke and suggested that language had been distorted and stripped of its emotional power through overanalysis and attempts to control it – and through it people, their thoughts, feelings and actions. In the *Essay on the Origin of Languages*, Rousseau used the analogy of music, which started off using the natural pitch in bones, reeds and gut as an extension of the human ability to communicate experience but, during the Enlightenment, was analysed and then manipulated, so that it reflected mathematically 'correct' pitch and harmony.[18] Music went from being an ordinary language, expressing individuality and emotion, to being a philosophical experiment, cerebral and exclusive.

---

17 William Uzgalis, 'John Locke', *The Stanford Encyclopedia of Philosophy* (Summer 2015 Edition), ed. Edward N. Zalta; http://plato.stanford.edu/entries/locke.

18 See Thomas Christensen, *Rameau and Musical Thought in the Enlightenment*, Cambridge: Cambridge University Press, 1993, chs 3 and 8. Also www.theguardian.com/music/2013/apr/05/mozart-bach-music-numbers-codes.

In the context of Hobbes, Locke and Rousseau, to some of his followers the work of Georg Hegel suggested that the meaning of language depended on coherence, on what was accepted within a particular group, and not on correspondence with any external point of reference. This interpretation inspired Karl Marx to go a step further in seeing language as a social construct used to control how people conceived of their world and communicated with others, to limit their choices and behaviour. Later, J. L. Austin and his pupil John Searle saw that scholars' obsession with analysing language and discovering the meaning of words missed the point: words are used to incite actions. In this sense, speech or text can only be understood in relation to the effect it was intended to – and did – have.[19] This is known as the speech–act theory.

Following the Empiricists, Rousseau, Hegel and Marx, some scholars understand religious language as that which binds members of a religion together (the word 'religion' might have originated in the Latin *ligare*, to bind). Its truth only relates to its efficacy, the extent to which the faithful share a way of looking at the world and act accordingly.

Note how the idea that language is composed of arbitrary signs pointing towards collections of similar experiences and, following on, the idea that the different use of signs and the distinctive way people choose to group experiences together can suggest something about an author and their experience of the world, underpins source criticism and redaction criticism, which developed out of it.

Taking a different direction, René Descartes, Baruch Spinoza and Gottfried Leibniz all saw the meaning of words relating to rational concepts, not external points of reference. As mathematicians they saw ultimate reality in the relationship between concepts, not in terms of the world of physical experience – although, of course, experience reflects concepts. For rationalists, a statement is true if it *coheres* with other statements that are known to be true, if it fits into the conceptual, rational system. For

---

19 For an interesting example of how this approach to language and meaning could be applied, see web.mit.edu/langton/www/pubs/SpeechActs.pdf.

example, Leibniz's famous principle of non-contradiction suggests that a concept is possible if it contains no logical contradiction and in some sense exists, whether or not there are instances of that concept manifesting in time and space.

In the late nineteenth and early twentieth centuries the rationalist approach to language was developed by A. N. Whitehead and Bertrand Russell, who tried to demonstrate the truth of all mathematical statements from first principles and the complete internal coherence of mathematics as a logical language.

At the same time, in Vienna, a circle of philosophers developed the Verification Principle, which divided all statements into three categories:

1   statements that are synthetically true and can be *verified* against sense experience, e.g. 'this is a hand';
2   statements that are analytically true and are *coherent* within a logical system;
3   statements that are *meaningless* because they are neither synthetically verifiable nor analytically true.

Members of the Vienna Circle were working on the basis of Kant's philosophy, as developed by Gottlob Frege, which suggested that meaning could only be *either* synthetic (dependent on correspondence with an empirically verifiable state of affairs) *or* analytic (depending on coherence with a logical/linguistic system). Later, in the 1950s, the American philosopher W. V. Quine attacked this whole either–or approach to language and meaning in his famous essay 'Two Dogmas of Empiricism', suggesting that the distinction between synthetically and analytically true statements was ultimately unhelpful and that philosophers should stop trying to understand meaning and focus instead on charting the relationship between words as signs and thus the relationship between concepts, describing the contours of the rational–linguistic world we inhabit.

Exploring the relationship between the internally coherent language described by Whitehead and Russell and the everyday world, at the turn of the twentieth century G. E. Moore developed the idea that ordinary concepts and terms that signify them – like 'hand' or 'door' – just have to be accepted; their meaning cannot be explained other than by referring to instances of the thing in question. When scholars dig away for meaning, at some point they hit bedrock, their spade is turned.

Ludwig Wittgenstein developed the idea that the meaning of language depends on its *usage*, not on *corresponding* with any static point of reference. A protégé of Russell and Moore who started his philosophical education in Vienna, during the First World War, while serving on the Eastern Front, Wittgenstein came to realize how different people have different ways of using language, even the same language, and without understanding their particular form of life it is impossible to understand what they really mean. The meaning of ordinary language depends on its everyday usage by the many and varied groups and even individuals who use German, French, Japanese or Swahili; we can only really understand the meaning of what is said or written through being immersed in the form of life within which it is said or written and through understanding the rules of the particular language game that is being played. Wittgenstein famously suggested that 'If a lion could talk, we could not understand him.'

In paragraph 23 of the *Philosophical Investigations*, Wittgenstein presents a list of common language games:

Giving orders, and obeying them—
Describing the appearance of an object—
Constructing an object from a description (a drawing)—
Reporting an event—
Speculating about an event—
Forming and testing a hypothesis—
Presenting the results of an experiment in tables and
diagrams—
Making up a story; and reading it—
Play-acting—
Singing catches—

Guessing riddles—
Making a joke; telling it—
Solving a problem in practical arithmetic—
Translating from one language into another—
Asking, thinking, cursing, greeting, praying.[20]

Note how, like the form critics, Wittgenstein saw the form within which any statement is framed affecting its meaning. Without understanding the rules implicit in the form, scholars have no hope of ascertaining the intended meaning of any communication.

Rudolf Bultmann, one of the most important advocates of form criticism, suggested that in searching for the meaning of Scripture we have to demythologize, excavate through strata of later explanations and interpolations that impose later world views on the original proclamation of Christianity – the kerygma – in each unit of text or pericope. In identifying the earliest kernels of text, we identify how witnesses received the gospel message, not the gospel message itself, and must expect the witnesses' expectations, experiences, culture and general form of life to have affected how they understood what they heard and saw. For Bultmann, research cannot take us to the historical Jesus or the truth of his message – that is only accessible through faith, which exists separately from evidence or argument and resists communication.

Religious Language is True for Us

In *The Postmodern Condition: A Report on Knowledge*, Jean-François Lyotard pulled together elements of Wittgenstein's work on language games, J. L. Austin's speech–acts theory and the sense that the Enlightenment view of truth had finally been discredited to put forward a new postmodern philosophy. Lyotard wrote that his work 'makes no claims to being original or even true', and that his ideas 'should not be accorded predictive value in relation to reality,

---

20   Ludwig Wittgenstein, *Philosophical Investigations*, trans. and ed. G. E. M. Anscombe, Oxford: Blackwell, 1958, pp. 11–12.

but strategic value in relation to the questions raised'.[21] As he saw it, truth could no longer be said to depend on correspondence with an objective state of affairs; the human perspective is necessarily subjective and inescapable. It follows that the meaning of a statement – religious or otherwise – can depend only on the extent to which it coheres or, more particularly, has 'strategic value' in relation to a particular form of life or task.

As Wittgenstein argued, the meaning of language is limited by the rules of the game in which it is used. As Austin suggested, words are not neutral but incite action, change things. Language is the means by which people play with other people, winning, losing, acting out and moving forward, shaping and changing the game. Paul Ricoeur explored what this approach might mean for reading the Bible through his essay 'Biblical Hermeneutics' (1975) and then his book *Essays on Biblical Interpretation* (1980). Drawing on Bultmann's work in form criticism, he suggested that the form or genre of a text defines the rules of the language game and so affects meaning and interpretation.

For postmodernists, religious statements are on an equal footing with other statements and are not in a different category. Truth and meaning are not single, static and unchanging but plural, various and dynamic. For religion, postmodernism is both a blessing and a curse – it provides a framework that enables a plethora of religions, denominations and interpretations to flourish but undermines the ability of any of them to claim to be right, to claim truth. If religions, their revelations, laws and insights are only true for members, and alternatives – even contradictory alternatives – are equally plausible, it begs the question: 'Why be religious at all?'

In the 1980s, philosophers such as D. Z. Phillips[22] and Gareth

---

21 Jean-François Lyotard, *The Postmodern Condition: A Report on Knowledge*, trans. Geoff Bennington and Brian Massum, Minneapolis, MN: University of Minnesota Press, 1993.

22 Claire McGraw, 'The Realism/Anti-Realism Debate in Religion', *Philosophy Compass* 3:1 (2008), pp. 254–72; see also D. Z. Phillips' *Contemplative Philosophy of Religion: Questions and Responses*, ed. Andy F. Sanders, Aldershot: Ashgate, 2007.

Moore OP explored the implications of the postmodern turn for religion in more depth. For both scholars, in their different ways, postmodernism prompts philosophers to re-examine the basis for any and all knowledge statements. It is no longer acceptable to assume a naïve Enlightenment model of truth. Statements are not EITHER true OR false – they are often BOTH true AND false. If I say 'Christ was raised from the dead', it may be true within a Southern Baptist community and false in a Sunni Muslim community. Biblical texts might be meaningful and true in very different ways in different Jewish or Christian settings and simultaneously meaningless and untrue in secular or atheist settings.

Gareth Moore OP ended his book *Believing in God* (1989) with the claim 'people do not discover religious truths, they make them',[23] echoing Voltaire's famous quip, *Si Dieu n'existait pas, il faudrait l'inventer* ('If God did not exist, it would be necessary to invent him').[24] People need God, need religion, need the Bible to mean what they think it means in order to reinforce their world view, so religious claims have strategic value and are true within the language game and form of life that generated them. People are in no position to make any further claims about religious truths. God may or may not have an independent existence, laws may or may not have some sort of a metaphysical reality, the Bible may or may not accurately relate historical events, Jesus might or might not have meant what Christians understand him to have meant. Human beings are in no position to know or claim to know the truth.

It follows from this that the truth of a biblical interpretation – or argument supported with biblical references – depends not on the extent to which it corresponds with the original intention(s) of the biblical author(s), the original reception or historical use of the text, but on whether modern consumers of that interpretation think that it is true for them, that it coheres with other aspects of their belief. Arguably this might lead to religious communities

---

23 Gareth Moore, *Believing in God*, Edinburgh: T. & T. Clark, 1989, last page.
24 *Épître à l'Auteur du Livre des Trois Imposteurs* (1770).

fragmenting, becoming atomized and containing more and more diverse extreme elements as smaller groups or even individuals start to pick and choose what they want to believe on the basis of what makes sense to them, for whatever reason, and others lack any solid standard of truth and meaning to appeal to, other than popularity or pragmatism.

Religious Language is Metaphorical

Not everybody interpreted Wittgenstein in this way. While the meaning of language might depend on the rules of the language game and the form of life within which it is being played, more universal forms of meaningful communication might still exist, although they would surely have their own rules.

In the 1950s Max Black explored the nature of metaphor as such a form of communication. He rejected the traditional idea that metaphors were just creative, flowery ways of saying what could otherwise be said directly, that metaphors could be substituted for ordinary descriptions. Like I. A. Richards, Black thought that there might be a language of metaphor with its own rules that might extend peoples' ability to communicate about things at the very edge of human understanding.

Following Black and Richards, in 1985, Janet Martin Soskice suggested that there is more to metaphor in religious language than making creative or arbitrary associations. When people 'speak of one thing in terms that are seen to be suggestive of another',[25] they recognize that they are at the boundary of communication and push beyond what it is possible to say in direct terms. A straightforward description cannot be substituted for a metaphor because the metaphor says something that cannot otherwise be said.

For example, when we speak of the camel as 'the ship of the desert', the ideas of swaying motion, a heavy and precious cargo, a broad wilderness, a route mapped by stars, distant ports of call and so on are brought to mind. Saying merely 'camel' does not bring

---

25   Janet Martin Soskice, *Metaphor and Religious Language*, Oxford: Oxford University Press, 1985, p. 15.

in these associations at all. Thus the metaphor of the camel as 'the ship of the desert' genuinely tells us something about camels that we would not have been able to learn without the help of the metaphor.

In the 1960s Ian Ramsey suggested that religious language consisted of qualified models that do not attempt to describe but rather evoke and disclose an insight we cannot otherwise communicate by pointing to something beyond themselves. A *model* for God might be love; God cannot literally be understood as a human emotion but the understanding of what love is or can be *points us in the direction of* what God is. A *qualifier* that would enrich the model of love might be 'infinite'. Saying that God is *infinite* love focuses and directs our thinking still further and enriches our understanding of God.

In a more general sense, in his recent encyclical *Laudato Si*, Pope Francis explains how the biblical narrative points beyond its literal interpretation to deeper truth; that Bible stories are metaphorical and symbolic, should not be taken literally and need interpretation:

> The creation accounts in the book of Genesis contain, in their own symbolic and narrative language, profound teachings about human existence and its historical reality. They suggest that human life is grounded in three fundamental and closely intertwined relationships: with God, with our neighbour and with the earth itself. According to the Bible, these three vital relationships have been broken, both outwardly and within us.[26]

Going much further, in *Beyond Literal Belief: Religion as Metaphor* (2015), David Tacey explains:

> There is an error in Christianity which has brought on this disconnect between religion and society. The religious story has been misinterpreted as history and fact. This worked while believers remained uneducated; in fact the claim that

---

26 Paragraph 66, www.thetablet.co.uk/UserFiles/Files/Laudato_Si_-_EN.pdf.

everything was historical added to its appeal. But as the West became more sophisticated, people abandoned religion in droves. They treated it with contempt, as an insult to their intelligence. The problem is not with the Scriptures as such, but with how they are interpreted. The original sin of religion is literalism, the habit of reading texts literally. This is not only an intellectual problem, which has given many a distorted view of the world, but is the cause of sectarian conflict and religious violence. Literalism engenders idolatry and aggression, and is the bane of civilization. It is the reason why the new atheists of the post 9/11 era are trying to get rid of religion. Getting rid of religion is an absurdity, but getting rid of literalism is something we need to seriously consider.[27]

Religious Language is Symbolic

That the Bible contains a great deal of symbolic language is obvious and has long been accepted by almost every Jewish and Christian scholar. The fact that Jewish and Christian scholars, including Augustine, embraced the many levels of meaning in each word and story is attested in previous chapters. In his *Dynamics of Faith* (1957), Paul Tillich wrote: 'Man's ultimate concern must be expressed symbolically, because symbolic language alone is able to express the ultimate.'

For Tillich:

Symbols have one characteristic in common with signs; they point beyond themselves to something else. Sometimes ... signs are called symbols; but this is unfortunate because it makes the distinction between signs and symbols more difficult. Decisive is the fact that signs do not participate in the reality of that to which they point, while symbols do. Therefore, signs can be replaced for reasons of expediency or convention, while symbols cannot.[28]

---

27   David Tacey, *Beyond Literal Belief: Religion as Metaphor*, Mulgrave, Victoria Australia: Garratt Publishing, 2015, p. xi.

28   See people.uwec.edu/beachea/tillich.html.

In essence he seems to be arguing that a universal symbolic language exists and enables people to express their experience of ultimate reality, God, in a meaningful way that transcends time, place and culture. Religious language should not be taken literally but it does not follow that there is no definite sense of what it means or that the sense is open to being defined differently by different groups or individuals. In Tillich's sense, religious language is a bit like mathematics – a universal language we have to learn but which seems to have an independent reality and enables us to communicate with every other mathematician, without fear of confusion or misunderstanding.

However, Tage Kurtén has argued that 'Although Tillich is writing here as if he were describing how things are ("God is ..."), what he is really saying concerns our use of language, not an ontology independent of our language.'[29] What does Tillich understand by ultimate reality? In what sense is God, for Tillich, real? Tillich is associated with Meister Eckhart's concept of God as the 'ground of our being'.[30] He wrote in *The Shaking of the Foundations*: 'There is no place to which we could flee from God, which is outside of God.'[31] This might seem strikingly close to Pantheism but is probably better understood in a medieval sense: just as Anselm saw God in being that could not be conceived not to be, and just as Aquinas saw God in the necessary ground underpinning contingent things, Tillich saw God as what our whole conceptual and physical existence rests upon. Can this be reduced to language? Maybe. Yet what is language if it is not a means of expressing what is real to us, and what is real if it is not real to us?

In the end the question of meaning and truth in language comes down to what we mean by reality. Is ultimate reality independent of human understanding or not? Does what is really real depend

29 Tage Kurtén, 'Internal Realism: A Joint Feature by Dewi Z. Phillips and Paul Tillich?', in D. Z. Phillips, *Contemplative Philosophy of Religion*, p. 100.

30 Paul Tillich, *Systematic Theology* I, Chicago: University of Chicago Press, 2012, p. 110.

31 Paul Tillich, *The Shaking of the Foundations*, New York: Charles Scribner's Sons, 1948; repr. Eugene, OR: Wipf & Stock, 2012, p. 40.

on the framework of space and time or is it timeless, spaceless, metaphysical? Philosophers' conceptions of reality translate into their understandings of what (religious) language means and why. Most religious philosophers see ultimate reality in broader terms than many atheist philosophers do, resisting the idea that 'human beings are the measure of all things'[32] and the argument that human beings cannot say what they cannot measure in any meaningful sense.

Conclusion

We hope that after reading *Bible Matters* you will accept that the Bible does matter, in lots of different senses, and more than that, that you will be inspired to read and find out a lot more about some of the areas we have introduced – archaeology or translation, ethics or feminist theology, maybe even the big philosophical question of truth. A book of this length and style could never hope to do justice to the Bible – a lifetime's study can't come close to doing that – but we hope we have achieved our aim in persuading you that it matters too much to ignore!

---

32 Protagoras.

Glossary

Acts (of the Apostles) Book of the New Testament, probably written by Luke to explain the development of the early Church following Jesus' death.

Aetiology Story explaining how things came to be the way they are in mythological terms, e.g. how the elephant got its trunk.

Allegory A story with a double, deeper meaning.

An other In postmodernism, how we relate to humanity as a whole in the person of another individual.

Anagignoskomena Eastern Orthodox word for biblical texts not regarded as fully canonical.

Ananias and Sapphira Early Christians who (according to Acts 5) failed to share their property with other members of the Church and were struck dead as a result.

Anaxagoras Pre-Socratic Greek philosopher, *c.*510–428 BC; thought that the organizing force in nature was *nous*, mind.

Anglicanism Denomination of Christianity that began with the English monarch rejecting the authority of the Pope during the reign of Henry VIII. There are now many Anglican Churches around the world, including the Church of England, the Church in Wales, the Episcopalian Churches in the USA etc. In some ways Anglicans share beliefs and practices with Roman Catholics and in others with Protestants such as Lutherans. Churches that protested against Anglican authority are known as 'nonconformists' (e.g. Methodists) – they are Protestant, but not part of the original breakaway groups of the reformation era.

Anthropomorphic 'In human form', particularly seeing God in human form as a sort of superhuman leader.

Anti-Semitism   Prejudice against the Jewish race and religion.

Apocalyptic   To do with the end of time and final judgement. Also a genre of biblical literature characterized by prophecies about the end of time and final judgement.

Apocrypha   Biblical texts regarded as not fully canonical and of secondary authority.

Apostle   Chosen follower of Jesus sent out to spread the gospel – traditionally 12 Apostles, although the lists in the Gospels vary and Paul is sometimes counted as an Apostle, although he never even met the living Jesus.

Aramaic   Language spoken across the ancient Near East, closely related to Hebrew and written in the same characters.

Archetype   Ancient story or image that is central to cultural understanding, definitive.

Ark of the Covenant   Gold-covered box used to store the tablets on which Moses inscribed the law and on top of which was the seat where YHVH's presence was said to reside. Was in the Temple, lost in or before AD 70.

Athanasius, Bishop of Alexandria   Important father of the Early Church, concerned to establish orthodoxy and stamp out heresy.

Babylonian exile   Period during which the elite of Judah were deported to Babylon following the sieges and falls of Jerusalem in 587 and 597 BC.

Baptism   Ritual washing or bathing in water; symbolizes purification, a new beginning, rebirth.

Bar Mitzvah   Coming-of-age ceremony in Judaism, commonly held for 13-year-old boys and involving each reciting a portion of the Torah in Hebrew to the synagogue congregation.

Base communities   Communities of poor Christians in South America with left-wing political and liberation-theological characteristics.

Biblical criticism   Close study of the Bible to establish the origins and correct interpretation of the texts.

Biblical inerrancy Belief that the Bible, when properly understood, contains no error.

Biblical literalism Belief that the Bible can be taken at face value and understood by most ordinary people with little explanation or study; that it contains no error and can be used as a guide to all aspects of life.

Black liberation theology Left-wing political reading of the Bible, taking it to support civil rights and a preferential option for poor African Americans and other oppressed minorities.

Bogomils Dualist sect from Bulgaria, tenth century AD.

Calvinism Protestant movement, following the work of John Calvin. Sometimes referred to as the Reformed tradition.

Canaan Ancient name for the land that is otherwise called Judaea, Palestine or Israel.

Canon Collection of authorized, authoritative books of Scripture.

Capitalism Economic system that assumes that a free market creates wealth and, ultimately, a fair society without much interference from government.

Cathars Christian dualist sect, particularly popular in Southern Europe between the twelfth and fourteenth centuries. Victims of a crusade.

Charismatic Charismatic Christianity emphasizes personal religious experience and a sense of joy and emotional well-being as a result of the saving power of Jesus.

Church of England Anglican Church in England. The Queen is the head of the Church of England, though the Archbishop of Canterbury is the most senior prelate in the Church of England.

Civil Rights Movement that seeks to extend equal legal rights to all human beings, regardless of race, gender, sexuality or religion.

Codex Sinaiticus Ancient biblical manuscript.

Communism Economic system that assumes that a fair society has to be planned for centrally, by government controlling markets and redistributing wealth according to need.

Comparative religions Approach to studying religions that focuses on the phenomena – external features – of religions, suggesting that much can be learned about religion through such an impartial comparative exercise.

Conservatism Right-wing or reactionary political or social position that prefers no change, avoiding risk and upholding traditions.

Council of Chalcedon AD 451 – important in terms of Christology, deciding the nature and importance of Jesus Christ and his relationship with God the Father and the Holy Spirit.

Council of Constantinople AD 381 – important in terms of confirming the Nicene Creed as a basic statement of doctrine for all Christians.

Council of Jamnia First century AD – hypothetical council supposed to have confirmed the canon of Hebrew Scripture. Today most scholars doubt it actually happened.

Council of Nicaea AD 325 – Important in establishing that Jesus Christ is homoousion – of the same substance with God the Father and was pre-existent.

Council of Trent 1545–63 – important in establishing Catholic doctrine following the Protestant Reformation, including authorizing the Vulgate translation of the Bible and the philosophy of St Thomas Aquinas.

Councils of the Church Meetings of the Church that made important decisions about orthodox beliefs and practices.

Counter-Reformation A period during which the Roman Catholic Church revived its traditions in reaction to the Protestant Reformation.

Creationism Belief that God created the world as described in the Bible.

Cynicism Extreme scepticism, such as doubts everything and ascribes negative motives to most people and actions.

Dasein Human existence, as in Heidegger.

Dead Sea Scrolls   Manuscripts discovered in caves near Qumran, an important archaeological site near the Dead Sea, after 1948.

Deism   Belief that God exists and created everything, but is so distant that God has no real role in everyday life.

Demiurge   In Neoplatonism, the demiurge was created by God and went on to create everything else. At a distance from God, the material creations of the demiurge are far from perfect.

Demythologization   The process of stripping away layers of tradition and belief to identify a kernel of original historical material, as in form criticism.

Denomination   Group within a religion.

Deuterocanonical   Catholic word for biblical text that is not part of the main canon, but is of secondary – deutero – importance.

Deuteronomist   Author of Deuteronomy who also seems to have redacted large portions of the Hebrew text, variously dated to the late pre-exilic, exilic or post-exilic periods.

Dialectic   As in Hegel, the process whereby truth emerges from discussion and debate between opposing positions.

Disciple   Follower.

Divine command ethics   Seeing that right and wrong are what God commands, either through Scripture or directly through ongoing revelation(s).

Doctrine   Set of official beliefs.

Documentary Hypothesis   Based on the Graf-Wellhausen Hypothesis, the belief that the first five books of the Hebrew Scriptures are made up of four source documents, J, E, D and P, edited together in a more or less complex process between the eighth and third centuries BC.

Double criterion of difference   As in Käsemann, material about Jesus that is neither plausible in a first-century Jewish nor an early Christian context is most likely to be authentic to Jesus.

Early Church Fathers   Important figures in the Early Church who contributed to the development of Christian doctrine.

Easter Letter of AD **367** Written by Athanasius – one of the first documents attesting to the Christian canon.

Eastern Orthodox Orthodox Churches in Russia, Greece, Serbia etc. These Churches are all independent and different to some extent but have many common features. It is a term like Protestant – nobody is a member of the Protestant Church but many Churches can rightly be described as Protestant.

Eastern Schism Eleventh-century dispute that led the Eastern (Orthodox) and Western (Roman Catholic) Churches to break away from each other.

Ebionites Jewish Christian movement from the first decades after the death of Christ – rejected Paul as an apostle and authoritative Christian teacher.

Eco-feminism Movements that try to link feminism with ecology, suggesting that patriarchy has encouraged the abuse of nature, whereas feminism restores a sustainable approach to nature.

Ecumenicalism Attempt to look beyond the divisions between denominations and work for common ends across Christian groups.

Editing Process of tidying a text, removing errors, repetition etc. Might involve formatting or otherwise joining several texts together to make a continuous narrative.

Eisegesis Reading beliefs into a piece of text, seeing it confirming what one already thought.

Ekklesia Church – also a term used by feminists to describe an ideal Christian community.

Elohist Author of the E source according to advocates of the Documentary Hypothesis. Possibly from Israel in the seventh century BC; refers to God as ELOHIM.

Empirical Information from the senses, i.e. sight, hearing, smell, taste, touch.

Enlightenment Period from the eighteenth century in Europe when scholars explored the implications of lessening church authority and made significant advances in philosophy and particularly in science.

Episcopalianism Type of Anglican Christianity.

Epistemological naïvety Assuming too much about what can be known and how.

Epistemology Branch of philosophy concerned with the nature and limits of knowledge.

Epistle Letter, particularly in the New Testament, as in Paul's Epistle to the Romans.

Eschatology The study of beliefs about the end of time, final judgement and afterlife.

Essene Group of Jews at and around the time of Jesus. The Essenes rejected ordinary life and lived in more or less monastic desert communities awaiting the end of time and final judgement.

Eucharist Ritual re-enacting Jesus' last supper with his disciples. Involves eating bread and drinking wine, representing Jesus' body and blood, and thus believers' partaking in Jesus' sacrifice and sharing in the benefits of atonement for the sins of humanity.

Evangelical Protestants Protestants who tend towards biblical literalism and reject both conservative and liberal Christianity.

Evangelist Gospel author.

Exegesis Process of reading and interpreting a text to tease out what it really means.

Exile See Babylonian exile.

Existentialism Movement that maintains that truth, while of absolute importance, cannot be known. Life must be lived in relation to truth but without certainty.

Falsification A theory of truth that regards any statement as meaningless unless it is mathematical or has content that can be falsified using empirical means – effectively this means in scientific terms.

Feminism Movement that recognizes the misogyny that has characterized society for millennia and seeks to address it, putting women on an equal and fair footing in all walks of life.

Fideism Faith that has no evidentiary support and can seem to rejoice in its irrationality.

First Quest Movement within historical criticism that sought to discover the 'historical Jesus' using all the tools of source criticism, form criticism, redaction criticism etc. to identify the genuine character and sayings of Jesus in the Gospels.

Form criticism Process that seeks to identify the genre and 'setting-in-life' (*Sitz im Leben*) of each separate unit of text, so clarifying its original meaning. Originated in the work of Gunkel, Bultmann and Dibelius.

Form of life As in Wittgenstein – cultural setting that determines the usage of language and the meaning of words.

Four-source hypothesis See Streeter's hypothesis.

Fragmentary Hypothesis Alternative to the Documentary Hypothesis; suggests that the Pentateuch is made up of multiple original sources.

Franciscans Followers of the Monastic Rule of St Francis.

Free-market capitalism Extreme form of capitalism – rejects all government regulation of trade and markets.

Genetic fallacy A conclusion is erroneously proposed on the basis of the history or origins of a thing, i.e. 'Can anything good come from Nazareth?', suggesting that because of the lowly reputation of a place, no person coming from there can be taken seriously.

German Confessing Church Church that arose in opposition to the German Evangelical Church; Karl Barth and Dietrich Bonhoeffer were members.

German Evangelical Church Official Nazi Church, sometimes called the *Reichskirche*.

Gnostic texts Texts produced by gnostic communities in the centuries immediately before and after Jesus. Characterized by a belief that secret, saving knowledge could be imparted to a select few through literature.

Gnosticism Group of sects influenced by Greek and eastern philosophies and to some extent by Christianity. Believed that secret, saving knowledge had been revealed to prophet(s) and recorded in texts.

Gospel Story of Jesus' life and ministry.

Gospels Stories about Jesus' life and ministry attributed to Matthew, Mark, Luke and John in the New Testament.

Grace God's saving action in the world.

Graf-Wellhausen Hypothesis See Documentary Hypothesis.

Griesbach Hypothesis Theory that Matthew was written first and Mark produced later as a simpler, abbreviated 'pocket' Matthew for less sophisticated converts in Rome and other cities of the diaspora.

Haggadah Jewish oral histories.

Haskalah The Jewish Enlightenment.

Hebrew Scriptures The books of Torah (Law), Nevi'im (Prophets) and Ketuvim (Writings).

Hegelianism Philosophy developed out of the ideas of Georg Hegel.

Heraclitus First Western philosopher to go beyond physical theory in search of metaphysical foundations and moral applications.

Heresy Unorthodox beliefs, denounced by mainstream religious authority.

Hermeneutic of innocence Reading and understanding texts at face value, without taking account of deeper influences and meanings.

Hermeneutical circle As in Schleiermacher, the process by which a reader must research and fully engage with the text and allow it to shape his or her understanding to better understand it.

Hermeneutics The philosophy of reading and interpreting texts.

Hermes Trismegistus Legendary figure purported to have imparted secret knowledge to Hermetic sects.

Hermetic Corpus   Works attributed to Hermes Trismegistus.

Hermeticism   Cult of Hermes Trismegistus – similar in some ways to Gnosticism.

Hexapla   Translation prepared by Origen in the third century BC.

Hexateuch   First six books of the Bible – the Torah plus Joshua.

High Church   Anglican Churches whose doctrine and practice is very similar to traditional Roman Catholicism.

Higher criticism   Historical criticism.

Historical criticism   Analysis of the biblical texts to ascertain their authorship, date, place of origin, stages of development, probable theological motivations and right interpretation.

Historicity   Extent of historical authenticity and/or accuracy.

Holistic   Reading the whole of a text rather than examining parts in isolation.

Homographs   Words that are spelt the same but have different meanings, e.g. 'bat' and 'bat'.

Homonyms   Each of two words having the same spelling but different meanings.

Homoousion   Of the same substance, as in the Nicene Creed.

Homophone   Words that sound the same but are spelt differently and have different meanings, e.g. 'bow' and 'bough'.

Human sciences   The study of human behaviour in all its forms, economic, psychological, sociological etc.

Humiliati   Italian religious order formed in the twelfth century and suppressed by Papal order in 1571.

Hussites   Christian movement following the teachings of Jan Hus, a proto-Protestant reformer.

Idiom   Local figure of speech.

Immanent eschatology   Belief that the final judgement and end of time will occur in the immediate future.

Inaugurated eschatology Belief that the final judgement and end of time has, in some sense, begun.

Incarnation God taking human form.

Indulgences Certificates granting time off what would otherwise be due in purgatory, usually granted in return for cash or gifts to the Church.

Infinite qualitative distinction Concept coined by the Danish philosopher Søren Kierkegaard and used extensively by Karl Barth. Refers to the extreme difference between the human and the divine.

Intelligent design Argument that an intelligent designer is a more probable explanation for certain features of the universe than pure chance.

Irenaeus of Lyons Early Christian Bishop of Lyons during the second century who is known for his refutations of Gnosticism and attempt to explain why evil happens to good people; saint.

Israel The name taken by Jacob after his encounter with YHVH. Later the northern part of the land that would come to be called Judaea, with its own royal dynasty and Temple based in Samaria between the death of Solomon and 721 BC. Later the name of the Jewish homeland established in Palestine in 1948.

Jahwist Author of the so-called J source according to the Documentary Hypothesis. Probably from Judah in or around the eighth century BC, though some argue for a later date. Refers to God as YHVH.

Jerome Early translator of the Bible, Saint.

Jesuits Members of the Society of Jesus.

Josephus Jewish military leader, later historian, taken prisoner and then employed by the Romans to write two accounts of how the wars in Judaea began and ended.

Judaea Roman name for the province that contained Judah and parts of neighbouring countries.

Judah Kingdom centred on Jerusalem – all that remained of David's kingdom after 721 BC.

Kerygma Central gospel message (Bultmann).

Ketuvim Books of writings in the Hebrew Scriptures.

King James Bible 1666 English translation of the Bible, highly influential in shaping Anglican faith – and indeed the English language.

Koine Greek Variety of Greek spoken by ordinary people in the first century AD, written in cursive, lower-case script, not in capitals as is classical Greek.

Kyriarchy Feminist term for a hierarchy dominated by men and male concerns.

Language game Wittgenstein's term for a context in which language is used in the same way, according to the same rules for the same end. It is possible for a single language to be used in multiple different ways in different contexts and for misunderstandings to arise when somebody uses language in a way that would be appropriate in one context within a different context or language game.

Left wing Political position that inclines towards government regulation of markets, provision of infrastructure and services and effective redistribution of wealth. Tends to have an inclusive approach to society, resisting nationalism and forms of prejudice such as racism, sexism and homophobia.

Liberal feminism Aim for political and legal reform, removing barriers to women's progress.

Liberal Protestants Protestant Christians who are moderate in their doctrine and practice, trying to be as inclusive and conciliatory as possible while working for a better, fairer society.

Liberalism Political position that sees guaranteeing individual liberty as the main aim of government. This can be manifest in different ways – some right-wing politicians claim to be liberal in that they want less government regulation and interference, thus allowing individuals the freedom to take care of themselves and do what they want, so long as others are not hurt. On the other hand, some left-wing politicians claim to be liberal in that they want to redistribute wealth and guarantee a minimum standard of living to everybody, making sure that nobody's liberty is effectively curtailed by a lack of means.

Liberation theology Left-wing movement within Catholic Christianity that interprets the Bible as calling for the poor to be liberated through faith and works.

Lingua Ignota Secret language – see Hildegard of Bingen.

Logos Greek for 'word' or 'saying'. In Neoplatonic and later Christian thought, the *Logos* is the creative aspect of God and that which could have been incarnate in the form of Jesus.

Lollards Followers of John Wycliffe, critics of the church hierarchy and its corruption – called for an English Bible to be made available.

Low Church Members of the Anglican Church who are influenced by Protestant beliefs and practices, for example by rejecting vestments and much ritual in worship.

Lower criticism Biblical interpretation.

Lutheranism Followers of Martin Luther – Protestants.

LXX Septuagint Greek translation of the Hebrew Scriptures.

Mandaeism Gnostic religion practised in the centuries following Jesus' death.

Manichaeism Major religion following the teachings of the Persian prophet Mani, from the third century AD.

Martin Luther Leader of the Protestant Reformation.

Marxism Doctrine espoused by Karl Marx – an idealistic version of Communism.

Masoretic Text Agreed scholarly version of the Hebrew Scriptures dating from the eleventh century.

Mass See Eucharist – but in Catholic or High-Church Anglican contexts.

Maximalism Belief that the Bible can be taken as historically accurate (among archaeologists and classical historians).

Mendicant orders Religious orders who prized poverty and called upon monks to travel from place to place preaching and serving the poor.

Messiah Hoped-for Jewish saviour who would re-found the house of David and purify the temple, re-establishing the covenant and, with God's favour, drive out the enemies of the people and establish an everlasting kingdom of God.

Metaphor Linguistic device evoking a meaning beyond itself, e.g. 'my love is a red, red rose'.

Metaphysical To do with matters above and beyond the physical world – ultimate timeless truth.

Methodism Following John Wesley, a Low-Church reforming branch of Anglicanism that split away and became an independent nonconformist Church in the eighteenth century.

Midrash Jewish interpretation of Scripture.

Minimalism Belief that the Bible cannot be taken to be historically accurate in any way (among archaeologists and classical historians).

Mishnah Early Jewish Rabbinic texts dating from after the destruction of the Temple in AD 70.

Misogynist Hater of women.

Modernity In Catholicism, those who wanted to embrace biblical criticism and change church doctrine and practice to suit society.

Muratorian Canon Early document listing the Christian canon.

Musar literature Jewish mystical texts.

Mysticism The study and practice of spirituality and religious experience.

Myth A story with a deeper meaning, often designed to explain where things came from or why they came to be as they are.

Nag Hammadi Codices Texts found in the upper-Egyptian desert in the late 1940s, containing many Gnostic texts.

Narrative theology Late-twentieth-century Christian movement that sees Christianity as a story or narrative that connects belief with culture, history, ethics and social practices. Many things can only be understood from within the relevant narrative, according to the story's internal logic.

Natural theology Belief that proof for the existence and nature of God and moral norms can be found through observation, interpretation and reason.

Neo-Kantian philosophy Revived or modified form of Kantian philosophy that was influential in the second part of the nineteenth century, particularly in Germany.

Neo-orthodoxy Dialectical theology – post-First World War form of Protestantism inspired by the work of Barth and Brunner.

Neoplatonic philosophy Third- to sixth-century AD developments of Platonic philosophy, associated with the work of e.g. Plotinus.

Nevi'im Prophets – Hebrew word.

New Testament Christian Scriptures.

Nihilism Belief that life is without objective meaning or purpose; there is no truth.

Non-propositional Faith that has no normal evidentiary support.

No-quest Period in between phases of the quest for the historical Jesus, when confidence in the potential of historical criticism was low.

Northern Kingdom See Israel – the kingdom centred on Samaria between the death of Solomon and 721 BC.

Noumenal Essential reality, beyond the temporal, physical world.

Objective The way things really are, independent of viewpoint or bias.

Old Testament Christian name for the books of the Hebrew Scriptures, rearranged and translated to suit Christian priorities.

Ontology The nature of being or the nature of existence..

Oral tradition Stories and sayings passed down by word of mouth without being written down.

Origen Early Church Father and great textual scholar. Influenced by Gnosticism.

Orthodox Mainstream, correct.

Orthodox (Jewish) Majority, traditional form of Judaism.

Oxford Group In the years leading up to the Second World War, a group of Christians who sought to address extremism through missionary work and the gospel message – Streeter was a member.

Palestine Name for Judaea derived from ancient Philistia, the name of the coastal strip running from Syria, through Lebanon and Israel into Gaza. This name was used by colonial powers and is still used by the native Arab people who seek to reclaim their land from the Israelis.

Papias Ancient Christian writer who referred to the authorship of Mark's Gospel.

Papyrus Plant-based paper used for some ancient manuscripts, especially in Egypt.

Pardes Mnemonic literally meaning Paradise – helps Jewish people remember the different approaches to interpreting a text.

Patriarchal Society dominated by (old) men.

Pentateuch First five books of the Bible (Genesis, Exodus, Leviticus, Numbers, Deuteronomy); Christian name for the Torah.

Pentecostalism Lively, charismatic form of Protestant Christianity common in Africa, the Caribbean and African American communities in the USA.

Pericope Extract from a text; usually used to refer to a biblical extract.

Phenomena Physical manifestations; things as we experience them.

Phenomenology Philosophical approach that focuses on how people experience things, not how they may or may not be in the abstract.

Philanthropy Literally the love of men – in practice a love of charitable giving.

Philo of Alexandria Influential Jewish philosopher from Egypt.

Pietism Form of Protestant Christianity that focuses on the individual's relationship with God; disavows learning and Church ministry in favour of personal spiritual experiences.

Porneia Sexual immorality of some undefined sort.

Post-liberal theology See Narrative theology.

Postmodern turn Change from Enlightenment values to postmodernism in European thought, sometime in the 1970s.

Postmodernism Movement characterized by a suspicion of organized systems of philosophy that claim to have truth or answers. Focuses on the many factors that shape individual perspective and make claiming objective knowledge an impossibility, e.g. race, gender, sexuality.

Priestly writer According to the Documentary Hypothesis, the last of the four authors of the Pentateuch, probably a priest at the Jerusalem Temple in the post-exilic period.

Promised land See Israel, Palestine, Judah, Judaea, Canaan – the land that Jewish people believed was promised by YHVH to Abraham as part of the covenant relationship.

Propaganda (Mis)information used to persuade to support a political position.

Prosperity theology Belief that God rewards faith economically, that wealth is a sign of God's favour and possibly a test, to see whether it will be used wisely.

Protestant Reformation Period in the sixteenth century when Protestants (e.g. Luther, Calvin, Zwingli) broke away from the

Roman Catholic Church, signalling a series of long and devastating European wars.

Pseudepigrapha Collection of non-canonical biblical texts ascribed to authors who are not likely to have actually written them; non-authentic texts.

Q Hypothetical lost sayings-source for the synoptic gospels.

Quakers Members of the Religious Society of Friends, a nonconformist Church that worships in silence, embraces pacifism and has no ministers or rituals.

Quest for the historical Jesus Application of historical criticism to discover the historical character and original message of Jesus of Nazareth in the Bible texts.

Rabbi Jewish leader; religious teacher.

Racism Prejudice against people because of their race/colour.

Radical Orthodoxy Christian movement that makes use of postmodern philosophy to reject Enlightenment values. Associated with John Milbank, Catherine Pickstock and Graham Ward in the UK.

Rationalism The view that regards reason as the chief source and test of knowledge.

Realized eschatology Belief that each person will be judged and proceed immediately to their reward/punishment on their death.

Redacting Enthusiastic editing! Could include rewriting or original interpolations into a text.

Redaction criticism The process of identifying where and how redaction has taken place as a means of identifying the 'original' text out of what remains. A form of historical criticism associated with Bornkamm and Conzelmann.

Reductionist An approach to understanding the nature of complex things by reducing them to simpler or more fundamental things.

Reformed (tradition) Protestant movement – see Calvinism.

Religious Society of Friends   See Quakers.

Religious studies   Branch of theology concerned with the phenomenological study of religion(s) and particularly the comparative religions approach.

Resurrection   Coming back from the dead. Jesus' resurrection took place three days after his death. Christians hope that they will each be resurrected to eternal life in the kingdom of God, though that means different things to different Christians.

Revival meetings   Protestant services designed to reinvigorate faith and effect conversions. Sometimes include public confessions and faith healings.

Right wing   Political position that tends towards freeing the market, reducing tax and regulations and reducing government provision of infrastructure and services – the role of the state is to police and punish crime and defend national interests, often to do with trade. Tends to have a narrow definition of 'normal' and can embrace nationalism and various degrees of prejudice, e.g. racism, sexism, homophobia.

Roman Catholicism   Majority Christian Church looking to the Pope in Rome as its ultimate authority.

Rylands Library Papyrus   Early fragment of the New Testament.

Sabbath   Jewish day of rest – sunset Friday to sunset Saturday.

Sacraments   Outward signs of inward spiritual change. Catholics have seven sacraments, Anglicans two – Baptism and the Eucharist.

Salvation history   (German: *Heilsgeschichte*) Seeks to understand God's activity within and through human history in order to effect his saving intentions.

Scripture   Holy texts.

Second Quest   Post-war (German) revival of New Testament historical criticism.

Secular   Non-religious.

Semitic language   Language from the Middle Eastern region with shared roots and characteristics, though no shared alphabet, e.g. Hebrew, Arabic, Aramaic.

Septuagint See LXX.

Seven rules Rules for textual interpretation attributed to Rabbi Hillel, a contemporary of Jesus Christ.

Situation ethics Protestant Christian approach to Ethics that puts people and Christian love (agape) at the heart of individual decision-making and dispenses with rules.

Sitz im Leben 'Setting-in-life' – original context for a unit of text (see Form criticism).

Socialism Left-wing political movement that, while not embracing the violent excesses of communism, works for a centralized, planned economy.

Socialist feminism Form of feminism that sees regulation, government provision of services – including full, free childcare and the general redistribution of wealth – as key to overcoming patriarchy and granting full equality to women.

Society of Jesus See Jesuits.

Sola Scriptura Belief that Scripture, the Bible, is the most important guide in faith and life.

Source criticism Form of historical criticism that identifies original source documents that have been edited or redacted together to form a biblical narrative. The Graf-Wellhausen and Streeter hypotheses are examples of the source-critical approach.

Southern Kingdom See Judah; the kingdom centred on Jerusalem after the death of Solomon.

Stemmatics Attempt to reconstruct the 'family-tree' of manuscripts, thus dating them and ordering them in terms of probable reliability.

Stoicism Greek philosophy practised by, for example, Marcus Aurelius.

Streeter's hypothesis The four-source theory put forward by B. H. Streeter in 1924.

Subjective Coloured by and relative to individual perspective.

Summum bonum The greatest good end, seen by Kant as a point towards which society is advancing.

Supplementary Hypothesis Alternative to the Documentary Hypothesis; suggests that the Pentateuch is made up of a core of original material that was later expanded in one or more phases by redactors.

Synoptic Gospels Matthew, Mark and Luke. Literally 'seen together', i.e. very similar.

Synoptic problem Why are three Gospels similar (Matthew, Mark and Luke, the Synoptic Gospels) and one so very different … answers to this problem vary!

Talmud Later Jewish Rabbinic texts from communities such as that in Babylon.

Textual criticism The detailed study of manuscripts to determine their original form and thus correct translation and interpretation.

Theism Belief in an active creator-God who knows and cares about people and can act in creation.

Third Quest Revival of New Testament Historical Criticism in the 1970s and 1980s, mostly in the USA.

Tolpuddle Martyrs Early trades unionists who opposed the lowering of agricultural wages in 1830s England and became popular heroes and an inspiration to the socialist movement.

Torah The first five books of Hebrew Scripture, the Law or Instruction – Genesis, Exodus, Leviticus, Numbers and Deuteronomy.

Totalitarianism A political system in which the state holds total control over the society and seeks to control all aspects of public and private life wherever possible. Opposite of libertarianism.

Tradition history A methodology of biblical criticism that related to form criticism, initially developed by Hermann Gunkel. Tradition history seeks to uncover the process by which biblical traditions arrived at their final form, especially how they passed from oral tradition to written form.

Transcendent The aspect of God's nature and power that is wholly independent of the material universe, beyond all physical laws. The opposite of immanence.

Tribes The twelve extended families that made up the ancient Israelite people, descended from the brothers of Joseph.

Trinity Doctrine that became the basis of mainstream Christian belief during the fourth century; asserts that God exists as three consubstantial persons or hypostases – the Father, the Son and the Holy Spirit.

Tübingen School Theological movement founded by Ferdinand Christian Baur at the University of Tübingen, applying Hegelian ideas to the study of Christianity and associated with the radical historical criticism of the Bible.

Two-source hypothesis An explanation for the synoptic problem; suggests that Matthew and Luke were based on Mark and a hypothetical sayings-collection called Q.

Unitarianism Christian movement that began in the sixteenth century and denied the doctrines of the Trinity, the divinity of Jesus Christ, original sin and predestination. Became popular in the eighteenth century in England; Samuel Taylor Coleridge was a Unitarian preacher.

Utilitarianism Consequentialist ethical theory that proposes that actions are justified if they result in the greatest happiness for the greatest number. Term coined by John Stuart Mill to refer to the work of Jeremy Bentham.

Verified Supported by empirical, sensory evidence. The Verification Principle suggests that any statement that cannot be so supported, and is not tautologous, is meaningless.

Veriditas **(viridity)** Term coined and used by Hildegard of Bingen to refer to spiritual and physical flourishing as an aspect of God's nature and human beings' relationship with the divine.

Virtue ethics An approach to Ethics that focuses on positive character traits – virtues – rather than on rules or the immediate consequences of actions. Traced back to Aristotle but increasingly popular from the mid-twentieth century.

Vulgate St Jerome's late-fourth-century Latin translation of the Bible that became, at the Council of Trent in the sixteenth century, the Roman Catholic Church's official Latin version of the Bible.

Waldensians A Christian movement from Lyon that spread across the Alps in the late 1170s.

Wo/man Term used by some feminists in an attempt to be more inclusive.

Wolfenbüttel Fragments Fragments of Reimarus' *Apology*, published by Lessing in 1774 and 1777.

Yale School Advocates of Narrative theology based at Yale University.

Young Hegelians Young followers of Hegel, implicated in the 1848 uprisings across Europe, e.g. Bauer, Feuerbach, Marx.

Zeitgeist the defining spirit of the time; general trend of thought or feeling characteristic of a particular period of time.

Index

Shakespeare, William xi, 27,
61, 265, 268
Shamai, Rabbi 253
Shapiro, Rabbi Rami 252, 253
Sicarii 49, 53, 59
Simon, Richard 30, 109, 123
Situation Ethics 215
Smart, Ninian 165
Smith, Adam 118
Smith, James K. A. 212
Socrates 96, 260
Sola Scriptura 193, 200, 202,
210
Soskice, Janet Martin 299
Source Criticism 80, 125, 152,
160, 176, 181, 293
Spielman, Doron 92
Spinoza, Baruch 107, 110–11,
122, 137, 201, 246–7, 249,
289, 293
Stavrakopoulou, Francesca 220
Steinberg, Rabbi David 251
Stemmatics 28
Sterne, Laurence 118
Stoicism 100, 150
Strauss, David 142, 146–50,
153, 154, 157, 161
Streeter, Burnett Hillman 166,
167, 175, 181
Streeter's Hypothesis 167
Supplementary Hypothesis
124, 135
Synagogue xi, 30, 47, 59, 229,
230, 246, 252, 256
Synoptic Problem 137, 152,
167

Tacey, David 300
Tacitus 96
Talmud 5, 7, 50, 59, 96, 256,
259
Temple (Jerusalem) 4, 5, 40,
42, 43, 45–53, 59, 60, 83,
85, 86, 88, 89, 90, 95, 124,
126, 232, 262
Temple, William (Archbishop)
214
Teresa of Avila 223–4
Textual Criticism 27–32,
106–7, 137, 158, 160, 176
The Simpsons 37
Third Quest for the Historical
Jesus 166, 175–6, 255
Thistleton, Anthony 78
Thomas, R. S. 274
Thompson, Thomas L. 134,
135
Tillich, Paul 301–2
Tobiads 49
Tolpuddle Martyrs 232
Tov, Emanuel 27–9
Tradition History 132, 135
Trinity (Doctrine of the) 174,
195, 212, 224
Tubingen School (University
of) 140, 148, 161, 168
Two Source Hypothesis 137,
144, 167, 181
Tyndale, William 15, 16, 25
Tyrrell, George 157, 161, 178,
199